THE RED ARMY MOVES

THE RED ARMY MOVES

Geoffrey Cox

Marble Hill London

First published by Victor Gollancz 1941
This edition published by Marble Hill Publishers in 2022
Flat 58, Macready House
75 Crawford Street
London W1H 5LP
www.marblehillpublishers.co.uk

Text © the Estate of Geoffrey Cox 2022

Geoffrey Cox has asserted his right to be identified as the author of this work in accordance with the Copyright, designs and Patent Act 1988.

All rights reserved

No part of this book may be reproduced or transmitted in any form or by any means, electronic, mechanical, recording or otherwise, without prior written permission of the copyright owner.

A CIP catalogue record for this book is available from the British Library

ISBN: 1-8383036-7-9

Printed and bound in the UK by Biddles Books
Cover design by Paul Harpin

To

MY CHILDREN

In the hope that they may grow
up to know struggle but not war

This book was written in the intervals between three campaigns. I began it when I first returned from Finland at the end of the war. I wrote a great part of it in Brussels in April and early May, while I waited for the blitzkrieg against the Low Countries to begin. One copy of the manuscript I sent off from Brussels by the last air mail ever carried before the city airport was bombed by the Germans. The other copy fell into the hands of the Gestapo in Lille, where I left my luggage during the Flanders campaign.

I worked at it again between spells of filling sandbags for the Chelsea Home Guard, when I returned to England after France had fallen. I finish it now under the grey skies and amidst the autumn mud which the Finnish troops had known in their time as they trudged forward on the Karelian Isthmus to face the Red Army. I wrote this book because I felt deeply that it ought to be written. I was, in Finland, one of the few spectators of an event which gave rise to great controversy, and which will continue to rouse such controversy. I find myself in possession of evidence about the Finnish war which no other observer has, and I feel that it should be brought into print before it is too late. As I worked at the book I have realised that parts of it will anger and hurt people I have been proud to count as my friends—people who were for Finland, and others who were for Russia in this war. To them I can say only one thing—so far as I have been able I have written here the truth.

CONTENTS

Chapter I.	November Night	*Page*	13
II.	The Helsinki Raids		18
III.	What Stalin Wanted		23
IV.	Invasion		31
V.	Kuusinen		38
VI.	Air War: Stage One		43
VII.	War in the Snow		52
VIII.	Forest General		59
IX.	Arctic War		63
X.	Troop Train		67
XI.	Wallenius		69
XII.	The Battle of Kemi River		75
XIII.	Road to Battle		82
XIV.	Battle Scene		87
XV.	Finnish Town		92
XVI.	Stockholm Christmas		103
XVII.	Volunteer Route		108
XVIII.	The Battle of Suomussalmi		112
XIX.	The Rattee Road		126
XX.	Kuhmo Front		134
XXI.	Why Russia Failed in the North		136
XXII.	Tolvajärvi Battle		139
XXIII.	Mannerheim		142
XXIV.	The Mannerheim Line		150

CONTENTS

Chapter XXV.	Air War: Stage Two	*Page* 156
XXVI.	Petsamo: Forgotten Front	162
XXVII.	Ghost Patrols	172
XXVIII.	Salla Front	175
XXIX.	The Volunteers	180
XXX.	Lottas	185
XXXI.	On the Isthmus	187
XXXII.	Ladoga and the 34th Tank Brigade	191
XXXIII.	Intervention?	195
XXXIV.	The Summa Offensive	200
XXXV.	Break Through	207
XXXVI.	Peace Treaty	211
XXXVII.	Foreign Aid	214
XXXVIII.	Why Peace Came	219
XXXIX.	The Last Day	223
XL.	Hango	232
XLI.	The Red Army	235
XLII.	The Red Air Force	248
XLIII.	The Finnish Army	253
XLIV.	The Propaganda War	256
XLV.	Cost of Defeat	262
XLVI.	The Press and Finland	265
XLVII.	Personal View	274

LIST OF ILLUSTRATIONS

between pages 138 and 139

i. General Wallenius
ii. Kemi River Supply Column
iii. Few had gloves
iv. Swedish help came - but never enough
v. Mostly peasant types
vi. It was like a scene from Napoleon's retreat from Moscow
vii. In time Rovaniemi Hospital was hit
viii. Ghost patrol

LIST OF MAPS

Finland	Page 15
The Battle of the Kemi River	77
The Battle of Suomussalmi	113
The Battle of Suomussalmi	114
Tolvajärvi Battle - the Finnish victory	141
The Mannerheim Line	151
The Petsamo corridor	163

CHAPTER I

NOVEMBER NIGHT

On the main platform of the Helsinki railway station not even a shaded light showed in the blackout. Porters, ticket collectors, passengers were huge looming shapes in the dense autumn night. But beyond the black shape of the station roof the sky was a flushed, glowering red, like a fading sunset in thundery weather. Then it darkened as black clouds of smoke rolled across it, followed by sudden spurts of red that could come only from some great fire. The whole atmosphere was ominous, heavy with menace.

I had been only six hours in Finland, and had no clear news of what had been happening throughout this last day of November in that year of wars, 1939. All I knew was that the Soviet-Finnish diplomatic crisis, which I had been sent northwards to report, was a mere crisis no longer. At Abo airport, on the south-western tip of Finland, we had learnt in the morning that Soviet planes had raided Helsinki airport.

Ignorant of the geography of the city (the airport is nine miles out) I nodded when the courier of the French Legation, who was pulling out his multitudinous canvas bags on to the platform, said, "Alors, they've hit a hangar at least." To neither of us did it occur that the Soviet might have bombed the centre of the city. We had agreed cheerfully, over lunch in the train, that if war had come to Finland, Helsinki would be about the safest spot. For reasons of policy alone the U.S.S.R. would surely never bomb a civilian centre. Moscow was shrewd enough to realise what a reaction this would have in the outside world, particularly among the forces of the Left.

I stumbled on into the dim granite hall of Saarinen's great station. It was crowded. In front of the booking offices waited queues of women, in ski trousers and heavy coats. Children stood by holding to the straps of baggage. Soldiers, rifles and steel helmets strapped on their backs, strode through towards the Viipuri train.

Some of the civilians were clearly wealthy. The women wore fur coats, and their luggage was of pigskin. Others had the tired, worn faces of the working class, and stood by wooden trunks, mattresses, cooking gear and matting baskets. A few had babies in their arms. I needed no telling to know what this scene meant. I had seen it only three months before on the railway stations of Paris; I had seen it in Prague in 1938, and before that in Spain. It was that flight under the shadow of the bomber which is one of the ugliest symptoms of modern war. Right up here, too, in this remote corner of the Baltic, it seemed more unjustifiable than it does in the big capitals whose rulers rule the world. This part of the globe was surely far enough away to have deserved peace.

I stared closely at these Finns, with their rounded, impassive semi-Oriental faces. Though they and their country were new to me, I could sense in this darkened hall an unmistakable atmosphere of fear. It hung in the reddened eyes of the women in the queues, who glanced to the lighted ticket windows, to the clock high up in the roof, to their waiting children. I could see it in the unsmiling face of one man, with a fur collar to his overcoat, who was saying good-bye to his family at the platform entrance. He had the same expression as I had seen on the face of a Jewish business man, whom I watched wave good-bye to his wife and children at the Westbahnhof in Vienna three days after the Anschluss.

This nervousness surprised me. I had not noticed the same in Paris or London stations during the late August evacuation. Was it possible that these people, a peasant stock, had worse nerves than hardened city dwellers, when it came to facing the risks of modern war?

I had not long for reflection. The courier and Morgan of Reuter's, who had travelled up with us, came back into the hall cursing because there were no taxis to be found. The square in front of the station seemed as dark as the bottom of a coal mine, despite the red in the western sky.

It seemed an age since our plane had touched down at Abo, and we had been told that we could go no farther because " there had been unexpected developments at Helsinki ". In the

FINLAND

airport café Finns had talked to each other rapidly, their faces strained and anxious. Then, as our bags were being cleared through the customs, had come the keynote of modern war— an air-raid siren. Abo was having its first alarm. With the wail still echoing above the pine forests we had climbed aboard a bus and set out for the railway station.

On the way we passed groups of sailors, evidently newly mobilised reservists, hurrying by with suitcases and bundles. Between the low wooden houses of the city two companies of troops, wearing grey Finnish army uniforms and steel helmets, and with packs on their backs, swung past singing. But there was no interruption with the train service and by two-thirty in the afternoon we were on the Helsinki train eating lunch in the dining-car. Butter in great chunks seemed strange after British wartime rationing. War seemed unreal again. On all the journey we had only one reminder of it.

We were moving through countryside that I was to come to know intimately in the next three months. Rolling, low hills covered with pines; brown, ploughed patches, covered with the first early snow; red-walled, white-windowed peasant houses. The road ran close to the railway. On it we drew level with a long column of lorries packed with troops. Men in uniform waved their rifles to the train. One group was singing. We could hear their voices above the steady click of wheels. A boy sitting against the back of the driver's cabin was paring some sausage with a knife. He waved the knife in the air with a stabbing motion and laughed. Men in the carriage with us laughed and waved back. We were watching Finland's reserves moving up. Other lorries followed, loaded with boxes of ammunition and supplies. Some had pine branches hastily stuck over the driver's cabin, for camouflage.

Still it all seemed rather unreal. Two days before I had been in Brussels, doing " over the fence " reporting on Germany, when my foreign editor had ordered me to get to Finland at once. I felt glad to have a chance to see Scandinavia; but that was all I expected to have to do. In Belgium, at least, no one expected that the Soviet Union would make war on Finland, and I shared that view.

I was lucky with plane connections, and got right through from Brussels to Malmo, through Copenhagen, without a hitch.

It was my first wartime journey across the North Sea, and I watched with some relief when the coast of Denmark moved towards us under the wings of the big K.L.M. Douglas machine. By eight o'clock the next morning I was in the Finnish plane, with a blue-and-white flag painted on the wings, flying out over the snow-covered outskirts of Stockholm. Below us children skated on open-air rinks and people trudged to work from blocks of gay white and yellow flats.

We went on over the blue, still unfrozen waters of the Gulf of Bothnia towards the scattered Aaland Islands, home of the Finnish clipper ships. Two Swedish military planes on patrol flew past to inspect us, and a Swedish destroyer moved along just within her coastal waters. Then we saw below the islands and the grey towers of Abo Cathedral and we were swinging down to land.

And now I was in Helsinki, with bomb fires all around. I still put them down to the airport blaze; my instinctive journalistic scepticism refused to let me be convinced that events had gone as far as full war. But in any case I knew I had work enough ahead. With Morgan I went into the Societetshuset Hotel, opposite the station, to telephone for a taxi. The porter pottered about, taking what seemed an age over the call. Impatient to get settled and get down to work, I asked him curtly to get me the number at once. To my amazement his eyes reddened and I realised he was on the point of tears. Embarrassed, I apologised. Slowly he replied, "It's really my fault, sir, but you see I have had a terrible day. I was here when the bombs fell in the street outside this afternoon, and my nerves are a bit on edge. A woman was killed very close to me."

"In the street." The words in his careful English rang in my brain. So the Soviet had bombed the city itself. That was why these people were pouring towards the trains. Surprised as I have seldom been in my life, I followed the man who had come for my bags and walked out again into the darkened roadway. Ahead of us the fires were leaping up again, red as the red flag.

CHAPTER II

THE HELSINKI RAIDS

The flames came chiefly from the north wing of the Technical High School, which had been hit by high explosive and incendiary bombs during the second raid on the city, made just after two-thirty that afternoon. I dumped my bags in the Hotel Kamp, and went out to look at the damage. Firemen were playing hoses from the square on to the upper windows of the school. In the debris of two apartment houses nearby the clearance squads were digging for bodies. Smuts, smoke, and the acrid smell of burning filled the air. Under foot glass from smashed windows crunched as you walked. For nearly half a mile round windows had been blown out by the force of the explosion. Even those of the Soviet Legation were spilt on to the pavement, and at the bus station, not five hundred yards from the railway, practically all the plate-glass windows had gone. Funeral wreaths from an undertaker's lay tumbled on the pavement, besides boxes of sweets and bundles of socks. Shopkeepers were busy covering the fronts of their premises with beaverboard and timber, but there was no sign of looting. For days afterwards I saw smashed shop windows with their contents intact.

That night, and the next few days, I pieced together from eyewitnesses, doctors and officials all the facts I could of this raid. I guessed then that this, the first Soviet attack on a city crowded with civilians, would have echoes far greater even than those of the Nazi attack on Guernica, in the Basque country. For the world was used to the idea of civilians being killed by Nazi bombs; but by Soviet bombs, well, that was a different thing.

The sirens had gone in Helsinki that morning at nine-twenty-five. Three squadrons of Soviet planes had flown over the outskirts of the city on their way to the Brando airport. They dropped there several high explosive bombs and some dozen incendiary bombs, but did little permanent damage. The chief airport buildings were untouched, and remained untouched throughout the war. Sirens were sounded as they went over, the first of the eighty alarms Helsinki was to know. It was the first hint the people of the capital had that they were at war. Many of them believed that the alarm was only a practice, and few went down into the cellars and shelters. Foreign journalists stared curiously from their hotel windows, and there was a lot of argument as to whether or not the anti-aircraft guns could be heard. Everyone took it in rather an offhand manner.

So that when the sirens went again in the afternoon people were still moderately unalarmed, and did not rush for the shelters which had been dug in the parks and squares. One girl I spoke to told me she finished a game of tennis and dressed leisurely to go home. Other people went into the squares to stare at the sky.

The city was not evacuated. In October, when the crisis first blew up, 100,000 people, about one-third of the city population, were moved out. The British Legation even got into a minor panic and moved the British colony to Sweden, a measure which shocked the Finns, who believed in British stoicism. Most of the evacuees, including the British colony, had drifted back in the weeks that followed, when no war and even no steady crisis developed. The schools in Helsinki reopened on the Monday before the fatal Thursday of the bombing. This was done, I understand, against the advice of Field-Marshal Mannerheim, who still regarded the situation as serious. But the politicians were confident. One high official of the Foreign Office told me that so little did he believe war was coming that, even though he knew the Russians had denounced the Treaty of Non-Aggression, and had broken off diplomatic relations, he took his own daughter to school on the Thursday morning without anxiety.

It was a bright autumn afternoon, with a scoured blue sky. Suddenly the sirens wailed, and then, ten minutes later, out of the blue came the roar of bombers. I have spoken with many eye-witnesses of the raid. They state that seven Soviet planes roared above the buildings, clearly visible, flying at approximately 3,000 feet. They went on steadily, outwardly harmless in appearance, bright in the sun. Then black specks appeared under them and almost at once the whole city seemed to rock with the explosion of bomb after bomb. Clouds of black smoke and dust poured into the air and rolled down the streets. On the Heikunkatu Street people, seeing the dust, shouted "Gas" and ran in terror. On the station square women flung their children on to the ground and lay over them, sheltering them with their bodies.

A moment more and the planes were gone. Behind them they left one wing of the Technical High School blazing in all its five storeys. In the street behind, two apartment houses, hit by high explosive bombs (the Finns estimated them at 500 lbs.), had had their insides torn out as if with a great hand, and hurled into a flaming tangle at the bottom.

Four floors, each of fifteen-inch concrete, were smashed through completely. The side of the house behind was torn away, leaving bed and furniture open as in a doll's house. One bomb hit a depot of the Butter Export Department of the Co-op. Four girls were killed there, and the manager had his arm torn off. Pieces of flying shrapnel and bomb splinters and glass pitted walls, beds, and furniture in other houses nearby and wounded people right and left. The chief casualties were among people staring through their windows.

The bombs had fallen in two chief groups, the one around the Technical High School, the other behind the Parliament House, close to the main city omnibus station. Here one bomb, falling on a granite rock in an empty section, exploded outwards against the wall of a seven-storey apartment house, pitting it with fragments. Incendiary bombs fell on a bus, setting it afire. Others set fire to a car in which a woman was trapped and finally dragged out, her hair blazing, almost unrecognisable as a human being.

Ambulances and police cars and fire engines raced to the bombed areas. With them raced three men who were to have an enormous influence on the outside world, the news-reel cameraman of Suomi Films (The Finnish Film Company) and two still photographers. They secured some pictures of the damage which are classics of air-raid photography. I saw all but one of the raids on Madrid, and no pictures were ever secured that were so vivid as these. Few of the photographs of London under fire have equalled them. One, showing a street of wreckage with a broken pram in the middle, was printed in papers in every part of the world.

In all, the Finnish authorities later announced, sixty-one people were killed and one hundred and twenty wounded.

These were by far the heaviest casualties suffered in any one raid in the Finnish war. In the High School one professor was killed. Many of the dead died from terrible wounds caused by flying bomb fragments or debris. Professor Palmen, the surgeon at the central city hospital, told me the next day that one girl looked as if a tiger had clawed her legs. He told me that six dead and fifteen wounded had been brought into his hospital alone, though it was half evacuated. One dying woman was brought in clutching a dead baby in her arms. One girl, Dolores Sundberg, twelve years old, had both her legs smashed to ragged stumps, and died on the operating table. To cope with the wounded, emergency beds were set up in the hospital corridor. Of the fifteen wounded, six were women, nine were men. The doctor himself had been carrying out an operation for appendicitis when the alarms went, and had had to carry on although the table rocked under the bomb explosions. He showed me a lump of shrapnel two inches by one inch he had taken out of one man's leg.

Why did the Soviet carry out this raid? Was it a deliberate attempt to stun civilian morale? The answer is known only to the commanders of the Red Army. All we could do in Helsinki was to collect the evidence. The first point is that the bombs all fell near military objectives. The first group, round the Technical High School, struck two hundred and fifty yards from the quays of the Sandviken section of the harbour. Here were cranes, warehouses and railways. This area was bombed again in the only other raid ever made on this part of the town. The Soviet may have believed there were ammunition dumps or valuable stores there, though it seems a strangely central place to store explosives. Eight bombs fell in the square two hundred yards short of the docks. One fell, incidentally, right at the mouth of a covered trench shelter, but did not damage it. There were only a few people in the trench, and they were all unhurt.

The other bombs fell four hundred yards from the Post Office, eight hundred from the railway station, and five hundred yards from the Parliament. They, too, could be fairly said to be close to military objectives.

It was not an example of indiscriminate bombing. There was no careless scattering of bombs regardless of targets. Nor was there any deliberate attempt to sow them in a purely civilian area—if such things exist in big cities. It could be described quite accurately as a raid carried out against military objectives—but carried out clumsily. And the hard fact remains that it was the civilians and not the docks or the Post Office which were hit.

The Russians must have been aware that this attack was bound to have a catastrophic effect on world opinion. They showed they knew this by later denying over the radio that there had been any attack on the centre of Helsinki. It is possible, of course, that the whole thing was a mistake. The Russians may have had a plan for war against Finland in which an air raid on Helsinki was one of the first moves. This plan may have just been dug out of a pigeon-hole and put into operation without revision. It is quite likely, for instance, that such a plan had been drawn up on the assumption that some third Power like Germany was using Finland as a base to attack the Soviet and that there was no need, therefore, to be over-nice about methods. Another explanation put forward is that Schadanov and the Leningrad high command, who had been advocating full-blooded war to crush not merely the Mannerheim Line but "the whole nest of Mannerheim Whites", started the war with a spectacular raid to make sure that there could be no return to the conference table for either Finns or Russians. For once Helsinki had been bombed and civilians lay dead in its streets no peace move would be easy.

What I believe to be the nearest to the truth is that the Russians made the attack for the same reason that they were to begin their invasion with inferior troops—because they thought the social structure of Finland was so rotten that one push would dislodge the present rulers. One raid like this would bring home to Helsinki and Finland the fact that the Russians meant business, that the Soviet Army was extremely powerful, and that if Finland resisted she would get no mercy. But, in fact, it had precisely the opposite effect. The Finns, with no unemployment, with prices still rising in their main export trades and with a sense of relief at being outside the conflict that had just started in the West, were more socially united than at any period since 1918. This sudden blow from the sky cemented cracks that still remained in that unity. Men of the Left who would have resented the return of Mannerheim to power were so infuriated by the brutality of this raid that they supported the war wholeheartedly.

Others who picked up pamphlets dropped by the Soviet planes saying that Finland's leaders wanted war and the Soviet wanted only peace were sickened by the knowledge that these were the same planes that had rained down the bombs.

The raid and the photographs it provided were used throughout Finland in the first month of the war as the main weapon of home propaganda. On every front I was to visit later man after man spoke angrily of this afternoon of November the 30th. I saw newspapers with photographs of the burning streets of Helsinki in peasants' homes and workers' flats all over the country. Not a little of the steel strength of Finnish morale in this war was due to the raid on Helsinki.

These Soviet bombs not only killed many men, women and children that afternoon; they killed a considerable body of potential friendship for the Soviet inside Finland which might have been a powerful help to Russia later.

CHAPTER III

WHAT STALIN WANTED

DIMLY LIT UP by the flames of burning buildings in Helsinki that night was a great dark structure, like an outsize Greek temple. It was the Finnish Diet. I had walked round there because I had heard that a full meeting of the Diet had been called. But I found the doors locked and a policeman turning the deputies' cars away. They were re-directed to a Trade Union hall in the suburbs of northern Helsinki which had been selected hastily as a secret meeting-place.

In this hall, the walls of which were still hung with rough posters advertising concerts and dances, the deputies sat in rows of chairs facing the stage. Several wore their uniforms as army officers newly mobilised. Just after seven-thirty A. J. Cajander, the Prime Minister, and his Cabinet, mounted the stage. The Premier made a short statement, saying that war had come despite the Government's efforts. He asked for a vote of confidence. It was taken by a show of hands. Every hand went up. Cajander then explained that his Cabinet now resigned, so that a new Government could be called. The present Cabinet was a coalition one, composed of Social-Democrats, agrarians and progressives, which were a liberal, bankers' group. He then led his Cabinet down from the stage and rang up President Kallio. The President said he would call on M. Risto Ryti, Chief Director of the Bank of Finland, to form a new Cabinet.

Cajander's Government, and particularly its Foreign Minister, M. E. Erkko, had carried through all the negotiations of the past six weeks which had led up to this autumn afternoon and its sudden Soviet raid. Tangled and remote, these talks had attracted little notice in the outside world. But in essence they were simple and straightforward.

Soviet Russia, the moment Germany's hands were tied by war with Britain and France, proceeded to shut and bolt the easiest approach to the Soviet Union—the routes along the shores of the Baltic and through the Gulf of Finland. Leningrad, the second largest city of the Union, lay right on the edge of the Gulf, exposed and vulnerable. Stalin himself knew how easily it could be attacked. In October 1919 he had, side by side with Trotsky, led the desperate fight of the people of Leningrad against the White general Yudenich, who had advanced up the south Baltic shore. Yudenich had in his army a British tank corps contingent under Colonel Carson. At the same time the British monitor, *Erebus*, working from Finnish ports was bombarding the fortress of Krasnoya Gorka. Seaplanes of the *Vindictive* attacked Leningrad harbour.

One route lay from East Prussia through Lithuania, Esthonia, Latvia. The second was through Finland and down the Karelian Isthmus, where the Finnish frontier was only twenty miles from the suburbs of Leningrad. Finland, as *The Times* wrote in 1919, is the key to Petrograd. The third route was through the waters of the Gulf of Finland, unless fortresses and a navy could block the sixty-mile entrance to the Gulf. Kolchak and the White Russians had regarded it as essential for the protection of "Petrograd" to have a base in the Baltic States and Finland. They let the Peace Conference know this definitely in 1919.

But the Soviet had none of these defences till Hitler went to war. Stalin had made some form of Baltic guarantee an essential condition of alliance with Britain and France. Mr. Chamberlain

WHAT STALIN WANTED

gave this in the House of Commons as one reason for the breakdown of the negotiations. The Soviet in the talks of the summer of 1939 had suggested that British, French and Soviet forces should occupy bases in the Baltic countries.

Hitler was less scrupulous or more determined than Mr. Chamberlain. He bought Stalin's support for his Polish war at the price of the Baltic and Finland. The Finns realised this as soon as Ribbentrop went to Moscow. They knew it doubly well when the Russians and the Germans remained good friends after the Polish war was over. The Finnish general, Wallenius, a Nazi in mind and sympathy if ever there was one, told me how he listened in, in the German Foreign Office, to Hitler's Danzig speech after the Polish war. He heard Hitler's warm friendly references to Russia. An official of the German Foreign Office turned to him after the speech:

"Well, General, wonderful, wasn't it?"

"Wonderful for you," said Finland's greatest pro-Nazi. "But not for Finland. I am going back there at once. That means war for us before the year is out."

Stalin lost no time in using the opportunity opened out to him. On September 24 the Esthonian Foreign Minister, M. Salter, was called to Moscow; by the 28th Esthonia had signed a pact of mutual assistance under which the Russians got a base at Baltischport, opposite the Finnish fortresses of Hango; they got, too, bases at Dago and Osel, and the right to garrison troops on the mainland. By October 21 the Red Army, equipped with tanks and heavy guns, was in possession. Planes of the Red air force were already on the fields near Tallin—the fields from which the first raids on Helsinki were to be made.

By October 2 it was the Latvians who were in Moscow. To settle things with them only three days were necessary. On October 5 Libava and Ventspils became Soviet naval and air bases. Again the Red Army moved farther west, pushing the Soviet frontier farther away from Leningrad. On the 10th of October Lithuania followed. Vilna, seized by the Soviet from the Poles, who had in turn grabbed it from Lithuania, was restored, and the Soviet got rights to keep troops and planes on Lithuanian soil. The south road to Leningrad was bolted and barred, and half the Gulf of Finland held too, from Libava and Baltischport. It remained only to close the Finnish road and the Finnish side of the Gulf. This was a task in quite a different category from that of securing concessions from the smaller Baltic states—and to Russia far more important. For Finland was not only a State, for her size, of considerable military strength, but many of her most influential leaders were deeply and bitterly anti-Soviet, and among the mass of the people there remained much instinctive anti-Russian feeling dating from the long periods of warfare between the two countries in the past. Mannerheim and the other chief Right-wing Finnish leaders had never made any secret of their detestation of the Soviet régime. In the days of the wars of intervention against the Bolsheviks their sympathy was clearly on the White side. Mannerheim himself had called for Finland to join Yudenich's drive on Leningrad in 1919. The Finns, incidentally, bear some responsibility for the death of John Reed, the American correspondent who wrote the classic of the Russian revolution, *Ten Days that Shook the World*. He was imprisoned in Helsinki on his way from Russia, and held incommunicado. He was not even allowed to let his friends know that he was arrested, and the American consul was met with a blank statement that no such man was held in prison. Reed only got word out of his arrest by smuggling out a false story that he had died in prison. This made such a stir that to disprove it the Finnish prison authorities had to produce Reed from their cells. But his imprisonment there had damaged his already shaken health.

Throughout the twenties and thirties this antagonism towards the Soviet was still a powerful force in Finland. Part of the Press was for years bitterly anti-Bolshevik. When Hitler came to power the close relations which had always existed between the Finnish and German General Staffs provided a link with the country which, right up till August 1939, appeared most likely to attack Russia. True, Russia and the Nazis were now slapping each other on the back in intimate style, but the moment this friendship collapsed and the Nazis turned against the Soviet there was no doubt that they could count on much support among Finland's conservatives. Even if that support was insufficient to carry the day against the mass of Finnish people, who would not want to be dragged into any war of Germany against Russia, the Germans would probably—as the case of Norway, Holland, Belgium and Denmark have shown—have been prepared to move in and use Finland as a base anyway. No one knew this better than Stalin.

But for all this relations between Russia and Finland were, in 1939, at about the most cordial stage they had ever been since 1918. The Finns were enjoying a period of comparative prosperity again, and there were no labour troubles that could make the employers angry about "Bolshevik influences". The horrors of the Polish war had made the Finnish people even more anxious to avoid being drawn into the present world struggle. They wanted neutrality, like all the small States of Europe. They just wanted to keep out. Even those who were violent crusaders against the Bolsheviks knew that this moment, with Germany allied with Russia and occupied in the West, was the last one in which to pick a quarrel with the Soviet.

On October 5 the Finnish Minister in Moscow, M. Yrjo Koskinen, was asked to call at the Kremlin. Molotov received him and said the Soviet would like the Finnish Foreign Minister or some other delegate to join the other Baltic visitors in Moscow to "discuss concrete political questions". Three days later, when the Finns had not made any move, the Soviet Minister in Helsinki, Dereviansky, called on Erkko and dropped some very definite hints that the Soviet was in an impatient mood. So the next day J. K. Paasikivi, one of the Finns who signed the Tartu peace in 1920 with the Soviet, was sent off to Moscow by train. He was met with a blunt demand for all the chief islands in the Gulf of Finland, for a rolling back of the frontier in Karelia for over thirty miles, so as to get the Finns' guns well away from Leningrad, for part of the Fisherman's Peninsula which would give Russia complete control of the ice-free port of Petsamo in the far north and, above all, for the peninsula of Hango, at the south-west corner of Finland. This, with its two naval fortress islands and its harbour, held the real key to the Gulf of Finland.

In return the Russians offered to hand over some territory just north of the Finnish "waist-line"—stretches of forest of no military value.

The Finns refused, primarily on the issue of Hango. That was the point on which they would not give way. Though they haggled over the others, they were prepared to cede the islands in the Gulf, to push back the frontier, even to cede the Petsamo area, but Hango—no. Their General Staff knew that the harbour here had won for them the civil war when German troops had landed there and hit the Helsinki Red Army in the back. Russian troops landing there again could take the Finns from the rear. In Russia's hands it was a pistol pressed into Finland's back. Russia wanted to keep 5,000 men there, with tanks and planes. With these they could hold the peninsula of Hango against any attack from the land, make the sea fortresses absolutely safe.

For a month Finnish delegations came and went to Moscow. Vaino Tanner, the Finnish Co-operative leader, who had known Lenin, joined Paasikivi. Stalin himself joined in the talks, smoked his pipe, joked with the delegates. Molotov tried to force matters by letting all the details of the negotiations out at a speech to the Supreme Congress of Soviets when the Finns were keeping them solidly dark. But every time it came back to the question of Hango, the Finns said "No". On the 13th of November their delegates finally left Moscow, and the talks were broken off. Russia was not to begin them again till Ryti and his peace delegation went to Moscow the next March.

Yet things still did not look like war. Stalin had wished Tanner and Paasikivi good luck as they left. The Finns expressed hopes that everything would be settled "in a way satisfactory to both parties". In Finland the evacuees who had left the cities in early October began to drift back. Correspondents wrote that the Finnish Foreign Office believed that merely a war of nerves was settling in. Moscow would keep Finland mobilised and at tension point till she crumpled under the strain. The Finns, a tough race, prepared not to crumple.

They had already called up the greater part of their army reserves. The first classes were mobilised as soon as the Russians invited a delegate to Moscow. By mid-October they had 300,000 men under arms. The Finnish army command was taking no chances and the politicians wanted their bargaining power strengthened. On the Isthmus the Mannerheim Line, begun just before the Czech crisis of 1938, was rushed to completion. The Karelian troops, always the pick of the army, were filled out with carefully selected men. War material was hastily bought abroad, Germany obligingly selling at profit much of that seized in Poland. Air-raid shelters were dug and roofed in with logs and earth in the cities. By the third week in November all men up to forty were under arms, except a big list of men in reserved occupations such as pulp works and the metal industry.

From November 13 the lull lasted right up to the last week of the month. The Finns awaited another call to Moscow, and pondered over what compromise they could offer at Hango. An island just off the coast, suitable for a naval base, from which Russia could close the Gulf of Finland but not dominate the Finnish mainland was discussed.

But no further invitations to Moscow came. Instead, on November 26, came a move ominously reminiscent of the opening stages of the Polish crisis. The Soviet Press announced furiously that Finnish artillery had fired across the frontier in Carelia near the village of Mainila, killing four and wounding nine Soviet troops. ¡The Soviet Government protested and demanded that the Finnish troops should move back fifteen miles. The Finns denied the charge, offered a joint investigation, and proposed a mutual withdrawal of troops from the frontier. The next day, Tuesday, November 28, the Soviet turned down this suggestion scornfully, pointing out that its troops would have to withdraw right into the outskirts of Leningrad. It then denounced the Soviet-Finnish Non-Aggression Pact. On Wednesday it formally broke off diplomatic relations with Finland. Alarmed, the Finns hastily suggested arbitration, and offered to withdraw their troops after all from the frontiers, though Soviet forces had already advanced over the frontier near Petsamo, at Pummanki. This was apparently to be overlooked as being "just a frontier incident".

But at dawn next day the Finns found that matters had gone beyond frontier incidents. On almost every road leading from Russia to Finland Soviet guns opened fire at dawn, and tanks rolled up to the customs barriers, smashed them, and moved on into Finland, followed by the peak-capped infantry of the Red Army. Within two hours, once the mist was gone from the flying fields, the first Soviet planes were on their way across the Gulf of Finland towards the Finnish shores, and the crowded streets of Helsinki.

Even so on the night of those first raids, the Finns made one last attempt to get the Russians back to the negotiations table. The resignation of the Cajander Government was, to a large extent, the expression of a desperate last-moment bid for peace. It is true that the Cajander would probably have resigned, anyway, to make way for the wider National Government essential for waging war. But on this night of November 30, as they drove through the streets lit by the flames from the bombs, the deputies were still thinking of above all getting peace. They had not expected war. The raid that afternoon was a direct shock to them and a terrible realisation of the possibilities ahead. They knew that the Moscow Press and radio were thundering that it was impossible to deal any longer with the present Finnish Government. If Cajander and Erkko resigned, and another wider Cabinet came in, perhaps the Russians might come back to the conference table? There seemed a particularly good chance of this if Tanner, the Socialist minister, who knew Stalin personally, were made Foreign Minister. At least that change might stop Helsinki being bombed again the next morning, stop the Russian bombers coming over the streets of the city again the moment dawn broke.

It was certainly worth a change of government to stop that. Even though Monsieur Ryti did not get his new Cabinet formed till the next afternoon both the Swedish and the United States Legations in Helsinki were informed that night, unofficially but unmistakably, that the old Government had resigned in order to leave no obstacle to a resumption of negotiations. Both Legations were asked to hand on this message to their Legations in Moscow and to have it brought to the knowledge of the Kremlin. M. Toivala, head of the Finnish Foreign Office Press Department, told an official of the United States Legation in front of me in the hall of the Hotel Kamp later that evening, that this was the real reason behind the Cabinet change. He asked him to see that the American Minister was informed at once.

Toivala then went even further. He decided to get into the foreign Press the information that Finland was still willing to talk. He therefore called several of us together and told us that the new Cabinet had actually been formed and that it was willing to resume negotiations with the Russians any time they liked. It was, in fact, inaccurate to say the Cabinet was formed. It was only in the process of being formed. But the basic fact that they wanted to talk was true. For the first thing the new Cabinet did the next afternoon was to let the Russians know, via the Swedes, that they would like to negotiate if possible. Several correspondents sent messages to say the Finns had virtually capitulated. The Russians, it seemed, would now be able to get what they wanted without further fighting. I sat down and wrote a message to this effect and phoned from my room in the Hotel Kamp at three o'clock that morning in front of M. Toivala, who was sitting there drinking a late-night whiskey with a group of us. He heard every word I said. He speaks perfect English. He agreed it summed up the situation. That message, incidentally, never got farther than Copenhagen, for not even this new war made the Ministry of Information in London keep the telephone censors working after midnight. (Later, in Brussels, I could not send the story of the German invasion for the same reason.) It matters little, it seems, if the British public is informed or not of what happens after twelve o'clock at night. They can wait until the next day. For the censors must sleep, it seems, even if journalists do not.

Yes, it looked that night as if the Russians were not merely going to win, but had already won. As my colleague Ronald Panton said from Copenhagen, this had been a one-day blitzkrieg. I went to bed exhausted, but with the feeling that there would be plenty of time to relax the next morning. Then I woke at nine and heard the wail of sirens, and I knew I was wrong. The Soviet planes were coming over again. And twenty-four hours later we had the final diplomatic confirmation that the time for talking was past. The Soviet Government had answered the Finnish offer of negotiation, handed on by the Swedes on the afternoon of December 2, with the curt reply that it recognised only one Finnish Government, the "People's Front" Government of Otto Kuusinen, set up at Terijoki, behind the advancing Red armies. It was war.

CHAPTER IV

INVASION

EARLY IN THE morning of Thursday, November 30, the Finnish Colonel in charge of troops on the road leading from the Soviet Frontier at Inari to the rail junction of Lieksa, half-way up the frontier between Lake Ladoga and the "waist line" of Finland, received a hurried call over the field telephone from his frontier patrols. They reported that at 6 a.m. five Russian tanks had crossed the border and were advancing down the road into Finnish territory. Infantry were following them. The Colonel at once rang through to the General Staff, then at its headquarters at Mikele, and reported the news. The officer who took the message was incredulous. The Finnish General Staff did not expect an immediate invasion at this moment. "Are you quite sure?" he queried. "It couldn't be just that they had mistaken their way?"

"No, my men report that they are definitely advancing steadily into Finnish territory."

The staff officer paused a moment. Then he replied:

"Well, you know what to do about it."

The Soviet invasion had actually started the day before at Petsamo. At Pummanki, on the Fisherman's Peninsula to the north of Petsamo, where the Finnish frontier guards had their barracks, Soviet infantry had advanced and opened fire in the afternoon. The Finns retreated by boat to the mainland, though more than fifteen were cut off. Three were taken prisoner. The rest fell fighting.

An hour after dawn it was clear that this and the Inari affair were not merely frontier incidents. On all six roads leading from Leningrad to the Carelian Isthmus; on the five chief roads north of Ladoga; at Lieksa and at Kuhmo; on the Rattee Road, and by another route that the Finns had not been aware of north of Kianta Lake, above Suomussalmi; at Salla and across the open fells just below Petsamo poured the Red Army. They advanced at every point where the road system offered a way through the jungle-like Finnish forests along the entire 500-mile frontier from the Arctic to the Gulf of Finland. The only point where no advance was made was at Kuusamo between Salla and Suomussalmi. Here there was an excellent road system on the Finnish side, but the approaches on the Soviet side of the frontier were not good.

In most of the areas into which the Russians marched the Finnish civilians had been evacuated and houses in the border regions burnt. Where this had not been done, the civilians were hastily taken out during this first day. Petsamo, for instance, was full of its normal population. It was completely emptied within twenty-four hours. At Suojoki, the buttonhook of territory hanging down into Russia north of Lake Ladoga, the civil authorities forgot to give the evacuation order. The civilians were there when the Red Army marched in. The Finns claimed that one wealthy merchant and his wife were shot.

On the Isthmus the people in several unevacuated villages rushed panic-stricken out of their houses when they heard the guns and saw Russian tanks rolling up the road. Some of them apparently ran across a Finnish minefield, exploding it. This is, I think, the most logical explanation of the story, put out by the Finnish Press Bureau at the time, that the Red Army drove Polish women and children ahead of them to blow up mines.

This frontier area on the Isthmus had been turned by the Finns into one huge minefield. In Terijoki, the former Czarist seaside resort, the Finns left the window of the co-operative store filled with food tins, but packed the building with mines. Red Army men who opened the door and forced their way in were smashed to bits.

The first official Finnish announcement of the attacks was made on the night of December 3, the fourth day of the war. It was read out in an upstairs conference room at the Hotel Kamp by Brotherus, a slight young man in the Foreign Office. The handful of us who were there took it down as he dictated it. The days of packed Press conferences, cyclostyled communiqués, an elaborate Press bureau, were yet to come. Looking into my notebook I find: "Bulletin. Soviet troops began war operations at dawn on Thursday, crossing the frontier in several places. Security detachments of Finnish troops fought them. Soon general fighting was in progress on all roads leading from Russia to Finland. The security detachments retired according to plan. Between six and nine tanks were destroyed. The main Russian attacks this first day were at Lipola, in Carelia, and Suojärvi, north of Ladoga. Russian planes bombed Viipuri, Helsinki, Abo, Lahti, Kotka, killing and wounding civilians as well as troops."

Later, in tents and dugouts on the front, I was to learn what the expression "security detachments of Finnish troops fought them" had meant in reality that autumn morning. North of Kianta, there were only sixty Finnish troops and one officer, Lieutenant Arno Irane, facing an entire Russian division, the 163rd. The Finns fought their way back for ten days against the Red Army advance guard. At the end fifteen of the Finns were killed and thirty-six wounded. Nine men alone escaped unharmed. At Salla one Finnish battalion was to fight a division over the main road for fourteen days. At Inari the Finnish troops had watched the first tanks with apprehension. The Captain commanding the frontier company saw that not one man wanted to make the first attack with the hand grenade. So he took the grenade himself.

"I was scared enough myself," he told us later. "But I knew that it was them or us."

So he flung the grenade at the caterpillar of the front tank.

"Fortunately the thing was only on a reconnaissance patrol, it seems, and it turned around and moved back the moment the crew heard the explosion," he went on. "As far as I could see, I didn't do the tank any damage. But my men got encouragement. They realised these things weren't invulnerable. An hour later another patrol of tanks came down. This time the Sergeant and two men at once took grenades and went for them. By the end of the day the bulk of my company had lost the first fear we all felt of these great lumbering brutes."

On the second day the Red Army came on again. The sirens I heard in the early morning at Helsinki were a warning for planes flying towards centres farther inland. It was the first of the four alarms of that day. I cursed when I heard the wail, but decided, after the news I had had the night before, to try to get some more sleep. At that moment there was a great pounding on my door. I jumped out, grabbed my dressing-gown, and opened the door to find standing there a tall, angular woman in the late thirties, wearing a very British coat and skirt and a thin greyish fur that looked right out of a country drawing-room. She was hammering on the door with a woman's shoe and shouting in English, "Air-raid alarm. Air-raid alarm."

As a journalist one sees strange sights, but this spectacle, in the heart of distant Finland, staggered me. I blinked, and the lady shouted in a very country voice, "Come on, come on. I'm a fully-trained air-raid warden. Downstairs."

Mentally noting that the export of air-raid wardenesses in wartime should surely be prohibited, I dressed and made my melancholic way down to the bar, which seemed the safest place. There was no coffee, but I got a glass of beer. With this I settled down wearily at a table and made another mental note that whiskey drunk at 3 a.m. can leave a horrible feeling in an air-raid alarm. The air-raid wardeness suddenly reappeared. "Now then, all against the wall. All against the wall," she shouted, in English. The patient Finnish women who had rushed in from the street stared in amazement. This, their expressions seemed to say, is clearly part of modern war. Strange women shout at you in strange tongues. With infinite dignity they let themselves be herded against the wall. I mentally underlined my thoughts about the export of air-raid wardenesses.

At midday the sirens went again. I was on my way from the first hospital, where I had talked with Professor Palmen about the wounded and dead from the previous day's raid, when I noticed the crew of a machine-gun on a barracks roof suddenly rush to their gun. Then came the wail.

I got into an open trench in the middle of a square. The guns sounded, and with them the roar of planes. It was a dull day with a low grey ceiling of cloud. Nine black bombers of medium size cut across the corner of the sky, flying at about 2,000 feet. Suddenly a guard on the pavement shouted, "One's down."

Half an hour later I got to its wreckage, in a patch of pines in the western suburbs of the city. The tangled smashed pieces were on fire. It was a two-engined medium bomber. The tail, with the letters "S.B." and huge dull red Soviet star, lay against a tree. Near was a bloody, tangled mess that had been the pilot's head and his khaki-clad torso. His hands were tightly clenched. I noted they were very small. The bodies of the two other members of the crew had already been carried away. Finnish guards came up with a piece of planking, dragged the smashed torso on to it and carried it away, too.

What had he been, this pilot, I wondered, whose life had finished like this? Young, eager to fight for Socialism, to build a better world? After adventure, or just a better job? It no longer mattered to him. His life was finished on this grey afternoon as he flew above the buildings of Helsinki. It could matter only to his family and friends and to the outside world now. Yet what had he thought, I wondered, when he received his orders to bring his plane and its cargo of bombs over this city? My mind went back to the air battles I had watched over Madrid when the snub-nosed Soviet chasers had meant salvation and freedom from the bombers. Crowds had cheered them as deliverers—crowds very like these quiet-faced Finns who now stared at this wreckage as they had stared towards the sky a few moments before. Did this war seem different to this pilot? Probably not. Probably he had shrugged his shoulders and obeyed orders, as millions of young men are doing all over the world to-day. When I saw that body lying there I realised, as never before, the enormous strength of any organised machine and how little the individual's feelings need count. Crowds of curious Finns gathered, picking up pieces of the machine as souvenirs. Two air officials, a film camera man, and a mechanic arrived. The propeller was carefully carried away. We interviewed a sixteen-year-old boy who had fired his rifle at the plane after it crashed. Three hours later—just to show how stories grow in wartime—I was solemnly assured in the dining-room of the Hotel Kamp that this boy had not only shot down the plane with his rifle, but finished off the pilot with his knife. In actual fact the plane had been hit by anti-aircraft fire.

This machine was one of seven that the Finns claimed to have shot down over Helsinki that day.

Colleagues of mine saw two others. They were both the same twin-engined medium "S.B." Soviet bomber, an American model built on licence in the Soviet. It was impossible personally to check all the Finnish air claims, but the British Military Attaché did so in these early days, and told me that he was certain that up to the figure of 250 planes brought down—reached about mid-January—every claim was justified. Bombs had fallen near the gas-works and the grid on the outskirts of Helsinki, and three workers' houses in the Munksnas suburb were hit. Other bombs had hit the porcelain factory Arabia and petrol storage tanks. The official figures were five dead and eleven wounded.

It was during this raid that the Soviet bombers were accused of swooping down and machine-gunning civilians on the roads. When I drove out to see the smashed machine, I noted the woods on either side of the road were filled with civilians in hiding. It was here the Finns declared that the people had cowered as the machines swooped down with their guns blazing. I pointed out to the Finnish official who told me this that it might well have been the bullets of Finnish anti-aircraft machine-guns. Later, however, an A.R.P. worker named Otto Tuli and a stretcher bearer declared that machine-gun bullets had smashed up the dust in the street opposite the S.O.K. Co-operative Buildings. A nineteen-year-old student name Taisto Saarinen declared that from the roof of an elementary school he saw planes come over and swoop down. Sparks then came from the telephone wires which swayed and were cut. This, he was convinced, was due to machine-gun fire. He saw the ambulances come and pick up people who had been wounded in the street. No bombs had been dropped there so it must have been bullets. Patients in the Diakonisa Hospital, so the Superintendent stated, were brought in suffering from machine-gun wounds. These witnesses and others gave their evidence later in greater detail to Sir Walter Citrine when he visited Finland with the Labour Delegation. Of course, the Russians may have been using their machine-guns against anti-aircraft gunners stationed on the house-tops and the civilians may have been hit in these attacks. The Finns had machine-guns on many of the chief buildings of Helsinki, and they had also excellent Bofors anti-aircraft guns, though very few of them.

The machine-gunning was, in fact, in much the same category as the bombing—the civilians may have been hit by missiles aimed at military objectives. But it does not make much difference to your civilian, if he is hit, what the bullet was really aimed at. The fact once again remained that the Russians had attacked Helsinki and had killed civilians there.

The seven planes brought down were shot down by Finnish anti-aircraft guns and not by fighter planes. The planes which made the attacks had been over the city within a few minutes of the sirens going. In the pockets of one of the pilots shot down Esthonian coins were found. It seemed clear that the raids were coming from the new bases near Tallin, twenty minutes' flight away across the water. The Soviet had apparently adopted the silent approach tactics the Italians had used when bombing Barcelona, a city situated, like Helsinki, beside the sea. They climbed to a height of fifteen to eighteen thousand feet, then shut off their engines, and swooped silently down over the city.

One of the machines had been brought down by an ex-world champion at pigeon shooting, Dr. Forselles. He had been serving with a machine-gun unit stationed on top of the green and white hundred-foot Olympic tower close to the heart of Helsinki, where the Olympic games were to have been held. The present world pigeon shooting champion was also serving with anti-aircraft gun specialists near Helsinki.

The sirens kept wailing alarms and all clears till dark came just after four. I hurried back to the Kamp to try to get a phone call through to London. When I got there news was just out that Moscow had set up in Terijoki a Communist régime under a former Finnish Communist, Otto Kuusinen. It threw a completely new light on the Russian tactics and aims.

CHAPTER V

KUUSINEN

TWO DAYS PREVIOUSLY, on the afternoon of November 29, the eve of the war, a very strange thing had happened on the frontier at Alakurtti, near Salla in Lapland. Up the forest road that led to the Russian and Finnish customs barriers, a Soviet military band suddenly marched. It came right to the barrier, halted and played the Internationale. After that it settled down and played a whole programme of Soviet military tunes.

The Finnish frontier guards rang up the commander of the area, Colonel Villamo, a genial warrior who had been commander of forces in Lapland since the last war. The guard held the telephone out of the window so that the music could be heard clearly.

"As soon as I caught those notes I told my officer to issue ammunition and stand ready for anything," the Colonel told me later. "The next morning came the first Soviet attack. Our first dead were killed right on the very barrier itself where the band had been playing. God knows what that concert meant. I suppose they wanted to put our men into a good humour."

The reason for this musical ceremony became a little clearer, as did the whole mysterious sudden outbreak of war, when the Moscow radio on December 1 announced that a Finnish popular Government had been set up at Terijoki, a little town just inside the Finnish border on the Carelian Isthmus. Its premier was Otto V. Kuusinen, a Finnish Communist exile and former general secretary of the Comintern. The band at Alakurtti had been the first propaganda move in his favour. The war was no longer one just for Hango or a change of strategic positions on the Isthmus. It was now to go the whole way to overthrow capitalism in Finland. Kuusinen, it was announced, had offered to establish diplomatic relations with the U.S.S.R. and had suggested a pact of mutual assistance. The Soviet had "replied" by recognising the Kuusinen Cabinet as the legal Government of Finland and agreeing to "lend assistance to that republic by armed forces with a view to the joint liquidation at the earliest possible moment of the very dangerous seat of war created in Finland by its former rulers".

This news was brought to the "former rulers" in Helsinki just as M. Ryti's new Cabinet had entered into office. Sir Risto Ryti (he was knighted in 1929 by the British) was a financier and head of the Bank of Finland. He had come out in 1924, like Dr. Schacht in Germany, as the man who stabilised the Finnish currency. His Cabinet, which he formed now, was described later, and accurately, as a bankers' and business-men's Cabinet. It was wide, including men from all parties except the I.K.L. Fascist Party and, of course, the banned Communists. Vaino Tanner became Foreign Minister. The Cabinet formation was delayed because Field-Marshal Mannerheim, it is said, was not very keen on Ryti. This is an interesting indication of the influence of the man whom Ralph Hewins of the *Daily Mail* aptly called the "uncrowned King of Finland", and who was now coming once again right to the fore.

Moscow's Kuusinen move immediately changed the whole aspect of the war. The Finnish "bankers' Cabinet", as the *Daily Telegraph* termed it, realised it was no longer conducting a war just over a question of military bases or frontiers. It was fighting for its very existence, for the existence of the system on which their whole society was founded. They knew now that they were fighting now for both their property and their lives. They realised that the Soviet were out for complete socialisation, or at least the formation of a semi-Socialist Government inside Finland. They determined to fight back hard.

This sudden production of a Communist régime, following so soon after the bombing of Helsinki, proved from a military point of view alone a great Russian blunder. It strengthened at once the fighting morale of the Finnish peasants, who made up sixty per cent of the Finnish population and the bulk of the army. Since the land reforms of the Lex Kallio of 1927 the bulk of the Finnish peasants were individual land-owners. They felt now that they were no longer fighting about some diplomatic trouble but were battling to keep their farms. The Boer War had shown Great Britain what "embattled farmers" could do. At the same time, Finland's owning classes suddenly found themselves facing not just a national war in which some compromise might be possible but a class war.

Nor did the appearance of Kuusinen as a Left-wing leader do anything to balance this by rousing stronger Left-wing feeling; indeed, it put pro-Soviet feeling farther back among the workers in the country. The mass of them were already angered by the bombing of Helsinki. Others, however socialistic in outlook, resented bitterly this Soviet invasion and the announcement by Russia that she had settled Finland's fate by recognising Kuusinen. The Finns, I found during the whole of my time in the country, definitely wanted the right to settle their own internal affairs. Even those who were well aware that their country was by nature of its trade greatly in the grip of the Western Powers, still resented direct Russian intervention in their internal affairs. They were against what one Finn described to me as "Communism by conquest". It would not work, he assured me, any more than Napoleon's campaigns to abolish feudalism all over Europe worked when the National factors came into play.

These two initial moves—the bombing of Helsinki, and the appointment of Kuusinen—solidified the Finnish people behind Ryti and Mannerheim in a way which seemed unbelievable when one thinks of the civil troubles which had torn Finland, not only in 1918, but during the Lapua Fascist movement in 1931 and 1932. That solidity was to remain till the end of this war.

Kuusinen was the chief Comintern expert for Finland, but he was not an ideal man for the job of winning over the Finnish workers to the Russian side in 1939. Fifty-nine years old, he had been an exile since the collapse of the Red régime in Helsinki in 1918. He had kept no great grip on the sympathies of the Finnish workers. From the University he had gone straight into politics in the old Finnish Social-Democratic Party after the war. In his earlier views he had swung between revolutionary and reformist standpoints. In 1905, when all of Finland joined the up-surge of revolution in Russia, he joined the November Socialists—a militant revolutionary group. But in 1911, after three years in the Finnish Parliament, he condemned violence as "a bourgeois method of fighting". In 1918 he was a member of the Finnish Government in Helsinki which fought Mannerheim and the Whites. After the victory of the Whites, he wrote a long and a very intelligent analysis of the civil war in which he declared that the greatest error of the Finnish Social-Democratic Party had not been to be outspokenly Communist. They should have proclaimed the slogan "Dictatorship of the Proletariat", instead of just "Democracy". The workers, he said, wanted to fight for more than their leaders were prepared to accept.

After 1918 he fled to Moscow, and became the first Secretary-General of the Comintern. In this post his name appeared as one of the signatories of the Zinovieff letter. He came into close touch with Stalin in Moscow, at the time when Stalin was Commissar for Nationalities. In the Communist politics during the troubled period of the twenties, he sided consistently with Stalin against Trotsky. When the British Trade Union delegation went to Moscow in 1924, Kuusinen was working as Stalin's secretary and sat in the same office with the Georgian leader when the delegation was received. Kuusinen himself came back from time to time, in disguise, to Finland. Aleksi Aaltonen, now secretary of the Finnish Social-Democratic Party, who had been in his day an exile in Russia from the white terror and later amnestied, told me that the last visit Kuusinen had made to Helsinki with his knowledge was in 1928. From that time on, though he kept in close touch with the underground Finnish Communist Party, he seems to have played a fairly modest bureaucratic rôle in the Comintern until Stalin suddenly thrust him under the glare of spotlights in Terijoki.

The Finns, in the official statement they issued at this time, criticised him chiefly in being a Left-wing careerist. "In Soviet Russia," the statement read, "he has succeeded in steering his way past the secret reefs on which many immigrés, among them many Finns, have foundered . . . when the Finnish Red Government was defeated several of its members fled to Russia. During the course of the time, however, these men have silently vanished from the scene. The only one who has avoided that general fate of exiles is O. V. Kuusinen." One of the delegates from abroad who attended the first meeting of the Comintern immediately after the war, told me that to his knowledge Kuusinen in those early days became the leading Finnish Communist in Russia by a process of rather rudimentary natural selection. One day late in 1918, the chief members of the Finnish Communist Party executive (then in exile after Mannerheim's victory) were holding a meeting in a building in Leningrad. Two Finns, who were either Fifth Columnists, or dissident Communists who disliked the line laid down by this exile executive, broke into a room and killed or wounded all except Kuusinen, who happened to be sitting nearest the door. He bolted out and got away.

Incidentally, it would be of interest, now the war is over, to find out if Kuusinen and his supporters ever actually went to the village of Terijoki which was nominally their capital, or whether they worked all the time from the greater convenience and security of the Comintern headquarters in Moscow. Finnish patrols tried to get through to the village and investigate, and claimed they found it empty. But the Russian front was pushed ahead and solidified too rapidly for further investigation. Planes bombed the village once or twice, but they were needed for more important tasks. Kuusinen's wife, who had remained in Finland, served throughout the war as a Lotta and his two sons, called up with their classes, fought on the Isthmus with the Finnish army.

The Finnish Press Bureau claimed that he was not even any longer a Finnish citizen, as he had taken out Russian nationality. But since Communism is a movement standing for internationalism this point hardly seems of importance. His name was very Finnish. It is by chance also that of a large Finnish drapery firm which has branches all over the country. One of the first things I saw when I got off the train at Viipuri was a big sign Kuusinen on a shop front; in Helsinki as I drove to the airport to return after the war I saw another sky sign which had had the "K" removed, and remained throughout the war "uusinen". It was certainly more Finnish than that of his Finance Minister at Terijoki, another exile from Helsinki, who had the name of Rosenberg.

Moscow at once began a formidable radio propaganda campaign for the Kuusinen Government. I found officials of the Finnish Press Bureau listening in to the first of these talks that evening in the Kamp. It looked as if we were to see total war, both on the front and at the rear. I stared out at the Finnish flag on the barracks across the street, and wondered if I would ever be in Helsinki to see it replaced by the Red Flag.

CHAPTER VI

AIR WAR: STAGE ONE

THE NEXT THREE days in Helsinki were days of air terror without air raids. The psychological shock of the mid-afternoon raid on November 30 was so great that, even though no other attack of such violence was ever made again on the capital during the war, an atmosphere of fear hung over the city at least until the beginning of the next week. It was intensified by a fever of rumours. These may have been deliberately spread by Soviet agents, or may have been due to genuine misinformation on the part of the Finnish authorities, or may have been just wild irresponsible whisperings of wartime. But everyone, not merely the uninformed, but even high officials, were convinced that there would be a mass air raid in which the centre of the city would be levelled as part of an attempt to finish Finland at one blow. Every minute of the daylight, from eight-thirty in the morning till four in the afternoon, the people who remained in the city these days waited to hear again the roar of planes. Death seemed always just overhead. When I look back on those days, the very physical atmosphere seemed to be affected by this feeling. The air seemed, as it were, darker, the sky low and menacing. At night the streets were dark gruesome canyons where fear lurked. Barbara Alving, the woman correspondent of the Stockholm paper *Dagens Nyheter*, who was by far the best Scandinavian journalist, howled out to me at this time that one's imagination tended to run no farther than the next morning at nine. You knew that then the sirens would go. On to what happened after that you simply ran down a shutter in your mind.

The strain in these days was worse than anything I knew in Madrid, though there, in the night raid on November 19, the damage was much greater and more spectacular than the Soviet had effected in Helsinki. It was similar in many ways to the strain of the first bombing of London. Yet the people of Helsinki were as tough and calm as the Spaniards. I put the difference down to the fact that the first Soviet raid was utterly unexpected. It came on a people psychologically quite unprepared for immediate war, and it knocked them, as it were, off their balance. Look at what had happened. There had been a sunny afternoon in Helsinki, some diplomatic tension about which the ordinary man or woman has only a confused idea; a morning alarm which passes off without any incident in the centre of the city; and then, suddenly, planes are overhead and death is in the street right beside you. It was as if the Germans had suddenly bombed London on the afternoon of the Godesberg talks. It showed, I believe, that if you launch a sudden civilian raid when your enemy is not expecting attack, you can have a devastating effect on civilian nerves. One military attaché in Helsinki who fought through the last war told me that he never felt so frightened in his life as that afternoon in the capital after the raid. "There was a kind of infectious terror," he said. London was to some extent spared this shock, though the attacks on Helsinki were only pin-pricks compared to the blitz on London, which is incomparably the greatest air offensive undertaken against any city in the world. For London was infinitely better prepared, not only militarily but mentally, to take it. We had been steadily hardened to the thought that one day we might die under an enemy bomb attack. Our ears were attuned, as it were, to the sirens. This would not have been so, however, if we had been suddenly attacked at the time of Godesberg or Munich, and it was not so in Helsinki. The result there was to give the bulk of the people a form of mild or bomb shock.

I saw evidence of it everywhere in the next few days. In the banks and shops people had tightly knit brows, strained eyes that showed they had slept badly. On the trams, packed with people heading for the railway or for bus stops, there were disputes over places, quarrels about baggage. In the lobby of the Hotel Kamp the porters were tired and irritable. The woman behind the cigarette stall in the corner looked worn out. When I went over to speak to her I noticed a tiny figure curled up under the counter. "It's my daughter," she explained. "I'm afraid to leave her at home, alone, so she stays here with me all day."

But steadily the Finns fought this sense of shock. They fought it in a typically Finnish way, by concentrating on the job at hand, which was to get their city evacuated.

Within four days, the Finns got two-thirds of the people out of the capital. At least 200,000 were moved out. From Helsinki there was only one railway line available and the roads were slippery with ice and fresh snow. On the first night of the raids, thousands of people fled on foot and on bicycle into the woods. Others stormed on to the trains. But the majority were moved out under careful evacuation schemes worked out by the city authorities. The town director, Baron Von Fraenkel, a burly shrewd man, explained the scheme of it to me later.

"We arranged a shuttle system of buses, taxis and cars, which the Automobile Association and private owner-drivers supplied. They moved people from fixed assembly points inside the city to places thirty-five miles out on the five main roads. Each driver took a full load, motored out at top speed, dropped people at intermediate villages if they had friends or relatives there, and then simply left the remainder in the first village after the fifty-kilometre stone. They turned round then and drove back for more. The people knew the assembly points in the city to go to in advance. Every district had been informed earlier by notices in the papers and by letters. At the assembly points and at the 'deposit centres', beyond the fifty-kilometre mark, the Lottas—the A.T.S. of Finland—ran coffee stalls and rest centres.

"In the reception villages we got all churches and schools heated. Into them went the people as they arrived. From each place the provincial authorities and the automobile clubs had arranged further distribution schemes. They drove in with their cars and buses, picked up loads, and carried them on to towns and villages prepared to receive them. You must remember Finland is largely a peasant country, and most people have a brother or a father or an uncle or a cousin on the land. Farm houses and farm tables are elastic things, and two or three related families fit in fairly easily. The farmers were often glad of the extra hands about the house, as most of their men were called up for service. Those people who did not have anywhere definite to go were billeted in schools, halls, cinemas—anything handy. We had no compulsory billeting scheme as you used in England, though many people volunteered to take evacuees. Paavo Nurmi, the famous runner, drove a car night and day ferrying people from Helsinki. Men drove three and four hundred miles a day along ice-covered roads, sleeping only a few hours between journeys."

In Helsinki in that first week-end of war I watched the face of the city change. Carpenters boarded up shop windows along the main streets. Hotel after hotel closed down. All churches were shut for the duration of the war. Dancing stopped almost completely, though Helsinki had been a city with little night life anyway. Orchestras disappeared from the restaurants. Women and men alike came out in ski trousers and ski boots.

There was no need for any propaganda to get these people to leave the city. The Soviet bombs had done enough to start it. Finnish discipline did the rest. Five districts of the city, those most liable to bombing, were closed to all civilians who had not special permits. Key men were not allowed to leave. One or two prominent bankers and directors of firms and school headmasters who had fled on the first day were summoned back ignominiously.

Yet after the first two days of raids and alarms, the third day, the Saturday, went off without a raid, though the sirens blew for one alarm at nine. It was a dull, cloudy day, with a very low ceiling. The Soviet, after losing seven planes the day before, either did not want to risk forcing any more down into the Finnish anti-aircraft guns, or had suddenly been halted by the wave of reaction against the first bombing in the outside world. On the Sunday, however, the first big scare rumour spread.

It started with the German 3,000-ton steamer *Donau*. She had come in to Helsinki the day before from Danzig to take off the German colony and the Soviet Legation staff, and was due to sail for Tallin, late in the afternoon.

Towards three-thirty in the afternoon I was in the hall of the Hotel Kamp. Its dreary, green-grey granite pillars and its dank, blacked-out waiting-room were already as familiar to me as my own home. It had been office, dining-room, meeting-place to me ever since that evening, which seemed weeks ago but was only four days before, when I arrived. As the clock moved towards four I noticed that the dining-room, usually crowded, had emptied.

I walked into the bar. It was clear. I asked the porter, a small, neat but rather irritable man (he was later arrested as a German spy), what had happened. He said, "It might be because the *Donau* is due to sail at four o'clock. They've moved off to a healthier spot."

So that was it. Helsinki was absolutely convinced that the moment that boat was clear of the harbour, with the Russian diplomats safely aboard, the raids would begin again. I don't know where the story started; it may have been the work of astute Russian whisperers. But everyone knew it. That afternoon on trams people asked, "Has she sailed yet?"

This "zero hour" technique is a very effective method of working on civilian nerves. I had noticed it in Madrid, when Franco dropped leaflets saying "We will bomb at four and nine to-night unless your Government surrenders". However tough your nerves might be, you could not resist watching the clock as the hands moved over that dread half-hour from three-thirty and eight-thirty. It is, I suppose, in a slight way what a condemned man goes through once he knows the hour of his execution. It would be a lot easier for him if he were just one morning suddenly taken out to the scaffold without a warning.

Actually the *Donau* did not sail at four that Sunday. The Finnish customs guards saw to that. They kept her as long as they could, going through every detail of baggage that the 180 members of the German colony took aboard. In his cabin Dereviansky, the Soviet Minister, sat with his secretary and a pile of his most important papers. The other thirty-eight members of his staff watched from the deck the handful of Finns who had come down to see the boat leave. Every now and then both Finns and Russians stared across the grey waters of the harbour to the south, where Esthonia and its air-fields lay. Slowly the line of Germans would pass the Finnish officials. It was like the *Bremen's* search in New York, just before war broke out. But it was not only the Finns who held up matters. The Germans did as much. For scores of them did not want to leave. They had lived all their lives in Finland; many were more Finn than German; many detested Hitler. Now their Legation was using all the Nazi weapons of threat to send them away. Hitler apparently wanted them for Poland.

Rumour followed rumour. She had sailed, but the pilot refused to take her out; she had sailed and turned back because some high Soviet official had been left behind; her engines were suddenly out of order; someone suspected sabotage; Moscow had sent an ultimatum saying that if the ship was not free in four hours' time they would bomb just the same; she had gone, scores of people had seen her pass the islands.

In Moscow the Finnish Minister and his staff were being refused their passports until the boat cleared port. Finally the *Donau* did not get away that Sunday evening at all, and we were all able to turn to writing our messages with the belief that no air raid just at dawn was likely.

But we were not to have a quiet night. Just after midnight came the gas bomb alarm. Ever since the start of the war the Finns had feared that the Russians would use poison gas on Helsinki. More experienced military men told them it was very unlikely, but after that first raid everything seemed possible, and the Finns had no civilian gas masks. Only a few officials had masks in Helsinki. Even the army was not fully equipped with them. The papers at once came out with instructions for temporary masks. You could buy kits with washing soda and cottonwool pads for use if necessary. My chambermaid had constructed an amateur one by filling a bag with charcoal drenched with soda. The newspapers advised you to urinate in your handkerchief and hold it over your face if the worst came to the worst. They said the Canadians at Loos had met the first gas attack that way. I had brought my British civilian gas mask with me. Now it was regarded with something like awe by the Finnish people I met. I always paid the cloakroom attendant at the Kamp extra to hide it in a cupboard.

These were generalised fears. On Sunday night, however, the Finnish secret police suddenly informed the Government departments and the foreign consulates that they had information that led them to suspect strongly that a gas attack might be launched at dawn the next day. This information came, I gather, from spies in Esthonia who reported gas bombs being unloaded from Soviet ships. It is possible that the spies were wrong, or that the Soviet deliberately planted the story on them to increase panic, or that the Finns deliberately spread the story so as to create extra sympathy abroad. I can hardly credit the last theory, for they offered to supply the foreign legations and consulates with something very precious in those days in Helsinki—buses and petrol to get their nationals out. They also warned their own officials, many of whom left the city and went to the outskirts.

That night I was working very late. About two in the morning I was coming out of my room in the Kamp when suddenly, running down the corridor, was the same air-raid wardeness of my first morning there. " Are you the porter, are you the porter?" she called. No, I was not the porter. Was I British? Yes, I was. Then would I help her down with her luggage. She had just had a phone message from the consulate telling her to go round there at once. A bus was to evacuate all British residents at dawn.

I talked it over with the night porter. Poor devil, he knew he had to stay till eight in the morning or lose his job. I had hesitated to tell him about the warning, because it seemed to me that I might just give him a night's anxiety for nothing. But I thought he might save himself if he knew. He was a burly man with peaked features, and was already looking nervously at the whispering groups in the hall. He had carried down, too, fourteen pieces of baggage for the air-raid wardeness. When I told him what it was all about he went suddenly pale. But he had a level head. He thought a few minutes and said, "I have a bicycle. My wife and children are gone. When I leave here I'll ride a little way out of town, and if nothing happens in the first hour I'll come back and chance it".

Meanwhile Toivala had sent round a police car to take us out of town and bring us back in the morning. We set off, driving along an icy road at about ten miles an hour. We had hardly got out of town before it began to snow. I realised no bomber on earth could get through that storm, but it was too late to turn back.

The British party duly left at 7 a.m. The air-raid wardeness started things off warmly by accusing a Legation secretary, who had been working for the last thirty-six hours without sleep, of "daring to speak to me with your voice reeking of whiskey". By dawn the snowstorm was thicker than ever, and the bombers had no chance of coming. Whether the blizzard stopped the raid, or whether it never existed outside some spy's imagination, I do not know. I decided that I would not send any word of it in my despatches. But the scare had been enough, and it had worn the thin nerves of Helsinki even thinner.

These first days of December built up a strange intimacy among the people who stayed in Helsinki. I got to know many Finns closely then. Under the danger which we all felt I suppose we opened up our private feelings more than we would have otherwise done, and the friendships I made then were to help me greatly throughout my later work in Finland. I found, too, companionship and cheerfulness from strangers which made me feel almost as if I were a Finn caught in this war myself.

I remember particularly one evening going, cold and rather melancholic, to buy some winter clothes in Stockman's, the big Helsinki department store. It was after hours, but a fireman let me in the back door and took me down to the basement. There an assistant manager, a volunteer A.R.P. staff, and several of the girls whose homes were far out, slept and ate. The assistant manager spoke English. He called out three girl assistants, and we started out on a tour of the departments, collecting the things I wanted on the way. All the girls had their husbands or brothers or friends at the front—one had even her father there. They had had no news of them since the fighting started; they had all been in the raids. But they joked as I chose my things and showed infinite patience in getting me fur caps and a ski jacket of the right fit. As I paid they said, "Keep the receipts till January 1. Then you'll get a bonus on them". Suddenly they looked grim. None of us expected that there would be much shopping being done in Helsinki by the end of the year by anyone but the Red Army.

But the manager interrupted to offer me a glass of whiskey, while the night watchman produced with great pride a wooden bar. He had, it seems, knocked out a burglar with it the night before, and cracked the man's skull.

These people were living in the most dangerous part of Helsinki. There were good targets—the station, the Diet, the post office—all within a few hundred yards. The building was big and solid, but it had only a glass dome over the centre.

"We are all right if it hits the sides," said the manager.

"And if it hits the dome?" I asked.

He shrugged his shoulders. We drank up our whiskey and left. I always felt grateful for that passing bit of friendship. Nothing particular had happened, yet that half-hour stands out in my mind as something warm and valuable. It is not everyone who stops to be friendly when the world is falling about their ears.

Then there was Mr. Spoof. He was a volunteer driver of the Finnish Automobile Association, and he acted for this first week as our chauffeur. He was just on seventy but he drove over icy roads at an average of over fifty miles an hour. When we protested about wasting time by skidding into ditches he gave us a look of utter scorn. We had still to learn that being ditched two or three times on a run is a normal part of driving in Finland. He spoke English, in which he cursed the Russians fluently, and he had a sense of humour. He told us with a chuckle that his daughter who lived in the south of France had changed the spelling of her name to Spoove.

His night driving was masterly. His headlights were too bright to turn on in town so he drove without lights on the wrong side of the road because there he could see the pavement edge better. We crept through pitch-black streets—no city in the world has ever had such a black-out as Helsinki in the winter—continually turning corners and coming face to face with furious drivers who were coming in the opposite direction, carefully hugging what was their legal side of the road.

One night Mr. Spoof got weary of this, switched his lights full on, and started off. We were stopped by patrol after patrol, each very angry. With one patrol we heard Mr. Spoof's voice rising to a new note of irritation, till he finally got into the car, banged the door, and hurled one word of Finnish out into the darkness and he let in his clutch and started off. I had just time to see one of the guards fitting a clip of cartridges into his rifle as we left. "What was that you said to him?" I asked.

"Oh, the damn fool said that if I went any farther with these lights he would shoot, so I just told him to shoot," replied Mr. Spoof calmly. "It's all right, he can't hit us even if he tries, because the road bends here." And true enough it did. In a moment we were away, without any shots following us, though the next night another Press car which tried the same game had both its back tyres riddled.

I met Mr. Spoof again later in the war. I asked after his car. "Ah, it is not good," he said sadly. "Three days ago I received a horse through the wind-screen when I collided with a sledge. I cut my arm and had to drive thirty miles with one hand and with a broken window in a snowstorm—it was twenty-five degrees below zero." Twenty-five degrees below zero—and Mr. Spoof was seventy. No wonder the Finns in their twenties fought like lions in the forests.

I shared Helsinki's feelings and many of its fears during those first days of the war. I got little sleep, and in war, as the blitz has taught us here, sleep is the finest of all drugs. These influences probably put an added note of bitterness into my despatches. With the Finns I stared at the sky, hating the bombers that came over and cursing the men who sent them, with a hatred that goes when I reckon up later the forces which caused this war and above all when I set them against the wilder, infinitely more ugly back-ground of the war in the Low Countries and in France and here in Britain.

The raid strain, too, gradually lifted. There was never to be another big raid on the centre of Helsinki. Whether the outcry about the first raid had had reactions inside Russia, or whether the Soviet realised how it had strengthened rather than shaken the Finnish will to fight, we cannot tell. There were raids on the outskirts, and one later raid on the dock area, but that was all—though the attacks were to be pressed home to the full on the provincial towns. But no one knew that that would be so in Helsinki in those first few days of "alert". When I watched families trudging out at night to sleep in the frozen woods and when I saw the strain that was on face after face, I felt that this suffering, whatever the cause of it, was itself definitely evil. After those days in Helsinki, I could always understand why the Finns fought as they did and why they remained solidly behind men like Mannerheim and Ryti, whom many of them had regarded all their lives as their chief enemies. No pamphlets or propaganda broadcast could undo the effect, at least for many weeks, of that first bomb raid and the days that followed.

CHAPTER VII

WAR IN THE SNOW

DOWN A TINY slope through the pine trees two men in white snow capes, rifles slung on their backs, swiftly moved on skis. At the foot they turned beside a man with a field telephone

WAR IN THE SNOW

who was sheltering behind a granite outcrop. He picked up the receiver and spoke rapidly. In the forest to the left a machine-gun stuttered suddenly, then stopped. Half a dozen rifle shots followed it, sounding like cannon in the stillness. Then there was silence again, the thick, almost tangible silence of the woods.

It was a week later. I was standing just behind the Finnish lines at Kuhmo, away out on the waist-line front in central Finland. Here, thirty miles in from the border, the Finnish troops were facing a Russian column moving in under a Soviet plan to thrust across the country at its narrowest point.

I looked at my watch and saw with surprise that it was only two-thirty in the afternoon. Yet dusk was already beginning. The cloudy sky had turned a leaden grey; the same shade seemed to creep over the snow-covered pines, their branches still and drooping under the snow, and over the snow road. As the light slackened further all perspective went. Trees, road and sky were one flat backdrop and the trunks and branches were mere pencil lines. This hour of dusk in the Finnish forests came to fascinate me. Now that I saw it for the first time I almost forgot the war.

But the line of men who turned a bend in the road ahead and came trudging towards us brought my mind back to it abruptly. They kept carefully to the side of the road, which curved through the pines like the drive of some great country house. Many of them trudged on skis; others rode in sleds drawn by shaggy brown ponies. All wore billowing white capes, with hoods, and smock-like white blouses and trousers over their uniforms. These were the "lummi puukus", snow capes worn as camouflage. The first impression was macabre. I thought of many things, mostly comic, as I saw this column—of penguins, and the Ku Klux Klan, and oversize pyjamas and pantomime dames. One man in front, with his cape drawn tightly over his bulky uniform, was like the figure on the Michelin tyre advertisements. Then I saw the faces beneath the white cowls. There was nothing comic about them. Brown, set, peasant faces, with dark, weary eyes and a thin stubble of beard, they had that set, fatalistic look of men who are on their way to or from battle.

A car, painted white as camouflage too, turned the bend in the road and two officers got out. They too had beards and their eyes were bloodshot as they came up to give a message to the man on the field telephone. In the woods ahead the machine-guns started again.

A young staff officer who had driven up with us explained that these men were on their way back from the outposts on the road five hundred yards ahead. There had been heavy shelling all morning; it had stopped only half an hour ago. They feared an attack when dark came.

We asked him if we could go forward to the front. "The front," he queried. "What front? There isn't one. This is the front, here —or half a mile ahead, or half a mile behind—anywhere where the patrols happen to be. We've got a couple of trees across the road just ahead, as a tank barrier, but I wouldn't even call that the front. All we have are our forest patrols, on the move all the time, and ahead of them the Russians. This is a war without fronts."

His words were true of all the fighting in this first fortnight of war, everywhere except on the Mannerheim Line. It was a time of ragged engagements between Russian advance guards and Finnish frontier troops. Each side was feeling out its enemy. The Russians, who had the initiative, were carrying out a manœuvre which was a type of gigantic infiltration, with divisions moving into Finland seeking out the weakest points. The Finns were striking back at them wherever they came, trying to feel out the enemy's strength before moving any of their precious reserves.

On these forest roads at Kuhmo the battle had been going on for eleven days now. These troops we watched marching back were being withdrawn for their first rest since the start of the war.

Under the trees by the roadside farther back the fresh troops were waiting to move up. Orange flames from a fire of pine logs were a slash of colour in the grey. The smoke drifted up through the trees, almost invisible. A plane would have had difficulty in spotting it. Around were the dark, circular Finnish army tents. They were surprisingly roomy, though they were only fourteen feet in diameter. They held twenty men, and had portable stoves which could bring the heat up to eighteen or twenty degrees centigrade. Stretched out with their feet towards the centre pole, some men were eating butter and hard Finnish bread and sausage. Others outside were harnessing the ponies which stood in a circle under the trees, eating hay thrown from the sledges. Rifles, skis and ski-sticks were piled in tripods, in rows. A pulka, a five-foot sledge, boat-shaped, really just a hollowed-out log, was being loaded with ammunition and a machine-gun. None of the men, I noticed, wore steel helmets. These were too heavy for use in the swift warfare of the forests. They had instead the Finnish army cap of grey fur, with ear flaps that could be let down, and a tiny blue-and-white army rosette badge on the front. Under their capes some wore a field-grey uniform, buttoning high on the neck, others khaki. The khaki was the old army uniform, changed in the late twenties. They all wore leather pull-on boots, coming to just below the knee with a curved "rhinoceros horn" toe, to catch under the thong of the skis. Most of the boots were new—a sign that these men were reservists. They were peasants from the districts round Abo, in the south, mostly Swedish-speaking. They carried a minimum of equipment—a rifle, bayonet, water bottle, light haversack. They had no entrenching tools. Every man had a puukko—a Finnish knife—swinging from his belt. Many of these had carved, painted handles and sheaths. Their ammunition was in pouches slung from the belt. They wore no overcoats, for these would have been too heavy for movement in the forest, but many of the men had sweaters over their uniforms; others wore leather jackets. Some had mittens, or gloves with a slit just under the first finger of the right hand to free it for trigger use. Others had gloves of fine wool that did not jam around the trigger. Some wore balaclava caps over their ears—it was twenty degrees centigrade below zero—but none had the flaps of their caps down. They wanted to be able to hear the slightest sound. In all my time in Finland I never saw a soldier with the ear flaps on his cap down, however bitterly cold it was.

On sledges were piled cases of ammunition; red cardboard boxes which I found contained the crisp, hard Finnish bread; sacks filled with round red "Dutch" cheeses. Two sleds carried big cans of milk. Each man in the Finnish army was allowed one litre of this a day. It supplied some of the vitamins which he would otherwise not have got. For the others he had to rely chiefly on butter. Vegetables were rarities at any time in winter Finland.

On a sled under the trees a field kitchen was being tended by two cooks. They lifted the lid off and showed me a great copper of stew—reindeer and veal. Another kitchen nearby was cooking up oatmeal porridge, a standby for every meal.

This sector was in the command of a regular army Captain. We found him a great burly man of twenty-seven, with a light beard. He was working in a bedroom in a two-storeyed wooden house—the only two-storeyed one in the village—in Kuhmo, a little straggling place of wooden buildings beside a frozen lake. A clumsy field telephone stood on the table beside him—the other end of the line we had seen in the woods. Spread out under his hand was a detailed map of the district. On it groups of ordinary pearl-headed pink and white pins marked the position of the troops. From the windows we could see across the white lake to the dark rolling hills that led to the Russian frontier. As we talked, faint, like a wood-pecker, came the tap-tapping of the distant machine-guns. The Captain looked dead-tired, like the officers in the forest. I asked him if the strain of fighting had been very hard. He grinned:

"I think I got five hours' sleep in the first three days of the war. We did not expect them to attack on this road and we had to rush our preparations. They have put in at least one full regiment on this approach alone. This means 3,000 men and about twenty field-guns and a great number of mortars and grenade throwing. When they first attacked they used armoured cars, but after two had been destroyed by hand grenades they sent back for light tanks. They used the first of these yesterday, and we managed to knock two of them out. We got the first one by tying seven hand grenades together. Then one of our men ski-ed up, rolled it over the tank and flung himself in the snow. The grenades broke the caterpillar right off the side of the tank."

I asked him how many men he had. He smiled again and said:

"That's the one fact I can't tell you."

But I doubt if he could have had more than two or three companies, between 200 and 300 men in all. That sounds fantastically small, I know, yet the first Finnish forces on this front were minute. Two companies was the regular frontier unit in the Finnish defence scheme, and it is likely that this was the force at first told off to watch this road. Throughout the war, for instance, two companies guarded the area from Oulu to Kuusamo, a great stretch of country running right across Finland. Two companies were all that held Suomussalmi village in the first weeks of the war. I noticed that when the Captain spoke of casualties on the night before he gave the names of the dead men. It could only have been a very small unit if he knew each man personally.

The previous night the Russian guns had put down fifty shells a minute on the front-line positions by the road. They concentrated the shelling chiefly on the road and on the machine-gun posts in the woods. It was difficult for them to get accurate fire, because they could not observe the results of their shooting in the forest. So far the Soviet had used no bombers. They had only sent over planes to scatter pamphlets over Kuhmo, calling on the Finnish troops to drop their arms and join the Red Army. The Captain grinned when he spoke of these pamphlets. They did not seem to worry him.

On this front the Russians had not used skis and they had no white snow capes. On their side the Finns had no artillery and no anti-tank guns. The Russians stripped all the Finnish dead when they could get to them. The Captain thought that they wanted the warm clothing and boots, though it was possible that they might use the uniforms for spies or for dropping saboteurs from parachutes. He had seen himself from an outpost the stripped body of a Finn lying in No-Man's-Land. The Finns brought it back during the night. Even the identity disc was gone.

The Captain told me that he had watched from the front, Russians shoot their seriously wounded when they had had to retreat. The Captain did not seem shocked at the idea of shooting the wounded. It was sometimes quite essential because you could not leave a man to freeze to death suffering terribly. "Morphine would have been more efficient but a soldier does not have morphine with him," he said.

The village of Kuhmo was by this time completely evacuated. Back on the road we had seen peasants waiting with their belongings for lorries to evacuate them.

"If we fall back behind this we will burn the village. It's the only way, for then the Russians will have no shelter when the real cold comes. It's the old way we've used against them for generations," he told me.

As we spoke the bell on the field telephone rang. The Captain picked up the clumsy receiver and listened. At the other end a voice was speaking quickly. The Captain gave two swift orders, put back the receiver and moved two of the pins on the left of his map.

"They are moving again," he said with a half smile. "But I think we have them well-watched." Then he turned to us again, and went on.

He asked me when Britain would come to Finland's aid. I shrugged my shoulders. I felt very much the same atmosphere in this frontier house as I had felt often in Spain in the fighting around Madrid. There was, I knew, a world of a difference in outlook between the rulers of the Spanish Republic and the leaders of Finland. But up here in the forest the feeling was tragically similar to that on the Madrid barricades. This blunt man, with his heavy, direct look and his weary eyes, and these troops who came and went from the headquarters looked very much like the men of the Communist fifth regiment during the weary days of the first fighting from Madrid. These men, too, saw themselves as members of a small Power attacked by a much larger Power. The odds were so unfair that it seemed to them that every country in the world must rush to their aid. They were not so much angered as amazed that no one showed any sign of helping them.

Down in the street beside our car, two sappers, telephone gear strapped on their backs, were preparing to move up towards the front. They showed me how they slipped the toe of their boot swiftly in under the leather thong of the ski and how they could be in or out of the ski in an instant.

One of them turned, swept down a little slope and jumped clean round at the bottom and trudged up. I was amazed at the speed they could make on the flat ground on their skis. They used them almost like skates.

Then they gathered up their gear, slung their rifles on their backs and said good-bye. Through the officer with us—for they spoke no English—one said:

"Tell the Englishman that we are pleased to see him here but we would like it much better if next time he comes he brought a few anti-tank guns with him."

Then they were off moving down the street. From the forest ahead, where they were going, I could hear the tap-tapping of the machine-guns, like a wood-pecker.

CHAPTER VIII

FOREST GENERAL

No INSIDE INFORMATION had led me to Kuhmo. I had got there purely by chance, by somewhat irregular methods. In the week that had followed the first tense days in Helsinki I had got severe "communiqué indigestion". All we had for news was official communiqué after official communiqué. At first I had not minded, for I had caught "Helsinki cold"—a heavy type of 'flu that hit practically every stranger who came into the Baltic winter damp of Helsinki. I took a day off, went out to the ski-ing hotel at Grankulla, twenty miles outside the city, which was now crammed with Legations, and slept for eighteen hours. But when I got on my feet again, and got back to the Hotel Kamp, I realised that we had no real knowledge of what was happening on the fronts. The communiqués were just a list of names, difficult to spell, sometimes impossible to find on the few maps we had available. There were no troops back yet who could tell us anything of the fighting. The military attachés had not been allowed near the war zone—indeed they were kept away from it for the first three months of the war, for fear the Germans saw too much and told their new friends the Russians. We needed both information and colour—but above all colour, for no one knew what this war in the snow really looked like.

The Finnish Press Bureau was already making difficulties about trips to the front. We were invited for one to the Mannerheim Line, and then told that only news agency reporters could go. So I decided to try other methods. Spain and the first two months of the Second World War had taught me that in every war there is a period in the early days when the control of the territory is still unorganised and when, if you like to take risks, you can get to surprising places. One Sunday in early October three American correspondents and I had driven out of Paris and by just showing our ordinary civilian police passes ended up right behind the Maginot Line casemates at Sierck, two miles from German territory. The authorities were very indignant, particularly when four other Americans followed over our tracks two days later and suddenly arrived at the headquarters of the troops fighting in Warndt Forest, but we got off with a wigging from the Deuxième Bureau and some rather public-school reprimands from the British Embassy. Walter Kerr, of the *New York Herald Tribune*, who had been one of our party on that trip, went one better a month later by taking a taxi from Luxembourg and driving up and down the Siegfried Line for half an hour without being stopped.

I saw I must try this in Finland and I saw the very person to try it with. That was Barbara Alving, the correspondent of the *Dagens Nyheter* of Stockholm. I knew from Spain and Czechoslovakia that she had more nerve than most men, and far more energy. We talked it over, enlisted one of her friends, a Finnish girl who spoke English and Swedish, as an interpreter, got a letter of credentials from Toivala of the Finnish Foreign Office. Then, saying nothing to the military Press Department, we got aboard the train the next Sunday morning and headed north. We had no clear idea of where to go, but we had heard rumours of fighting around Kuhmo and Suomussalmi. A young officer on the train told us that there was an army staff at Oulu, the junction for that region, so we decided to try our luck there.

It held in amazing fashion. At ten on the Monday morning we were eating breakfast in a warm Oulu hotel while an astonished Adjutant examined our papers and telephoned his General. By one o'clock we were motoring over the white snow roads towards Kajaani. The next morning we were in the back seat of a great Chevrolet that flew the blue-and-white pennant of General Tuompo, Commander-in-Chief of all fronts in the north, racing towards the Kuhmo front.

When we got back from Kuhmo we were told that the General himself would see us at headquarters. These were in a villa on the outskirts of Kajaani, camouflaged with pine branches. A sentry in a goatskin coat, and with fixed bayonet, stood at the door. Field telephone lines, hoary with frost, led in from the roadway. The General himself we found in a small upstairs bedroom that had been converted into an office. I expected to find a burly, aggressive man expressive of the truculent peasant characteristic of the Finns. I found instead a quiet figure of medium height who looked like a schoolmaster. He had horn-rimmed spectacles, brown boots, grey stockings that were pulled up to the knees of his breeches, and a double row of medal ribbons on his chest. A photograph of shaggy President Kallio, who had given the Finnish peasants the land, hung on the wall. Beside it was a map on which General Tuompo had sketched out what was happening in the three sectors of his immediate front—Lieksa, Kuhmo, Suomussalmi.

Kuhmo was the centre of the fan-like series of attacks that the Soviet had launched towards this Finnish "waist-line". To the north, two divisions—the 163rd and the 44th—were moving towards Suomussalmi village. If the Russians once held the road junction there, their right flank would be guarded and they could move down safely towards Kajaani, the paper-pulp manufacturing town eighty miles to the south. Kajaani was the main Russian objective in this sector, for it guarded the approach to the Limingo Plain and the road towards Oulu, on the Gulf of Bothnia. It was also on a railway line running across-country to the west.

Simultaneously to the south another full Russian division was hitting for Lieksa, on Lake Pielinen. This attack was aimed at cutting the north-south railway there. After that, the Russian plan was apparently to drive north to link up at Nurmes with the Kuhmo troops for a final move on Kajaani. Papers captured on Russian officers on all three main points of the front confirm this.

The Russians were aided in this offensive by the Tsarist construction of the Finnish railways. They had been built on the same broad gauge as the Russian railways, as part of the Imperial Russian transport system and all ran on the eastern—that is the Russian—side of the Finnish lakes. The Tsarist General Staff had demanded this, for they wanted the lakes to lie between the railway and any enemy coming from the west. But now that Finland's enemy was coming from the east the railways were endangered at once.

If you look on the map of Finland you will see that nearly every railway curves round the right-hand eastern side of the main lakes. Those that do not, have been built since 1918.

"The Russians started with one great advantage," General Tuompo said, as he turned back from showing us this map. "They had concentrated their forces right on the frontier, though under the non-aggression treaty with Finland there was to be a neutral belt twenty miles deep, observed by both sides. This gave them a flying start. They came in at once with full materials, tanks, armoured cars, artillery."

Then he made a remark that at the time I found very strange. He said: "But we have had ten days of fighting now and in that time our troops have developed the necessary aggressive spirit. We have had losses, of course, but there is a price you have to pay for that essential sense of aggressiveness."

It seemed rash for a General commanding part of a small army very much on the defensive to talk about "aggressive spirit". But that was the principle of the whole of the Finnish defence—counter-attack. They fought a war of movement, of repeated attacks on Russian communications, which necessitated the utmost aggressive and fighting spirit from their men. Later on the Rattee Road, Suomussalmi and at Kemi River, I was to see how essential this aggressive spirit was for sheer defensive purposes. In Finland attack undoubtedly proved the best defence. There was no Maginot Line mentality in northern Finland—and very little on the Karelian Isthmus too.

The General turned to the question of the Red Army. "It is too early to judge the quality of their men. They have attacked so far in masses, but after all they have masses of men. The advance guard at Suomussalmi was made up of Finnish-speaking troops from Russian Karelia. We noticed that they fought much better than the ordinary Russian troops. Some we took prisoners. They said that there had been Finnish Communist exiles amongst them. They have sent some Finnish exiles in as spies. Two of them, on skis, came through the woods and hailed an army car outside Kajaani yesterday. They pretended to be peasants and asked a lot of questions of the officers in the car. One of the officers got suspicious, and asked for their papers. They had none.

"We have been hitting back with our own patrols. Last night three men got through the forest and burnt two planes on an aerodrome on a lake just the other side of the border. They got away on their skis without being caught."

I asked him if gas had been used. The Finns had announced officially that gas shells had been used at one point on the Isthmus, but I was never able to check that story. General Tuompo said the only suspicions they had had was when the Russians used a type of grenade. It had a bakelite centre an inch across, which he took from his drawer to show me The men near there when the grenades had burst had been taken ill and vomited. The centre had smelt strongly when it was first picked up. It was now being sent to the laboratory for examination.

As we left the General said, "I'm sorry I can't tell you much at the moment. Come back in a month's time and I might have something interesting to show you." He said it laughingly. I laughed too. It seemed to me pure wishful thinking.

We had come on to his headquarters from the hospital where we had talked with many wounded men and their story was no cheerful one. They were almost all hit by shell fragments. Every one of them had talked of the way the Russians came on, on, in crowds. "When they came out on to the ice of Lake Kianta, they were like a dense black crowd," one wounded man told me. "We waited until they were only 200 metres off, and fired right into them with machine-guns and rifles. When they broke their dead were heaped on the ice."

None of these Finns had any respect for the Russians individually as fighters. Their shooting was bad—they shot chiefly from the hip when advancing with little or no covering fire from support sections. But all had echoed one statement: "There are so many of them, so many." Their eyes seemed to darken as they spoke. You could see rising up in these men's minds the vision of great masses pouring down these snow-covered roads and of the gigantic forces ranged behind them over there in the Soviet Union.

CHAPTER IX

ARCTIC WAR

FROM THIS SUOMUSSALMI region, which was later to become the most celebrated battleground of the Finnish war, I went on northwards to Rovaniemi and the Lapland front. I was lured on by a desire to see war in the Arctic. I wanted, in journalistic parlance, an Arctic Circle dateline. I wanted to be able to write "From The Arctic Front". When I got there I found that I was to stumble into one of the most vivid and critical battles of the whole northern war—the smashing of the first Russian dash for Kemijärvi and the Swedish border.

For at the very moment when I began the lurching, bilious drive across the snow from Kajaani towards Oulu and the Arctic train, this Salla front had suddenly become the most serious proposition for the Finnish General Staff. One full Russian division of the 11th Army, with tanks, artillery and motorised supply units, had forced its way across the border opposite the White seaport of Kandalaksha, and by December 10 had captured the important road junction of Salla. Two days later, divided into two columns, it was moving with almost German swiftness westward.

The Finns had always expected that, if the Russians tried any invasion in the north, it would come at Salla. It lay opposite the point where the Murmansk railway ran most closely to the Finnish border. Supplies could be brought up the White Sea canal from Leningrad and concentrated at Kandalaksha, which provided also the essential base town for winter operations. On the Finnish side the border country was hilly, and heavily wooded; but 110 miles in from the frontier lay a railhead, the northernmost in Finland, Kemijärvi. This is a small timber town on the edge of Kemi Lake. The single track railway, which terminates there, runs south to Rovaniemi and on to the Swedish frontier at Tornio. One main tourist road also links up with the Arctic Highway twenty-five miles north of Rovaniemi.

If the Soviet could get right through to the Swedish border they could cut at Tornio the only railway linking Finland with Sweden, a railway which was to become the vital route in the spring when Allied help was discussed. Even if they did not get that distance, Rovaniemi alone was a prize worth having. Once there the Russians would have cut the Arctic Highway, the one road that the Finns had to supply their troops in Petsamo. The Finnish troops south of Petsamo would have had to give up and retreat over the Norwegian border. The top of Finland would have been lopped off like a dead branch.

Realising this, the Finns had long made of Rovaniemi, the capital of Lapland, a military centre. It had a two-storied, modern building, specially fitted for staff headquarters and big barracks. Manœuvres had regularly been held in recent years along the roads leading in from the Russian border. In front of Kemijärvi defence lines, mile-wide swathes of trees cut off to form anti-tank barriers, with barbed wire and mines spread amongst them, had been started by troops during the summer. Strong posts were set up on the frontier, and the command was placed in the hands of an old warrior called Colonel Villamo, who had been administrator of Lapland for years, and was known locally as the King of Lapland. Though now greying-haired and in his early sixties, he was still regarded as one of the strongest figures in the country. Like several other Finnish officers, he sported sideboard whiskers, which gave a curiously cherubic expression to his lined, hardened face. He looked like Charles Laughton portraying a nineteenth-century blood. He had lived for the past twenty-two years in Lapland, in a house in Rovanie where he had the curious hobby of collecting dried animal penises. It was to Villamo that the frontier posts telephoned on November 29 with the news that the Soviet military band was playing the Internationale just across the way. At dawn the next day the guards were on the wire again, to say that the attack had started. Headed by tanks, the Russians advanced steadily down the one main road leading in towards Salla.

To meet this attack, made by at least one full division, Colonel Villamo had one battalion of troops and frontier guards—about 1,000 men. They went into action at once, fighting a delaying battle along the road. "They fought every inch of the way, without a pause, for a fortnight," he told me himself later. "Many of them were so weary that they fell asleep on their skis. When they woke they went back to the fight. I had no reserves, no artillery, no anti-tank guns, only a small supply of anti-tank grenades, which was rapidly exhausted. Against the tanks we had then to use ordinary grenades and machine-gun fire."

By the ninth the Finns were back in the outskirts of Salla. The village itself, and the great white concrete-and-plaster tourist hotel, where honeymooners had cursed the August mosquitoes and all Helsinki had come to ski, was fired and destroyed at Villamo's order. Only black smoking chimneys and ruins were left to shelter the Soviet troops. Those gaunt chimneys which were to be the symbol of Finland in resistance appeared first here on the pine-covered slopes of the 300-foot hill called Salla Mountain. The population had already been evacuated.

By the 10th the Soviet supply column was parked outside the

ruined hotel, and the division was divided by its commander into two striking forces. One was to move towards Kemijärvi by the direct road through the forests of Märkajärvi, across Joutsi Lake, and on to the town. The other was to take a new road to the north only finished the year before. It led straight west to the Kemi River, crossing it at Pelkosenniemi, thirty-five miles north of Kemijärvi. From there it ran due south, on the west shore of the river, to the rear of Kemijärvi town. By the eleventh the columns were on the move again.

Down south the General Staff took alarm. If Kemijärvi fell their position was serious. Villamo was wiring for reinforcements. His immediate chief at this moment was General Tuompo, whom I had seen at Kajaani. Not expecting any big thrust in the centre, the Finnish command had thought that all the area from Lieksa right north to Petsamo could be safely co-ordinated under the one command at Kajaani. But the Russians had concentrated now at least 120,000 men and one corps of light tanks on the whole length of this front. They were formed up in three army corps each of two divisions. One corps was operating opposite Kuhmo: one opposite Suomussalmi: one opposite Salla. It was clear that Tuompo, fighting the battle of Suomussalmi, was too far away to cope with this new threat. So Mannerheim divided this northern front into two, taking Kuusamo as the boundary. South of this Tuompo was left in charge. The northern sector, up to Salla and on to Petsamo, was made a new military district. Mannerheim looked around among his Generals to find a man capable of winning this losing battle. It was a job for someone exceptional. He decided to take a chance on General Wallenius, a hardened old fighter who had been once Chief of the General Staff, but who had been living in virtual disgrace, almost exile since he had staged an abortive Fascist putsch in 1932. It was a gamble to send Wallenius north. He had many personal enemies; he was no longer young; he lived hard. But Mannerheim knew the situation required a desperate remedy. On December 14 General Wallenius stepped out of a military plane at Rovaniemi and drove in by car to the headquarters building. Villamo, his oldest friend, was waiting for him. By dusk he had taken over the front completely, and was working out his plan of campaign.

CHAPTER X

TROOP TRAIN

That same evening we too by chance arrived in Rovaniemi. By this time our party had enlisted a new member—a slight bespectacled Finnish officer, called by the somewhat Gaelic-sounding name of Mackinnen. It is, however, thoroughly Finnish. He was a Finnish journalist, a Social-Democratic news-agency man in peace-time. He had picked us up at a railway junction outside Kajaani where he had been sent by the General Staff the moment their indignant Press Department at headquarters realised what we were up to. We were not pleased to see him. He symbolised the end of our days of freedom. That made me at first intensely critical, but I later came to like him personally and respect him professionally. But for Mackinnen's efforts, for instance, it is very unlikely that the story of Suomussalmi would have got one-tenth of the publicity that it did. Yet he lacked pull at headquarters and to the end remained only a minor figure in a Press Bureau dominated by sluggish professional officers who regarded every journalist fundamentally as a spy.

We had made our way across country to Rovaniemi by troop train.

We drank tea and ate hard bread and cheese with the Commander, a stocky, bespectacled, reservist Major, who in civilian life edited a paper at Abo. An Olympic Games competitor in weight lifting was one of his men. These were all Army Service Corps troops, and the train was a long line of wagons of shells—Molotov's headache pills, the Major called them.

There was one other passenger—a huge man with his arm in a sling. He had fought in the first engagement of Suomussalmi and was sent back home on sick leave with a broken elbow bone. He told us, via Mackinnen, that he had been out on a ski patrol and almost run into a group of Russians as he came down a slope. About twenty of them were apparently getting a pep talk from a commissar under some trees. He jumped off his skis and opened fire with a sub-machine-gun. He kept up the burst and claimed to have killed or wounded all of them. The rest of his patrol came up and finished them off. But one of the wounded men by this time had flung his rifle at him and hit him on the elbow, breaking it.

I was sceptical when I heard this story. It sounded to me very exaggerated. But later when I saw the conditions in which these patrols fought, I believed it to be true. The light sub-machine-gun, the Suomi pistol that the Finnish patrols used, gave them an enormous advantage over the Russians.

From Kemi the train wound slowly northwards, branching off upon the main line where the express for Sweden was waiting to pull out towards the frontier. At one window of it stood a blonde woman in a smartly-cut mink coat, and with plucked eyebrows and a red mouth. She stared out at the trucks and horses, the vans with the grey-capped troops, the shuttered munition wagons. The officers stared back at her. She was suddenly a glimpse of another world, a world of shaded lights in drawing-room corners, of jewels at the shoulders of evening dresses, of music and colour. Then she was gone and we were left only with the snow and the grey dusk sky as we moved onwards towards Rovaniemi and war.

In the wagon ahead the troops began to sing slow, half-mournful peasant songs of the south. They seemed quite unworried by these unequal fights they clearly had ahead. I felt in myself a deep sense of the tragedy of this small army going out to what looked like certain destruction. But I found no reflection of this among the Finns. They fairly spilled confidence. One showed me a fancy puukko—dagger—at his belt. It consisted of two knives, one normal size, one a tiny minnow-like affair. He pulled out the small one. "That's for tickling Russians. The other's for finishing them off," he grinned, drawing it through the air across the front of his throat. Another officer, a thin, intellectual-looking boy with spectacles, showed me a heavy revolver with a rifle-like butt. It had belonged to old Svinhufhud, first President of Finland and in his day the country's crack rifle-shot, who won a shooting competition at the age of seventy-five.

It was six o'clock when we reached Rovaniemi. I saw a low wooden station, a waiting-room crowded with children with leather-covered caps and women in heavy coats. From a poster on the wall, a vast London bobby stared at us as he pursed his lips round a whistle, advertising a David Hume detective novel. He seemed to grin as we argued with Mackinnen about a car. Outside in the dusk, I glimpsed low wooden buildings looking on to wide, snow-covered streets, like a picture of Alaska in the gold-rush days. On the horizon loomed the curve of the hill of Ousnawara, from which for two nights in the summer you can see the midnight sun. But now it was pitch dark. The car stopped in front of a grey modernistic concrete building. I went in through swing doors and felt as if I had stepped into a Selvator Dali dream. Here was no Alaskan saloon, but a great modernistic hall with grey walls and a white steel balustraded gallery. In one corner was an automatic lift. But at one side Red Cross nurses were dressing the wounds of troops who waited by a huge leaping fire in this lounge. Ahead the tables of the restaurant were crowded with people dining. There were girls in ski costumes and girls in smarter frocks. This was Pohjanhovi, the main tourist hotel of the north, which was to be my headquarters for the next five weeks.

I had little time to study the Pohjanhovi. For we were told that General Wallenius could see us at once. We dropped our bags and turned to the car.

CHAPTER XI

WALLENIUS

GENERAL WALLENIUS, LIKE Mr. Winston Churchill, had been a war correspondent in his time. He had, too, Churchillian audacity and informality. But he had other less attractive characteristics. He was heart and soul a Nazi and had a long record of Fascist activity that had qualified him to be an intimate friend of many Nazi leaders. At this moment he had just come back to Finland after reporting the Polish campaign and visiting the Siegfried Line when the war started. He had also seen a lot of the war in China, on which he had written a book. His articles were published in Helsinki papers but his journeys were also probably undertaken to provide the Finnish General Staff with information. Another object was to let the flames lit up by his Fascist past die down a bit.

I found Wallenius, like Colonel Villamo, a stocky figure with a deeply-lined face and sideboard whiskers. At a first glance he looked completely unreal, like a film actor portraying a Crimea General. In his early sixties, his hair was thin and greying. He had small blue eyes, a scarred nose, and a curiously bony handshake. He smoked a pipe with Baldwinian regularity, and smiled a great deal; in fact, he smiled too much. He had a habit of meeting any awkward question with a smile which wrinkled further his lined face. I found in his manner something of the Sam Weller touch—I had been reading the *Pickwick Papers* on the train coming north. He seemed in these early days prepared to grin at whatever difficulty cropped up. Later I came to think that this cheerfulness covered a certain sense of uncertainty towards the world.

I went to see him with a frank sense of antagonism. I detest Fascism and I hated having to give publicity to a man who was so thoroughly Fascist. Before I went on to his headquarters I looked up his career in Hampden Jackson's book on Finland—incidentally a masterpiece in its way. I used it continually. Hampden Jackson, I found, certainly had no good opinion of him. Wallenius was chief of the Finnish General Staff until 1925; he had become by 1931 Secretary-General of the Lapua movement. This was a Fascist movement which had grown up in 1929 as a Peasant-Lutheran priest-capitalist reaction to the world slump, which had hit Finland, with its dependence on one crop, timber, particularly hard. It drew its name from a village in what one might call the "kulak area" close to Vaasa. There a troup of peasants had beaten up a trainful of red-shirted Socialists who arrived to hold a meeting. This incident had started a nationwide Red hunt that led to the banning and arrest of the Communists, and a long series of attacks on individuals and papers. A great deal of repressive legislation passed through parliament. M.P.s were kidnapped, mass demonstrations held in Helsinki at which Government officials attended. Then the Lapuans stood by ready to take control the moment certain Finnish industrial interests felt sufficiently endangered to call in the terrorists to their aid, as the Thyssens and the Krupps were about to do with the Nazis in Germany. Amongst its chief backers was the Neutral

Co-op Movement which hoped to crush the rival Socialist-progressive Co-operative, and the timber exporters who wanted to get wages down. Among its leaders was Wallenius.

In 1930 the General first came vividly into the picture. With a group of terrorists he kidnapped the ex-President, Stahlberg, and his wife. Stahlberg was a mild-minded progressive who was due to stand for President at the next election. For this Wallenius was arrested. Three months later a complaisant Helsinki court found him not guilty. So he retired to Lapua, raised a private army of civil guardsmen and in March 1932 somewhat precipitately marched on Helsinki.

But the orthodox Right found they did not need him. Already the depths of the slump had been plumbed, and prices and trade were rising. Just as in England Mosley was let drop after a section of the big business had kept him going "just in case", during the years 1933-34 Wallenius went to the wall when the normal conservative forces found they could defend their position by more constitutional means. Svinhufhud was brought from retirement to make a radio speech against the Lapuans: Mannerheim kept silent and gave them no support. Wallenius's troops were surrounded at Mantsala, north of Helsinki, and melted away without firing a shot. The General himself was arrested and bound over for three years. He thereupon took the train north to Lapland and disappeared from sight as manager of a fishing company in Petsamo till the Chinese war gave him an opportunity to get right away to his favourite hobby of war.

Now he was back, gold lace, clinking highboots and all, at a desk in the white-walled room of the General Staff building in Rovaniemi. He put his pipe down on the desk and began to talk rapidly as soon as I had taken my place. There was hard fighting round Salla, he said, "sehr harte Kampfe". He spoke good, harsh German. He had been a member of the Jaeger battalion, the Finnish cadets trained in Hamburg to be one of the forces to break up Russia from within during the Great War. Unlike most of them he had not taken part only in the fairly static trench warfare on the Riga front, but had been fighting actively with German units on the Bulgarian front against Russia when 1917 and the Independence movement in Finland came. He returned and was soon in charge of the White forces in Lapland, pushing back the scattered Red Finnish troops who were there.

He grinned when I asked him of that period. "In May 1918 I was waging war against British troops, or rather Finnish Communists commanded by British officers on this very Salla front—but in Russia," he said, "Maynard, in charge of your Archangel expedition, had enrolled the Finnish Reds who had escaped to Russia into a militia which was commanded by a Colonel and two lieutenants; they held the front opposite us, for at that time they were frightened that the Germans under van der Goltz, who had helped us in the War of Independence, would drive through and cut off the Murmansk Railway.

"But I don't think those officers of yours were very keen on the troops they had to lead. One day in July 1918 they sent over a messenger with a white flag suggesting a short truce, and asking if they might come over to pay us a visit. They came, stayed three days in our Mess. On the last night the Colonel got up and said, 'Gentlemen, I give you the toast of His Majesty King George of England'; I didn't mind. I drank the toast, and all my officers followed. The next day they went back to their lines and we started fighting again."

The General took the pipe out of his mouth and grinned again. Then he went on to tell me that after the 1918 armistice he concentrated on seizing Petsamo for the Finns. "I was sent up there with an army to take control of the port in 1919," he said. "Well, I say an army. It was a force of sixty-four men to be exact. We worked from Ivalo as a base. When I had established my lines of communication and left men to guard them, I found I had only eighteen men left. So with an army of eighteen I took Petsamo and held it till the Bolsheviks drove us out in 1920."

I switched the conversation to the present war. At once Wallenius came out with a remark which was very significant. "We calculate on a one-year war," he said. One year. I almost smiled with astonishment. The outside world was thinking in terms of days, at the most weeks. Here was an ex-chief of the General Staff talking of one year. "After that we will either have got help, or it will not be worth fighting further," he said.

"This first month is the most important. For after that the weather should come to our aid. The Russians have chosen the best time, from their point of view, to attack. The snow is still not deep enough to let us ski properly, while it is cold enough for ice roads to be built easily. Winter gives them an enormous advantage for organising communications. Every river becomes a road, every lake an airfield. If we can hold on till the end of this month, then heavier snow will come in January and February, and we should be able to hold them all right. We are more used to the cold than they—look at our children tumbling about everywhere in the snow."

And the Russian army? "It is too early to judge yet, but certain things are clear. They do attack in the steam-roller, mass style. I believe it is psychological. There are two armies in the world which still attack in mass, the Russians and the Chinese. They feel braver in a great body. They hate moving about in small quantities.

"Their arms vary. Their planes so far seem to lack manœuvrability, but they have ample artillery, and are using tanks even up in Petsamo."

Wallenius said other things which I never used. They struck me, standing as they did without proof, as being intentional "plants". He spoke of troops on the Suomussalmi front who had shot their political commissars; of machine-guns set up behind the advancing Red Army. Once, in the company of an Italian correspondent who struck me as exceedingly irresponsible (his colleagues thought the same) Wallenius told us that men on the front claimed that some Russian tank crews were locked in their tanks. "We found the same in Spain," cried the Italian. It was a typical Fascist lie. Why lock a crew in the tank? If something goes wrong then they have no chance of trying to make even the simplest repairs.

Wallenius claimed too that once General Putna (since liquidated), the Soviet Military Attaché in Berlin, told him that during the fighting against the mutineers of Kronstadt in 1923 the Soviet did put belts of machine-gun fire down behind their troops.

Wallenius spoke German because, except for some scraps of English, it was the only foreign language he knew. That was symbolical. He was deeply pro-German; in fact, he was more, he was deeply pro-Nazi. He was in every way the type of man from whom one section of the early Nazis was recruited—a Finnish Goering, as it were, energetic, an able soldier with a real love for campaigning, who had never been able to find in peacetime any job which gave him the same sense of activity and purpose that fighting gave him. He liked war, I believe (this was the seventh he had been connected with), because then he felt full of confidence and self-respect. His sense of uncertainty went. I noticed this again and again in Rovaniemi. He loved the Press conferences he later gave, at which he explained the day's fighting with pride, pointing out on the map with his pipe-stem "hier harte Kampfe, hier zwei Tanken zerstort ". He loved marching up the hall of the Pohjanhovi hotel with every officer springing to his feet and bowing stiffly: he loved driving off in his three-quarter length white goatskin coat towards the front; liked stamping round under shell fire setting new positions, talking with his officers. I really believe, too, that he liked killing Russians. This may have been partly a blend of an old Swedish-Finnish hatred of Russia (for Wallenius is a Swedish, not Finnish name. He came from the old Swedish land-owning class, like Mannerheim); it may have been partly the sense of satisfaction of the leader of a small army hitting back at a huge opposing force, the cries of David as he gets an effective stone home on Goliath's forehead; it may have been bitter anti-Bolshevist feeling; it may have been one more expression of some sense of inferiority triumphing. But his eyes lit up when he described to us at Joutsijärvi the way the Russians were mown down on the ice night after night; "they lay there in heaps, great heaps", he cried. Another time he showed us one of the many curious Russian gadgets captured—an officer's sword with a bayonet scabbard fixed to it. The bayonet was the long grooved French type. "The blood runs down that groove, right down it," he said, smiling yet again, and there was something terrible in his smile this time.

I sensed and saw all these qualities in him in the north, and his critics stressed them to me in the south. In the final days of the war, when, deprived of a command for his errors on the Isthmus, he sat drinking with us in our hotel bedrooms in Helsinki, argumentative and sometimes maudlin, they all came out as if under a magnifying glass. Then only Wallenius the Nazi was to be seen. But at this time in the north the unequal fight he was engaged in gave him a completely different air, one of courage (of which he had masses), and dignity. Leading a tiny army against an overwhelmingly large enemy force, he reflected the endurance and sacrifice of the men he led. I realise now that when I saw him in those days I never saw just Wallenius the General, but beyond him I saw the men in fur caps and white capes battling inch by inch along the Salla road; wounded men dying the terrible death of the frozen forests; men on patrol earning a virtual V.C. half a dozen times a night, holding off the teeming Russian army. The strain of the work, too, the need for prompt decision, for long hours of effort, tightened him and sloughed off much of the fake attitude of Nazism. He had no time to worry about taking out any feelings of uncertainty. For the moment the Nazi was lost in the General. And the General was certainly urgently needed, for the Russians were sweeping down towards Rovaniemi now almost as fast as they could move.

CHAPTER XII

THE BATTLE OF KEMI RIVER

THE RUSSIANS DID not wait long at Salla village when they had seized its ruins on December 10. Their commander had sent his two forces ahead at once. Half a division, with tanks and artillery, went straight on towards Kemijärvi by the south, direct road. The other half drove in the same direction, along the north road, heading for the frozen Kemi River and the village of Pelkosenniemi to hit Kemijärvi from the north.

With only weary troops ahead of them, the advance started off according to plan. Night after night the Moscow radio announced, with perfect truth, that their troops in the north were moving in and occupying the country without meeting any effective resistance. The Finnish patrols fought them on both roads, but the main forces were drawn back to be re-formed. On the south road the troops took up a position at Joutsijärvi, a small frozen lake across which the road ran. Here they had a comparatively good position. Though dominated by the hills opposite, they had machine-gun posts and trenches amid the houses of a farm, and the lake provided a wonderful field of fire. Behind, between Joutsijärvi and Kemijärvi, were the five wide defence belts, half a mile broad, of lopped-off trees, barbed wire, mines. These great swathes, like some jungle on the moon, some incredible dead fossilised waste under their covering of snow, formed the main northern defences. Even with a small body of troops they could be held for some time. But to the north things were far more difficult.

For here only the Kemi River provided any real obstacle. It was wide, frozen, open. Troops in trenches opposite the Pelkosenniemi ford might be able to hold up any direct crossing, unless they were outflanked by forces crossing further up or further down stream. But once across the fight would be much more difficult. The road ran almost dead flat to Kemijärvi. A branch road from the Pelkosenniemi crossroads gave an alternative route to the Arctic Highway. And by the fourteenth, when Wallenius took over, the Russian advance guard were already moving into the village of Savukoski twenty-eight miles further east, the last place between Salla and Pelkosenniemi.

Wallenius decided that he must stop at all costs this thrust before it got beyond Pelkosenniemi. He had against him, he knew, a force with at least twenty tanks, and approximately 6,000 men, of the 569th Regiment of the Russian Army. He had asked for reinforcements, and one fresh battalion was, I believe, sent up to him. It was composed entirely of reservists, who had never fought before, though some of their officers were old campaigners. He therefore decided to leave his right wing, on the Joutsijärvi road, very lightly held, and to throw everything he had against Pelkosenniemi. On the south road he left two companies—two hundred men. In all he had then as a force for the north about 1,000 men. Certainly not more. He may have even had considerably less. I could not get the exact figures in wartime; they will be available only when the Finnish war archives are prepared.

This force he got ready, and into position, only at the last moment. The fresh troops actually arrived at Kemijärvi railway terminus on the afternoon of December 18. They were put into lorries and rushed up the thirty-five miles to the front. There was literally not even half an hour to lose, for the Russian advance guard was already across the Kemi River.

Picture the setting for this, the first battle of the campaign in the north. A country of rolling, almost flat pine forests, with

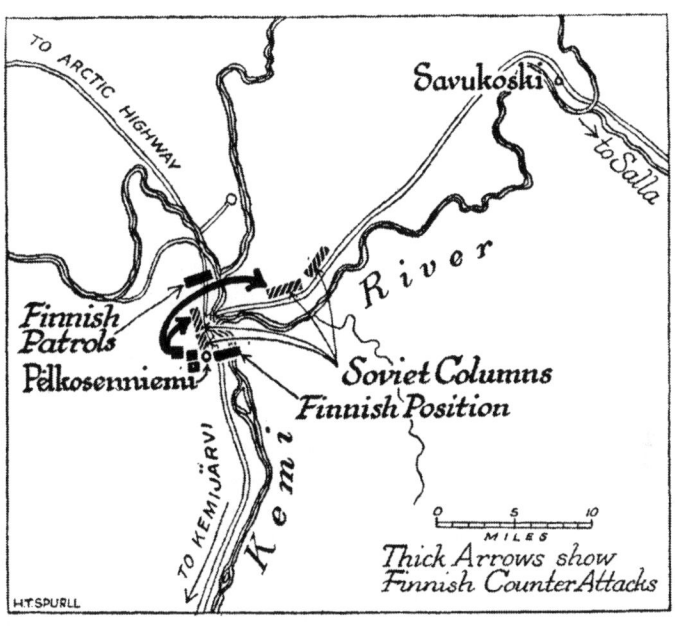

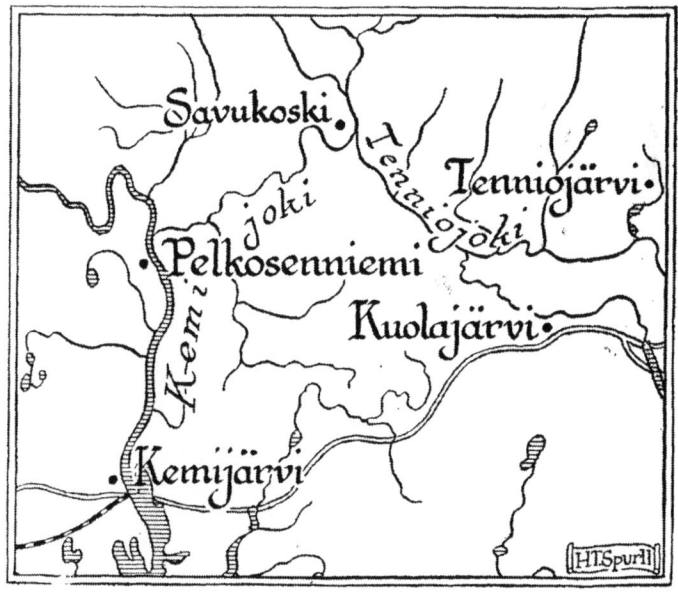

THE BATTLE OF KEMI RIVER

roads and woods alike coated with a foot of fresh, dry snow. Through this winds the wide white band of the frozen Kemi River, fifty to sixty yards wide, with sloping banks twenty feet high on the western side. The village of Pelkosenniemi, a scattering of wooden houses, stands in a wide sloping clearing a quarter of a mile back from the river bank. From the village, with its towered wooden church, the wide snow-covered road runs through a forest of small trees for a mile till it meets the connecting road that goes toward, the Arctic Highway. Then it turns abruptly to the right, runs another quarter of a mile to a group of farm-houses on the river bank, and down towards the ford. Across, through a narrow gap in the black forest, it carries on towards Salla.

Late on the afternoon of the 18th the last Finnish patrols retreat across the ice and take up their posts in the farm buildings. They are not wearing skis. There is not snow enough yet. They lie and wait. In the forest opposite there grows a strange, unreal roar. A light tank, nine and a half tons, moves cautiously down to the opening opposite the river, like a beast coming to drink. No one in sight. It turns and goes back to report. A minute or two later, and dark figures appear on the roadway and in the trees close beside it. Their peaked caps stand out in the dusk. They are the Soviet advance-guard.

Back in the village of Pelkosenniemi Colonel Villamo is waiting with his officers. His troops, in two main bodies, are grouped in the woods just behind the village. A screen of scouts cover the entrance to the village itself. They wait for word from these scouts with the impatience of gamblers. For they have decided to gamble.

The Finnish patrols have brought in accurate information about the strength of the enemy. They report that the main supply column has halted about two miles the other side of the river, and is settling down, apparently preparing to spend the night there. Behind it a further force of infantry—at least one full battalion—is still marching up. Another force, probably a full regiment, is preparing to come on across the river.

Wallenius and Villamo have two immediate problems to decide. There are two roads the Russians can take. One to the right towards the Arctic Highway, one to their left towards Kemijärvi. The Finns have not men enough to hold both. They decide to gamble on the Russians moving towards Kemijärvi, and to keep all their men ready to thrust against them there. On the Arctic Circle road they leave one patrol. "How many men did you have in it?" I asked Wallenius later. "Three," he said curtly. "Three held that road for me. I remembered from my experience in Bulgaria that the Russians do not easily break away from a rigidly prepared plan. They were clearly aiming for Kemijärvi. Otherwise why should they have divided their force neatly into two halves to come on both north and south road? Even if the Arctic road was wide open to them, and offered a way right into Rovaniemi, which was practically unprotected, I believed they would not suddenly dash for it. They would keep to their preconceived plan. I knew, too, that they could never discover that that other road was open, for they had not any effective patrols. It was cloudy, and their aircraft could do little scouting. In any case, all our men were hidden in the woods. The Russians were completely blind, while we knew every one of their moves, almost minute by minute, for we had a screen of scouts moving through the forest alongside their columns all the way. We convoyed them into the position we wanted."

Even so, the Finns passed an anxious afternoon. For if the Russians had by chance turned down the Arctic road their position was outflanked. Just before midday the Russian scouts came across the river and moved slowly and confidently up to the cross-roads. The Finnish patrols waiting there lay silent in the snow. The Red infantrymen, numbering about two hundred, paused while their officers consulted their maps. Then they moved steadily off—down the Kemijärvi road.

A Finn rushed back to a field telephone, told Villamo, who told Wallenius. At once came back Wallenius's orders, long prepared. His force was divided into three groups. One was put in position in the village, to bar the direct road to Kemijärvi; this was the smallest unit, perhaps one hundred and fifty men. The second was sent through the forests to the west to wait close to the cross-road, ready to attack the Russian advance-guard in the flank; the third, the largest force, set out on a twelve-hour march in a huge three-quarter circle to cross the river north of the Russians, move through the forest, and hit at their supply column.

Wallenius was gambling again. He told me later: "I have

always worked on the principle of having more men behind the enemy than in front." Here his front, the main road to Kemijärvi, was held by one thin line of troops. His others were moving through the forest. If they lost their direction in these thick, pathless pinewoods; if they were late; if the Russians discovered their approach, and prepared for attack; the whole strategy would collapse. But Wallenius trusted his Finnish troops, and his knowledge of the country. They brought him victory.

Zero hour for the flank attacks was set for 2 a.m. on the morning of December 19. Both were to be delivered simultaneously. But already in the afternoon of the 18th the fighting in the village had started. Finns opened fire on the Russian vanguard. From positions on the main village slope, around the church, their machine-guns suddenly poured fire into the Russian advance. The Russians sent back word asking for fire from their batteries. Late in the afternoon the shells began to slither through the dusk across the river from Russian guns in position near the supply column. The Finns were forced back into the village itself. Around the church the fighting became intense. Grenades, bayonets, knives were all used. But by nightfall the Finns were still holding their positions.

Then, exactly at 2 a.m., the two flank forces struck. Just on the Finnish side of the river Russian troops and supply wagons suddenly found themselves hit by machine-gun fire out of the forests that a moment before had seemed dead and empty. They fired back, but their enemy was invisible. Their officers sent back scouts to ask for help. But it was too late, for already the main column was under fire.

The second flanking force had crept up to a position within two hundred yards of the road where the Russians were encamping for the night. The column was strung out for half a mile. In the front were five tanks, then officers' cars, then supply lorries. Under the trees were over a hundred horses, partly used for the handful of cavalry that accompanied the column, but chiefly used for the supply sledges. The men slept in the lorries, or in little lean-to shelters they had hastily constructed by the roadside. Many of them had dug weapon pits close to the fires, and filled the bottoms of them with straw. They had learnt enough by now, too, to build pits for their fires so that they would not be seen by the Finns.

THE BATTLE OF KEMI RIVER

I talked later with Finnish wounded who had taken part in the attack. They said that in the dark they moved up, working by compass only, and were almost on top of the column before they realised it. They suddenly heard Russian voices. At once they got down into position. They had had a twelve-hour march, and none of them had fought before. Their commanding officer, a Captain, had fallen through a piece of rotted ice when crossing the river, and his clothes, soaked, had frozen on him like boards. He could not change them, so he fought on for eighteen hours with them in that condition. He later died of the pneumonia he inevitably contracted.

When the first fire order was given, suddenly madness swept into the Russian column. The horses went down in one shrieking, kicking mass. Men who rushed to get their rifles fell. But after a few minutes the Russian infantry settled down to fire back. From their pits they opened fire with heavy machine-guns fitted with tracer bullets which lit up the woods, searching for the hidden Finns. Farther back the reserve body of infantry had time to get into position and open fire in steady order. The battle soon developed into a major fight at two points, one around the supply column, the other against the main infantry position about half a mile behind.

It lasted until midday the next day. The Russians tried to turn the supply lorries, but Finnish snipers picked off the drivers. Gradually the Finns closed in. A first rush towards the open road was beaten off, but soon they were at work with grenades among the lorries. The Russians retreated down the road to join the reserve infantry. But here, too, the fight was nearly over. Unable to see the Finns, who had always the cover of the forest, and who moved with trained swiftness, the Russians had a great disadvantage. They were on the road, visible; the Finns were in the forests, invisible. The Finns had surprise; the Russians were off their balance from the start. By midday it was clear that there was nothing for them but to retreat. The vanguard had been driven back from the village, leaving ninety-eight dead—the Finns counted them carefully—around the church; the other section had retreated across the river, routed. The Commander of the main body could do no more. His advance tanks had been captured near the supply column left. He gave the order to retreat, leaving his guns and all his supplies behind.

By midday such lorries as had got away were already back at Savukoski. The north Salla road was safe.

It had cost the Finns dearly. Wallenius had lost more men than the Russians did. He had certainly not men enough to cut off the retreat completely. New reserves came up the day of the battle, and were flung into the pursuit, but they numbered only a couple of companies, and had not even anti-tank grenades. Yet now the Finns had stopped the advance on Kemijärvi. From that moment on, December 19, more than half the Russian threat to Rovaniemi and the north had gone.

CHAPTER XIII

ROAD TO BATTLE

WE CAME ON the first of the dead at the curves on the still forest road. As we drove towards them they looked like mere bundles of rags. We got out and bent over the first man. Stiff with the frost he had fallen, spinning under the force of a bullet in the stomach, into the ditch under the pine trees. He was a Finn, a tall boy in a new grey uniform. His boots, with their upturned toes, were still yellow with newness. They had already gathered up his rifle, but his body lay there, face down. He must have been killed towards the end of the battle, pursuing the Russian advance-guard as they retreated from the village towards the Kemi River crossing.

It was the day after the battle, December 19, at one in the afternoon. We had come up by car from Rovaniemi, driving out from Pohjanhovi in the dark of early morning. The trip had come unexpectedly. For days I had harried General Wallenius for permission to go towards the front, even if only to Kemijärvi. Each time I met the same smiling but negative reply. Then suddenly, the night before, we had been told we could go.

With our headlights picking out the snow, we motored across the two railway bridges of Rovaniemi on to the Arctic Highway. Above us the stars were still brilliant points in the grey dark sky. Wide and straight ran the road on its 250-mile stretch to Petsamo.

ROAD TO BATTLE

An occasional supply lorry roared towards us, hesitated, and then crept by on the narrow passing space that the Finnish roads give. Through the dark pines by the roadside the first red glimmerings of dawn showed. Inside the car the heaters kept our feet fairly warm; but our breath froze solidly on the windows, coating them with a genuine, impervious frosting. Henri Danjou, of the *Paris Soir*, scraped a hole with his knife, cursed when it froze over within five minutes, and relapsed into sleep.

After thirty miles we turned off eastwards on to the Kemijärvi road. Toivala, son of the Press chief of the Foreign Office, an eighteen-year-old boy who was acting as a member of the Press service, unbuttoned his revolver holster. No one knew where Russian patrols might be. The chauffeur stared towards the sky. It was time for planes to come over, and Kemijärvi had already been twice bombed.

By the roadside ahead we saw, at one bend, a lone car. We slowed down to pass it carefully. In front a man was slumped over his wheel. Shot? But it turned out that he was only sleeping. He told us he was an army chauffeur and he had only five hours' sleep in the last four days, and that he had pulled up to get at least an hour's rest before pushing on. Toivala got out and drove the car on for him, while the man curled up in the back seat and slept on.

The sun was already red behind the pine hills when we came down the last slope into Kemijärvi. A soldier in a goatskin coat stopped us, examined our papers. By the roadside I noticed five tanks, five heavy machine-guns and piles of rifles, guarded by a sentry. They were the first booty of the Pelkosenniemi battle. Then we were in the main street of Kemijärvi.

At the chief cross-roads all was bustle. Soldiers drove sledges, pulled by rough-coated horses, and loaded with cans of milk, boxes of supplies, ammunition. Three peasants were herding thirty to forty Finnish cows, small, grey, dispirited beasts. They came from the evacuated regions around Salla. This trip in the cold, when they were used to the shelter of barns and to warm hay and beets, was killing them. Two had collapsed by the roadside. A peasant was trying to drag one to her feet. Another had already had her throat cut, and two soldiers were skinning the carcase.

In front of a block of one-storied wooden offices a boy in civil guard uniform and an elderly man, already well into the fifties, were standing on guard, rifles in their gloved hands. Girls, their cheeks flushed with the cold, and with red Balaklava caps on their heads, went past briskly on their way to the boarded-up shops. A group of Lottas in grey uniforms came down the steps of the hall that served as a troop canteen. One, who could not have been more than eighteen, had perfect features and a clear, pale skin that gave her a look of real beauty. From the fire brigade quarters next door five men wheeled out the local fire engine and stationed it in the street. It was nearly ten o'clock, and at ten the first alarm of the day usually came to Kemijärvi. Almost frantic with the cold, I stamped up and down, watching the colours of the sun spread slowly over the surrounding hills. Everywhere lay the snow. It covered the streets, turned the ice of the lakes into huge open fields, lay caked and frozen on the drooping boughs of the pine trees, banked the roofs. Besides the wharf of the Kemi Lake—for Järvi is the Finnish for lake—half a dozen motor launches and lake steamers were drawn up near the shore, immobile in the ice. On the streets, lines of troops on skis moved from their billets towards the station. They passed a cinema that was turned into a stable; brown horses stared up from their straw at posters advertising Joan Crawford and Hedy Lamarr. On the wall of the little hotel the thermometer showed twenty-eight degrees below zero.

Kemijärvi was to me always one of the most beautiful places in the somewhat monotonous Finnish landscape. The hills, low and covered with dark-blue pines, ringed the sky. They were larger than most Finnish hills, and had indeed earned the title of mountains—the Summa Mountains. This morning, under the cloudless sky, coloured pale gold and red and even green in the rising sun, they held a mysterious, distant look, as if they held the secrets of some strange, unknown land. Yet I knew that in their fastnesses at this moment men were fighting and dying. Somewhere amid those dark pines shells were bursting and men were waiting, grenade in hand, to face tanks.

This part of Finland was very like my homeland, New Zealand. True, New Zealand is a land of wild mountain ranges which, beside these swelling hills, was a stormy sea of rock. But the colouring and atmosphere were very similar. There were the same simple colours—dark-green of forest, pastel-blues and gold in the sky, white snow; the same clearness which brought out every detail and made each horizon a veil hiding mysterious things and peoples, just as the horizons of southern New Zealand had led Samuel Butler to his imaginings of *Erewhon*. In this Finnish country, too, was the sense of hardness and strength which makes New Zealand the stern, vivid land it is, hard with a masculinity which has always made the soft, breast-like hills and the fluffy hedges of southern England seem to me essentially feminine.

I was drawn from my contemplation of the scenery and from my efforts to keep warm by a horrible screech from the tower above the fire-brigade station.

Kemijärvi's siren, which had a note of its own (it was worked by hand, by a small boy), was coming into action. Immediately, from houses on every side, women and girls appeared, carrying blankets and cushions and bundles towards the trench shelters in the fields on the outskirts of the town. In a few moments the streets were deserted.

The hum of planes sounded over the northern hills. Then three tiny specks were up above us, white against the blue. A machine-gun opened fire from the ground, but the tracers dropped well short of the bombers, which went on their leisurely way towards the east side of the town and dropped their bombs with thuds that shook the wooden buildings and threw up clouds of smoke and dust. "They're trying to hit the positions behind Joutsijärvi," said an officer standing beside us.

We watched the planes circle and drop a second stick of bombs. The machine-guns were silent. Whatever may have happened on the ground at Pelkosenniemi, there was no doubt who had the mastery of the air.

As the All Clear went Toivala came to tell us we could start for the front. We had a quick cup of coffee in a basement café run by Lottas, where a gramophone played "In the Chapel in the Moonlight" and soldiers stared at De Maitre of the *Petit Parisien* with his monocle and grey Swedish cap, and Henri Danjou of *Paris Soir* in a leather cap that made him look like a smiling brigand, and particularly at the riding trousers of a Swedish woman correspondent. When we went outside our driver was pressing a clip of cartridges into the magazine of his rifle. Even his unexpressive Finnish face looked worn and shocked. From Toivala I learnt the reason. "They have just told him that his brother was killed in yesterday's fighting," he said.

On the road we slowed down to inspect the captured tanks. All five were light adaptations of Vickers' models. Three were amphibian, with propellers, rudders and side floats. In the driver's seat of one were two dirty shirts, and of another a broken bag of rice. Curious Finnish soldiers stared at them, banging the armour plating with their rifle butts.

On the Pelkosenniemi road we passed no one, and saw no one around the shuttered farm-houses. The district had been evacuated. Only in one small village did we see a group of soldiers working around a great yellow van, which we learnt was the corpse van used for clearing dead from the battlefields. We went on past the forty-fifth kilometre stone, beyond which Wallenius had warned us to be careful of Russian stragglers. At a little bridge ahead we suddenly stopped. The sentry on it held up his hand, and signalled with a jerk of his rifle towards a hut, from which five men, pulling on their white capes, hurried out. Clipping ammunition into their pouches, they hurriedly talked together. The sentry had seen a dark figure in the woods at the edge of the stream.

Crouching, rifle in hand, parting the branches and peering through as if they were hunting wild animals, they moved off into the forest. I felt sorry for any Russians in there.

Our chauffeur, clutching his rifle, had gone off with the others. If anyone doubts that revenge can be a great driving force in war they need only have seen the look on that boy's face as he too went into the wood.

In the hut, still decorated with two photographs of the foresters in army uniform, and with half-washed plates on the table, we waited. It was deadly still. Then once again there were white figures on the road and, amongst them, the dark shape of a Russian. His hands held above his head, his face grey with terror under his peaked Soviet cap, he stumbled along in front of two soldiers who held their rifles at his back. All the ugly reality of war was written on that peasant's face as he marched, exhausted and hungry, towards what he was certain was death. I thought of the bombs on Helsinki, and the frightened child cowering under the tobacconist's counter, and the people trudging in the snow to escape from bombers, and I remembered that this horror was spread on both sides. I pondered a little on the way in which, generation after generation, the people of different countries fight each other in wars the causes of which they rarely understand fully, so that war seems to a great part of mankind not something caused by man but just an event of nature, like a typhoon or an earthquake. On that Finnish forest road as I watched this prisoner being led away I realised, too, something which all my generation has had to learn—that there is no good just recoiling from the horror of war because we have known how good peace can be. War is here for our time, for what are to many of us the best years of our lives. It is useless bewailing it. All we can do is make sure that the price it exacts is not paid this time in vain.

Another mile, and we were in Pelkosenniemi village. On the outskirts were the first signs of battle—a shed hit by shells, equipment scattered in a ditch, a broken lorry. The bulk of the houses and the wooden-towered church remained untouched. In front of the mayor's office soldiers were gathering war spoils—saddles, rifles with long Russian bayonets, boxes of ammunition, telephone wire, and, heaped in front, the instruments of the Russian military band which had played opposite the frontier the day war began. They were stacked just as they had been taken from the Russian band lorry—horns, trumpets, drums. I noticed they were not made of brass, but of some alloy. They lay now in the snow, spoils of victory in the village into which they were to have played a triumphal march of entry.

CHAPTER XIV

BATTLE SCENE

IT WAS AFTER the village, where the open fields suddenly narrowed down to one road edged with pines, that we found the first twisted corpses. Scattered in the ditches, or on the road itself, they were a ghastly trail that led us to the low cliff above the Kemi River. Here the fight had been around a group of farm buildings. The log walls were shattered like the skeletons, where shells had smashed through. Horses, smashed wagons, and more dead lay twisted beside the road. The horses, their coarse blood spilled among the snow, seemed almost more tragic than the men. They had certainly had no hand in this ghastly business, yet here they lay.

On the ice itself a lorry stood where the Russians had left it, right in mid-stream. Beside it lay the bodies of two men. Farther off, half-way to the shelter of the pines on the bank, was another crumpled figure, killed by some Finnish sniper's bullet as he ran. We drove on across the ice to the narrow entry of the Salla road that dropped, still and white, to the edge of the river.

The ruins of the column lay three-quarters of a mile farther on. We scraped past another great van, loaded with more bodies of the Finnish dead, being gathered up to take home to their families. For in Finland till the end all dead were sent home for burial. Then ahead I saw a line of what looked like junk cars drawn up in some empty allotment on the edge of a city. At the head was a staff car; behind it three tanks; then lorries, some straight on the road, others swung into the ditches.

Still gripping the wheel of the staff car was the driver, his forehead smashed by a bullet. Alongside lay the body of a Russian officer—the first of the dead who were strewn everywhere. How strange were these bodies, on this road where it was already so cold that if I took my glove off to write I could keep my hand in the air only a minute. The cold had frozen them into the positions in which they fell. It had, too, slightly shrunken their bodies and features, giving them an artificial, waxen appearance. The whole road was some huge waxwork representation of a battle scene, carefully staged. Even the dark brown-red stain that was spilt on uniforms and on the snow was paint rather than blood. Dead that I had seen in Spain had usually been slumped, shapeless bundles of clothes and flesh, that still had about them the horror of decay as well as death. But this scene here struck in me, I found, no horror. It was hard to believe that these figures had ever been men. Yet men lay with hand grenades in their hands, poised to throw; one man leant against a wagon-wheel with a length of wire still in his hands; another was fitting a clip of cartridges into a rifle. Until you got right up to him you could not tell that he was not still living. Others had spun into ditches, and fell there, still giving an impression of movement. It was this incredible effect of the cold which gave the Finnish battlefields their fake appearance, for the very action seemed to be frozen into stillness. It was as if one moment of the battle time had suddenly stopped on this road near Kemi, halting the scene for all time.

There was a line of thirty-eight trucks, all Fords made in Russia, with hinged sides. The tyres, with chains on one rear wheel, looked of poor quality rubber. They lay amid the spilled gear, the endless gear of war. Gas masks, telephone wires, machine-gun belts, sausages tied together like ropes, a spilled barrel of frozen fish, a pile of old leather shoes, a poster of a girl advertising a Red Cross fund, two curved swords, and amidst this, the dead, like so much more gear. Here a shattered arm; there a leg covered with snow. Wooden boxes that had held ammunition lay everywhere; horses, their guts smashed and open, artificial pink, lay under the high wooden arch of the sledges.

The Russians apparently cleaned out anything left by the Finns in evacuated houses along the way. I saw an ancient sewing machine, a butter churn, even a bundle of silk stockings, two silver teapots and some girls' underclothes—the rather pathetic looting of men who have few "consumers' goods" in their lives. Some of the Russian dead wore steel helmets; some peaked caps. They all had heelless felt boots, which are wonderfully warm when the snow is dry, but hopeless if it is wet. Some had overcoats that were adequately thick; others had thin coats, and I saw that their padded uniforms were rotted. Few looked adequately clothed for this terrible temperature.

You could follow the course of the battle as you walked from man to man. Here three men had spun and fallen as they charged for a machine-gun pit; there the horses were piled in one great hillock of flesh where they had been mown down, farther on half a dozen lorries were half turned, as their drivers had tried to get them round and move off. Other lorries were on their side. And everywhere I turned back from the material to the men. Russian dead lying face down, as if weeping, in the snow; curled on their back, eyes closed, as if asleep; clutching stomachs, sides, heads; gripping the sides of lorries; stumbling forward, gun in hand; running back, gun thrown away; everywhere the dead. In one place two men, Russian and Finn, lay frozen together in their final death struggle. Over most of the bodies frost and light snow had already put a faint hoary coating.

The Finns were easy to distinguish. They all had white snow clothes over their grey uniforms, and their boots were of new, yellow leather. Every man's face had been covered by his comrades with a piece of cloth or a fir branch. I drew away the branch from the face of one man, huge in his grey uniform. It was a typical Finnish peasant face, rounded, with almost slit eyes and strong, curving sweep of jaw. In his death he looked very young—just in the twenties. I had seen enough of this uniform now, in my three weeks in Finland, to realise what this death was going to mean when word of it got back to some red-painted peasant shack in the forests of the south.

And the Russians? I went from body to body, staring at the faces of these men fallen here, in their peaked Soviet caps with the dull red star on their front. The faces underneath were Oriental, simple, a little brutish, those of peasants from southern Russia. One man, a huge fair figure, had completely Mongoloid features; another the dark, sharp look of a Tartar. But the mass had the broad nose, narrow forehead and wide dark eyes of the peasant.

I tried to think of what this slaughter would mean to their families and lovers in the collective farms and the dusty peasant villages from which they had come. But, though I have visited Russia, I found this difficult, for these people and their lives were, I realised, strange to me. Then, fallen across the body of a dead horse, I saw one man who brought it home to me abruptly. He clutched still in his hand a tiny suitcase from which had spilled a child's broken doll, two pairs of black children's gym shoes, and a child's frock. He had clearly picked them up from a Finnish peasant's house. The man was young. You could see how carefully he had gathered these things, thinking of the day when he would be able to go back to his home, and his daughter would run out to meet him, and he would give her this doll, and these precious clothes. Now here he lay, outstretched on this forest road in Finland, beside a horse with its entrails scattered in the snow.

The sun was already almost gone, and the sky behind the pines was a brilliant, lovely yellow that made the scene more fantastic than ever. Through the small pine trees on either side of the road patrols moved looking for survivors. A band of peasants was piling saddles, rifles and other gear together, and carrying corpses to the huge yellow wagon that had returned for yet another load.

I poked round among a bundle of papers. From a volume on which a Swedish journalist picked out for me the words "Stalin. The principles of Leninism" a photo tumbled out. I have it still. It showed a group of Russian army officers, roughly dressed, standing and sitting together like a football team. They had simple, sincere faces, some intelligent, some sympathetic, some rather dull. Here, too, one man was completely Mongoloid in type. There were other snaps of men taken on manœuvres, snaps of friends together, posed pictures of young soldiers in their uniform. A propaganda film lay spilled from its case in the snow. There had been a complete wagon with cinema projection apparatus and printing presses for the field newspaper. The paper heads for the field newspaper had on them coloured pictures of Red Army men dragging big guns by tractors. The whole thing gave an atmosphere of rather informal friendliness. You felt that it had been rather good fun to be an officer in this division. There was a sense of informality and simplicity about the whole affair. But that had not been enough to save them from this disaster. And success is the only thing that counts, ultimately, in armies.

It would have been better if they had left some of this propaganda gear behind, and brought white snow clothes and skis and warm food. This column seemed to show that the Red Army was not designed for this type of sudden raid into another country. It had been developed for different purposes—to bring arms and aid to a people already in revolt, or to defend the soil of the Soviet Union. That red flag, stretched in the snow, was ultimately meant to be their greatest weapon. When it was raised the armies of the enemy would gradually melt away and come to the Soviet side; the Internationale from those band instruments would break down the enemy walls as the trumpets had broken down the walls of Jericho. But these weapons had proved of no avail in this war in Finland, for the Finns did not see this as a war of liberation. For them the red flag was something to fire at, not to hail. After I had seen that battlefield of Kemi River I believed that it was going to cost the Soviet heavy to carry out, with this huge, unadapted army, this move which was essentially, from every military standpoint, a smash-and-grab raid.

In the gathering dusk we started back for Kemijärvi. Our young chauffeur drove with his eyes reddened. He talked quickly in Finnish to Toivala. It seemed he had walked deep out into the woods, and seen everywhere bodies, bodies. You could see that each dead Finn had been to him his brother. Outside Pelkosenniemi village we stopped to take aboard an officer wrapped in a blanket, a feverish, shivering figure. It was the Captain who had fallen into the river at the start of the attack. He was already in the first stage of the pneumonia which was to kill him.

It was dark when we reached Kemijärvi. We changed cars, for the chauffeur had asked if he could remain behind. He wanted to see for one moment the body of his brother, whom they had brought in for burial that afternoon. Still impassive, he drove away while we changed cars beside the shadow of the captured tanks and raced back to Rovaniemi.

It was not till I settled down at the typewriter to write that I noticed the date on a Finnish paper lying there. I saw it was December 21, the day by which, the Finns declared, the Soviet Generals had determined to win the war, for it was Stalin's birthday.

CHAPTER XV

FINNISH TOWN

WHEN THE SIRENS began it was so dark behind the blacked-out windows of my hotel bedroom, covered as they were with thick brown paper, that I could not tell whether it was day or still night. There seemed to be two of these banshees, wailing in turn. I looked at my watch and saw that it was just ten o'clock. I pulled open the window and a blast of Arctic air came in, but I had had time to see that it was day and the sky clear for the first time since I had been in Rovaniemi. I pulled on my clothes, and moved out into the corridor. This hotel, close to the bridge, seemed to me a peculiarly unhealthy place to be in in an air raid, and what better military objective could there be than the bridge leading towards Kemijärvi?

Outside, the people of Rovaniemi, mostly women wrapped in

fur-collared coats, carrying rugs and cushions and bundles, were hurrying across the snow to the shelter. Its wooden doors, flung open by an A.R.P. official, gaped black in the white of a little field in front of the Pohjanhovi. Boys on skis slid along the street, piled their skis outside the shelter, and went down. Nurses and Lottas were helping the wounded, on crutches and sticks, across from the floor of the hotel that served as hospital. On the ice of the far bend of the river black figures were running for the woods; men were frantically whipping their sled horses. Above the low green hills the sky was pale and beautiful with the first colours of the sunrise-sunset glow which was all we saw of the sun these mid-December days.

The hotel stood on a bush-edged bank twenty feet high above the river. Soldiers and civil guards, pulling on white cloaks, took up their posts in the bushes. On the roof of a hut two men, like penguins in their white clothing, fitted a belt of ammunition into a machine-gun. Wallenius, wearing a short white fur coat, came out of the hotel and drove away in his car. The sirens stopped, and a complete stillness took their place.

Down in the dark shelter trench it was surprisingly warm. Soldiers, waitresses from the hotel, Lottas, nurses talked and joked. A seventeen-year-old boy, the air-raid warden, kept watch by the entrance. Gradually, away beyond the low hills, we heard the hum of planes. They came closer and closer, clearly flying very high. But they avoided us by at least three miles, and droned on south towards Kemi railway junction. Our one anti-aircraft gun, hidden in the forests over the river, held its fire. The All Clear went, and one more alarm was over. We trooped out of our shelter, back to breakfast.

This scene was to become as familiar to me as anything I have known, for in the next five weeks I was to experience it morning after morning. This little town where it happened became a place that I came to love. In Rovaniemi I really grew to know Finland. I entered into its life in a way which would never have been possible in Helsinki. I got away from that international hotel atmosphere which hangs round all modern journalism and is the curse of it, and absorbed, unconsciously rather than intentionally, the life of these northern Finns day after day. When I think of Finland it is to Rovaniemi that my mind instinctively turns.

GM

Rovaniemi in normal times is the home of some thousand people. It is the northernmost town of Finland, for between it and the Arctic there is, apart from the big village of Ivalo, nothing but wild wastes and tundras. It is the marketing town for Lapland. Here the Lapp reindeer proprietors, the peasants and the timber workers come to spend their money. In the summer the Petsamo road and its position on the Arctic Circle bring it a substantial tourist trade, chiefly from Sweden. Its life was very typically that of any small Finnish country town.

The Pohjanhovi, though unusual in appearance, was only one of the modern hotels that the Finns had built in the north to develop their tourist trade. True, it was the most elaborate of them. Built of grey concrete, the windows which ran right along one side gave the tourists a view across the river and to the hills beyond. In front, seven flagpoles, now bare, carried in normal times the flags of all neighbouring nations. The only absentee had been, I was informed, the Red Flag of Russia. It had very good modern fittings—steel bedroom furniture, telephones, great brick fireplaces in the hall and on every landing, and the lift so proudly advertised as "the most northerly lift in the world".

Its porter was a burly Finn with, of all things, a strong Australian accent when he spoke English. He had emigrated to Australia after the last war and had been for a time a kangaroo hunter. The best Finnish fur caps were, incidentally, made of specially imported kangaroo hides. He controlled two minute assistants, who even up here wore complete "buttons" uniforms, and acted as everything from air-raid wardens to telephone operators. Around his desk advertisements still told of bus rides to Petsamo, and of the permanent wave that you could get at the barber's in the main street.

The barber in Rovaniemi was a woman—they often are in Finland—and a very good-looking woman, too, dark haired and chic in a way that looked very sophisticated beside the rounded, simpler faces of the other Finnish girls. She had two shops, one for men and one for women, both fitted up as smartly and modernly as anything you will see in the biggest British provincial cities.

Seven miles northward, on the Arctic Highway which ran for 240 miles to Petsamo, a signpost marked the Arctic Circle. Local gossip had it that the Circle should actually hit about the centre of the town, but that the taxi drivers had managed to get the post set just a good fare's distance from town.

The rest of the town was made up chiefly of one-storied wooden buildings, spreading out from a crossroad where the snow was by mid-December already banked by the pavement edges. There was, however, a big two-storied co-operative store, and a series of offices of new, modern design, and the inevitable sauna, the steam bath. This was one of the genuine primitive models. The steam came from a series of blackened, heated stones in an oven high up in the wall of the small steam chamber. You took off your clothes in a cubicle in a dressing-room, then took your towel and walked past groups of curious Rovaniemians and soldiers back on leave, till you got to the steam room. Here an ancient hag, steamed down till she was nothing but a skeleton with a covering of skin, hurled a beaker of water on to the stones. Immediately the room filled with choking hot steam.

The hardened bathers climbed up a wooden stair which led to bunks set in on the opposite side of the room, right under the roof. Here the steam was at its most intense. You lay there till the sweat drenched you. Then you took a bundle of leafy birch twigs, which were standing in a bucket of cold water, and beat your legs and back and shoulders. It sounds ultra-masochistic, but the leaves always softened the blows, so that it was no more than a hard scrubbing. Afterwards your whole body was fresh with the smell of birch leaves.

Well steamed, you went next door and lay on a wooden bench while the old woman soaped you and washed you from head to foot as if you were a child. This was an essential part of the sauna treatment. It was psychologically, I suppose, a simple reversion to childhood, to the Saturday night tub in your mother's hands. It is an interesting fact that the Finns, who in this war were to show the world what they had always known themselves, that they were one of the toughest races on the earth, should have made this rite part of their main relaxation.

The washing over, you sluiced yourself down with cold water, or rolled in the snow. In the country districts, in saunas on farms, rolling in the snow was the only practical cold douche. But in Rovaniemi it was hardly regarded as the thing. The first time I went, however, the Swedish correspondent who was showing me the sauna technique insisted on it. To the amazement of the two women attendants, we ran out into the only snow available—the main street outside—and rolled there in the freshly-fallen drifts. Fortunately it was dark. Otherwise we would have been frowned on, for Rovaniemi, like all the country districts of Finland, was sternly religious, and tolerated no nonsense.

Before it went to the sauna, Rovaniemi went ski-ing. Or rather, in times of peace it went ski-ing, trudging across the frozen river to the pine slopes of the Ousnawara or to the great ski jump to the east. But now almost all private skis had been handed over for army use, and it was rarely that we met anyone on the ski trips which we took in the afternoons. This Finnish ski-ing is, incidentally, very different from the swift alpine runs most British people know. For the Finns, skis were a means of getting over comparatively flat snow country quickly. They used them almost as snow-shoes. They could move on them at incredible speed, running on the flat in quick jog-trot that most Austrians or Swiss would have regarded as excessively exhausting. Cross-country ski races, over undulating areas with little downward slopes, were a major sport. I found on these trips that a downhill run of say half a mile through woods where you had to turn and twist almost every five yards, was regarded as luxury. On the other hand, they were all expert at complicated turns, and as ski-jumpers they were in the front rank of the world.

During the greater part of the five weeks that I was in Rovaniemi the thermometer set on the outer wall of the Pohjanhovi showed temperatures of minus eighteen to minus thirty degrees centigrade. People often ask me if this cold was not terrible. But the truth is, when I look back on Finland, I do not have any great recollections of overwhelming cold. I remember long car drives, when, half car-sick on the bouncing roads, I sat back with my feet so cold that they seemed past pain; I remember wind stinging my nose, frosting my eyebrows, till I had to rub my face with snow as protection against frostbite; I remember the sharp, cold air that rushed into your lungs as you stepped out from the hotel. But to deal with winter the Finns had worked out proper types of clothing and housing. I wore ample clothes to guard against it—double sets of underwear, two and three sweaters, a wool lined canvas coat; a leather cap with fur flaps; gloves. Even on the fronts, to talk with officers we went usually into the warm arctic tents, where stoves gave a temperature of up to twenty degrees; we travelled in cars with heaters which kept much of the cold down; the trains were warmed throughout the war; and at the end of each journey there was always the Pohjanhovi, with its ample food, its central heating. Another great factor was that the air was dry. It was a dry cold, so that you could walk in the snow without getting your feet wet, and the powdered snow on your boots rubbed off like dust.

Food, in the Pohjanhovi, and in all the other restaurants I ate in, up and down North Finland, was always ample. The standard foods—butter, milk, biscuit-like bread, sausage, reindeer meat, herring were always available. As well, you could get soups, cold smoked salmon, steaks (sometimes of bear), eggs, tinned fruit and any amount of fresh apples. I have never felt so well for years as I did on the rudimentary regime in Rovaniemi. Until the very end there was never any lack of foodstuffs in Finland. It must be one of the rare cases of a country which finished its war without one person suffering any degree of malnutrition.

On my first day in Rovaniemi I walked in the growing dusk to a yard where the skis of the villagers, stacked into heaps, were being waxed ready for use by the troops. Held before an open fire, whose flames were a splash of golden colour in the drab grey setting, they were rubbed with wax by ski experts. All the industry of this little town was, in fact, linked to the war effort with that ant-like efficiency which characterised all that the Finns did. The Lapps had given up making the bright red and blue and yellow-edged hide gloves and leggings for tourists, and turned to making simpler ones for the army. Old Lapp women, with tiny wizened faces, smoking pipes as they worked, sat in warm sheds sewing the hides. In other sheds nearby, the purple meat of the reindeer, the staple food of Lapland, was stacked for military use. It needed no refrigerators. Killed in the first frosts of late October, it would keep in any shed until April. It was used in small shreds or in tiny squares, for it was very tough, and needed a great deal of cooking.

In a school building the local Lotta association was packing up parcels for the troops for Christmas. It seemed almost absurd, I thought when I first saw them, to be sending off Christmas parcels in this war in which the tiny Finnish army was bound to be routed, but still they were doing it. Brawny workers' wives stood side by side with more obvious members of the local bourgeoisie, all in their grey Lotta uniforms with the blue swastika badge at their necks. The uniforms were prim, with high necks, puritanical and stiff. I looked among these women for any sign of condescension on the one side, or of truckling on the other, but I could see none. They seemed to treat each other as equals in this work at least. I spoke with the working woman through an interpreter on the war. She seemed unsaddened by the war, but her spirit was one of defiance rather than tragedy. She saw it as something which must be won; defeat did not apparently enter her mind.

Never once in all those five weeks in Rovaniemi did I come across any sign of antagonism to the war, or of feeling that Soviet Russia, and not a Mannerheim-led Finland was the true spiritual home of these peasants or workers. True, Lapland is an economically primitive and inherently conservative part of Finland. But I had here always a sense of solid communal spirit of resistance right till the end; even the war weariness that ultimately came, never showed itself in any manifestations, personal or public, against the war policy of the Government.

For all its unity, Rovaniemi was as full of social differentiations as any small town in, say, the American Middle-West or Australia and New Zealand. The leadership of the Lottas was safely entrusted to the wife of one of the bank managers. On Saturday nights in normal times the middle classes of the place gathered to eat and dance to the radio in the Pohjanhovi; even in wartime the bank managers, the daughters of the chief shop-keepers, the heads of the police, and the army officers ate there, talked to the journalists and listened, through the shriek of Moscow jamming, to the news bulletins on the radio. All dancing had been stopped during the war. For the Finns war was almost a religious act, to be taken with its requisite grimness. It was a terrible tribute to the blood-letting that their previous wars had brought.

In peace time, the other people gathered to dance in the hall of the fire brigade. The fire brigade held in Finland as privileged a position as the "pompiers" in France. Like them they were apparently required to act as everything from doctors in street accidents to searchers for lost children. Every Saturday night the chairs in the hall above the engine shed—the brigade was, incidentally, purely voluntary—were pushed aside, a local jazz band got busy, and the dancing started. It was frequently surrounded by a high degree of heavy schnapps drinking, and ended in occasional fights in which puukkos—daggers—were used.

The Finns fought with puukkos in earnest. The technique, as explained to me, was this. You seized your puukko by the blade, leaving half an inch of the tip free, and demanded from your opponent, "How much can you take?" If he agreed on the same amount you then went at it trying to gouge each other's legs and arms and stomachs. But I doubt if this careful ritual often went into play, though there seemed, by all accounts, to be fights enough in the country districts.

If you killed a man in a puukko fight you got only imprisonment, and not a very heavy sentence of that. There was no death penalty in Finland. If you killed a man in a drunken fight you got an even slighter sentence. For a crime passionelle it was less still.

A simple, hard people, these Finns. Certainly not people to interfere with, as Arthur Mencken, of Paramount News, found one night in Helsinki when he interfered in a quarrel between a screaming girl and four soldiers in a back street. He was in hospital for a week with a badly injured ankle where he had been kicked by one of the Finns. The U.S. Military Attaché was also attacked in the black-out as a suspect parachutist. The only night I went to Helsinki's one dance hall—called the Café de Paris, of all titles—we were cleared out because one soldier had shot another in the middle of the dance floor. But these things happen in wars. If the French censors had not been so strict the world would have heard amazing stories of the outbursts of crimes passionelle in France during the first six months of the war.

In Rovaniemi wages were low. The waitresses in the Pohjanhovi were paid five hundred marks a month—about two pounds ten. Yet the town had a full life. There was no unemployment. There were two cheap popular restaurants, one with neat modern tables and shaded lights, the other at the rear of the Pohjanhovi, where you could get a full meal for a shilling. There was ski-ing on Saturdays and Sundays in the winter, athletics and swimming in the summer; the sauna on Saturday nights; ample food; books—in French, English, German in the local booksellers.

There was even a British circle which studied English and English literature. There were two cinemas, small halls, showing talkies, in programmes that change twice a week. I saw some good films there—Lydia Barova, in an old Czech film; some modern German propaganda pieces.

Until the bad raids which came at the end of January, life in Rovaniemi was little affected by the war. It was only as the fighting wore on, and you passed again and again a coffin being dragged through the streets on a sled, and noticed how more and more women were wearing mourning—their black was like a blow against the white snow—that you could feel the price of it. I felt in the end I knew it all well; the grey-haired station master; the dark girl in the station ravintola, serving coffee and beer at a table under the poster advertising David Hume's detective novels; the wealthier peasants who wore vivid blue Lapp coats, with red and blue edgings, and their wives in the curious coloured Lapp hats, like a cross between a squashed-in opera hat and a mortar board; the six-months-old bear, tied up to the corner of a reindeer-meat shed. He used to try to scramble up the edge of the shed if you frightened him.

In the market-place a photographer, of all people, did constant business. Soldiers about to leave for the front and their girl friends posed before his painted back-drop. Nearby a line of wooden single-room shops formed a local Petticoat Lane, with cheap wool-lined coats, felt boots, black astrakhan caps for sale.

On the outskirts was the local Klubbi, the meeting, and drinking-place of the wealthier citizens. It was the one place where you could get alcohol during the war, for Rovaniemi was in one of the war zones in which prohibition was rigorously enforced. We used to drink milk and an orange drink called ironically enough in these Arctic regions "Valencia". The Klubbi I found a somewhat melancholy place with a walk home that seemed always half a mile too far.

Rovaniemi lived fully. There was a local saying that you could have no private life, because everyone could tell from the footprints in the snow where you had been last night. But the inhabitants seemed to manage despite that. On Sunday evenings, even with the temperature twenty-five below zero, you would see the same strolling pairs of girls, the same loitering groups of boys at the street corners, that you will see on the streets of any small town all over the world.

These youths, and the girls too, did their share of the war work. Many of the boys were already drilling. I would come back from a walk in the morning across the ice of the Kemi River to see, swinging down the road from the wooden houses, a line of troops, singing as they went.

On the frozen bend of the river, men cut green cubes of ice three feet square, and dragged them off on sledges for summer refrigeration; through dark holes in the ice others fished; husky dogs barked and turned in the snow; the air was piercing cold on your nose and eyes as you ski-ed down the slope behind the power station from the shooting range where the anti-aircraft gun was hidden, and where the crew slept in the old ski-er's hut.

One of the last days that I was in Rovaniemi I went up to the ski jump that stood, like some strange mechanical toy, on the edge of the hill four miles from town. It was used as a look-out for aeroplanes. At the foot was a tiny hut, with two Lottas making coffee before going up to take their two-hour turn as watchers on top. I climbed the 200 feet up the swaying, whistling wooden stairs. On the top the wind was icy cold, and felt as if a fully-grown man was pulling at your sleeve. On the upper platform, where the ski-ers began their run, a seventeen-year-old girl, her cheeks flushed with the wind, her fair hair thrust under a grey fur cap, stood wrapped in a great goat-skin, Robinson Crusoe coat. She was from Viipuri. Caught up here when the war began —she had been visiting her sister, who worked in the local stationer's—she had volunteered for this look-out work. For eight hours a day, doing two hours on, two off, three days a week, she watched from this tower, ready to phone down to the hut below if she saw planes through her glasses. A fourteen-year-old boy with a rifle was her sole guard against any plane that might care to machine-gun her.

From the top of the swaying jump the view was magnificent. Dark-green and white, the forests, the frozen river, the fields, the lakes stretched away on every side. A mass of match-boxes scattered by the two spans of the bridges were the log huts and wooden houses of Rovaniemi. A thin grey column of smoke rose from a train in the station. It would not be hard to pick out your objective in this snow, I decided. Far from the snow hiding it—if it were a building—it silhouetted it. And every man was a clear black target, if he were not in his white clothes.

As I stood there at midday the sun came up, sending long dark shadows along the forest rides. Dark pines stretched away to the northern horizon, towards the Arctic Sea, distant, mysterious. The white slope of the ski run was suicidally attractive, like a cliff drop. I held back from it, but the boy guard walked to the very edge, without even holding to the rail. I thought with considerable respect of the men who had built this structure, hammering and cutting timber, away up here in these winds. Behind the trunks of the pines below us, the sky was a deep, rich primrose-yellow, a pure colour that made one think of an Arctic peopled with fantastic creatures, like figures from a coloured cartoon of a fairytale. Planes with bombs, and men with guns, moving to kill seemed impossible. Yet from this look-out, the signals for four air raids, in which over a score of civilians had been killed, had already been given.

We turned to go. The girl was laughing at something our guide had said. She called "Huyva paivaa" to us—"Good-bye". Her yellow hair blowing, her teeth white, she leant back with the sky blue behind her. The boy by her side stood holding his rifle. There was much that was courageous and fine about them both, much of the really fine things that are in the strange, roughfibred spirit of Finland. That same spirit was in the men, the brothers and friends of this boy and this girl, who were even then battling in the distant dark forests to the east over which we stared. I know that is not the only side to the Finnish character. Weeks I spent later in Helsinki were to remind me vividly that in Finland, as in other countries, business and political interest can count more than the people themselves. But when, back here in England, people talk to me of Finland as a country made up entirely of White generals and timber bosses, with a mass of brutalised peasants and workers driven by these leaders into war, I think of the men in the north I saw so often trudging forward to battle and of that boy and girl. For they, no less than Wallenius and Mannerheim and the other bosses, fought this Finnish war with their hearts. That is the truth. It does not fit in with the reading of the Finnish political situation put out à la Kuusinen —but nor did the course of the war. It does not fit in with the theory that the Red Army came into a country where the people were waiting to greet it as a liberator. But it is true, all the same. One of the undeniable facts which anyone who was in Finland during this war must record for history, is that the country fought with a unity seldom equalled by any nation in war. That was true in the north which I saw at this stage of the war, and it was equally true of the more industrialised south, as I was later to realise.

CHAPTER XVI

STOCKHOLM CHRISTMAS

THE BATTLE OF Kemi River not merely gave me a vivid picture of this war in the snow; it gave me a touch of severe colic, the symptoms of which I shall not describe, but which were very unpleasant. I decided that, rather than risk being hospitalised in Rovaniemi, I would go down to Stockholm for a break of several days, and get some full medical attention.

I crossed over the narrow, snow-covered frontier bridge at Haparanda, where millions were made in the last Great War by Swedes who supplied Russia with war materials, and where members of the Finnish Jaeger battalions ski-ed at night over the ice of the Gulf of Bothnia to get to Germany for military training. The streets beyond the boundary were filled with Swedish soldiers, huge blond men in white three-quarter length sheepskin coats and white caps with the three crown badge of Sweden on the front. They filled the dining-room of the main hotel. There were street lights and an illuminated Christmas tree—strange sights after the black-out of Finland. Military lorries swelled the usually meagre stream of traffic; the train for Stockholm was hours late because of troop-train traffic.

The next morning I woke in my sleeping-car half-way down the long route south. I stared, practically blinking, out of my window. What was it that made this scene, ordinary enough in any snow country in winter time, seem so strange? Here too were pines, snow lakes, red houses, as in Finland, and ruddy-cheeked children ski-ing. Then I realised that the difference lay in the light. After the semi-dusk of the mid-winter days of Rovaniemi the colours here were like a Van Gogh picture beside a Corot. That brilliant fresh-washed blue of the sky, that purple-green of the pines were shades deeper, more definite than the colours of Finland in winter. Even the Finnish snow seemed grey in comparison with this sparkling frosted coating.

Stockholm on Christmas Eve was sheer beauty. From every window Christmas trees, bright with lights, showed in the blocks of flats and houses of the suburbs through which my train ran. The yellow buildings round the quays had their coating of white snow, and ice already blocked the harbour, packing in the ferry boats and the grey naval vessels. At night the modern buildings beyond the royal palace were jewelled masses of brightly-lit windows. Beautiful girls—is there any other city in the world with such a high average of feminine beauty as Stockholm?— went past with flushed faces under their fur-edged bonnets. In the incredible Moorish décor of the Royal Restaurant, I sat with Walter Duranty while a jazz band played for the teadance. The dining-room tables at the back were being loaded with Christmas smorbröd; the men and women were well-dressed. It was the richest city I have seen. There was, it is true, a late 1890's, somewhat parvenu air about it all. It was the kind of atmosphere that Oscar Wilde must have delighted to shock. But it was rich. Then as I sat there my mind went back to Finland. I thought of men lying in snow dugouts for days on end. I thought of the patrols working through the woods in temperatures of twenty to thirty below zero; and this wealth seemed a little disgusting. For much of this prosperity I knew was based on war—on other people's wars. Kiruna iron ore, Bofors guns and other armaments not only had brought Sweden wealth now, but had done so during the last war. I knew that other countries lived just as much from armaments and that the Swedes could point to the fact that they had not mis-spent their gains. Their clean cities, healthy people, magnificent blocks of flats, showed that. But the impression remained. I found that every one of my colleagues, without exception, felt this faint antagonism to Sweden when they came from Finland. Some put it down to a trace of surliness in the Swedish men, some rationalised it into a dislike of Sweden's attitude over Finland. Yet no one, coming from Finland during that winter, and having lived in that atmosphere of spartan, almost religious exaltation of struggle could fail to be struck by the contrast of this fat Sweden.

This feeling was far from being confined to foreigners. Many Swedes felt it deeply. Stockholm, that Christmas, had by no means an easy mind with which to enjoy its prosperity. It was torn by anxiety about the Finnish war, by a blend of fear that the war would spread to Sweden and shame that they were not already fighting in it. It reminded me instantly of the Britain I had returned to from Prague just after the Munich settlement. There was that same miasma that hung over us after we had secured "Peace in our time". The younger Swedes stared out over their harbour at the flag on the King's palace, watched the guard go by with the drums at their head, and talked of the days of Gustavus Adolphus and of their great military past. You could feel them searching in themselves for reminders that they had been fighters in their time, had not always been spectators getting rich, that their spirit was not rotted away. Crowds gathered outside the volunteer recruiting offices for Finland. Full-page advertisements in the papers cried "Finland's fate is yours". Bands of volunteers went off nightly from the Swedish station for Haparanda, waving good-bye to people standing in the snow.

By this time 20,000 volunteers had, so the Help of Finland Organisation stated, been registered. But it was doubtful if more than 3,000 had left for the north. These had, amongst them, several prominent Swedish military men. Colonel Viking, who had been the Swedish military adviser to Haille Selassie in the Abyssinian war; Lieutenant-Colonel Dreyssen, director of the Swedish Military Academy; Captain Malcolm Murray, a descendant of one of the Scottish families who had gone to Sweden to fight under Gustavus Adolphus and remained; Lieutenant-Colonel Ehrensvard, a veteran of the Finnish White armies of 1918, had gone off with the first batches. Officers and men serving with the Swedish regular army had been told they could volunteer if they wished. In some barracks commanders called their men on to parade and gave them a chance to volunteer. Thousands stepped forward at these meetings. But the flow of volunteers was being rigidly controlled by the Swedish General Staff. They insisted that the number of volunteers allowed out of the country must be kept down to one-tenth of the mobilised force of the Swedish army. This was at the moment 70,000 men.

Seven thousand men available for Finland would mean barely half a division. I knew that to secure effective aid, at least two or three full divisions of, say, 50,000 men would be required.

The Swedish General Staff did not take this decision because they were not in favour of helping Finland. Most of them were passionately anxious to intervene. It was only hard military facts which prevented them from doing more. For Sweden was ill-equipped and ill-prepared for war, and above all, she lacked trained reserves. During the years of the twenties and thirties, her full drafts had not been called up, because the Government wanted to save money on equipment. Only one quarter of the men trained had, moreover, done any training for winter fighting. The peacetime army had varied in strength from 34,000 to 60,000 men, the larger figure forming the summer draft. The period for training for the infantry was only twenty weeks and for the artillery and specialists just on thirty weeks. Above all the Swedish air force was weak. The programme announced in Parliament was for only 250 first-line planes in 1941. The bombers were chiefly Junkers and the fighters Gloster Gladiators, a machine which was to prove excellent in this cold weather in the north. This force was quite inadequate to deal with any threats from either Russia or Germany. Although the Swedes had few big cities which could be easily destroyed, and though their main armament factories were well protected by their excellent Bofors anti-aircraft guns, they knew that in the air they were not in a position to go to war. Air power in the case of Sweden, as in the case of Finland, was to prove decisive.

Sweden has been bitterly criticised for adopting this negative attitude in the Finnish war, an attitude which never got beyond "non-intervention". But she did not act by fear. Her attitude was one of careful calculation. For it was not Russia which determined Swedish policy at this moment, it was Hitler. It was the shadow of a Nazi invasion looming over the south of Sweden which paralysed her chances of moving in the north. It has never been confirmed that the Prince du Vweid, the German Minister in Stockholm, directly threatened to intervene in the south if Sweden moved to help Finland, and it does not matter much if he did or not. For the threat, even if unspoken, was always there. The Swedes were afraid that if they got into war with Russia Germany would always intervene. The Swedes were menaced on two fronts and they had to choose which enemy was the more dangerous. They chose to conserve their forces to face Germany if necessary. This decision enabled them to keep out of war when Norway was attacked. A Sweden weakened by war would definitely have been overrun and seized by the Germans during the Norway campaign. A Sweden engaged in a long bitter struggle with Russia would probably have been overrun by the Germans to get the iron ore mines. To avoid this her Government preferred to balance on the slippery pole of neutrality.

There was, however, one thing the Swedes could do. They could strengthen their defences as much as possible. Stockholm amidst its atmosphere of Christmas and peace thought and practised war. Troops on skis carried out practice attacks in parks near the Zoological Gardens. From the restaurant there we used to watch them crouching behind trees and rushing across the open fields. Air-raid shelters were laboriously blasted from the granite on which Stockholm is built. Other shelters were built of wood and covered with earth, in the main city squares, side by side with the little skating rinks which were flooded for children. Men in white coats tramped into the woods with skis for musketry practice. A civil defence force, a type of Home Guard, was advocated. The output of war material was rushed. Correspondence courses were even started by newspapers on "How to be a soldier in Three Lessons".

One scene of those last days in December 1939 will always typify the Christmas Stockholm for me. I had gone to visit Barbara Alving at her flat on the outskirts of Stockholm. Her modern sitting-room was full of the atmosphere of the creativeness of peace—newly-designed Swedish furniture, books, magazines, modern lighting. Her baby played round the Christmas tree which was still lit and standing by the window. Outside the voices of children tobogganing in the woods in the dusk came up shrilly. Headlights of cars taking people to concerts, theatres, restaurants, showed on the snow below. Then up through the darkness came three great shafts of light—searchlights. They swept the sky slowly, menacingly. Had they formed the letters by sky writing, they could not have said more clearly, W . . . A . . . R . . .

CHAPTER XVII

VOLUNTEER ROUTE

On the Haparanda-bound train no one was in two minds about Finland. Mack Halton, of the *Toronto Star*, found that out rapidly. Almost every moment of our way back to Rovaniemi we were carried along on a tide of interventionist fervour.

We left Stockholm on December 30, in the evening. On the snow-covered platform, where wind sent gusts of flakes swirling around the paper stand and the refreshment barrow, young Swedes, unmistakably volunteers, leaned from windows among their admiring friends. As we dumped our rucksacks in the sleeper, a tall man with clipped grey moustache watched us closely.

"Aviateurs Italiens?" he asked me, smiling.

"Non, nous sommes des Anglais," I replied.

"Ah, the Royal Air Force. So England now sends aviators into Finland. Bravo. I thought you were Italians, because I travelled north last week with six Italian airmen. One was a colonel who had shot down seven planes personally in Spain."

When I explained that we were mere journalists, he looked as if I had gone out of my way to deceive him personally. So I hastily asked him what Sweden thought of the Finnish war. He had no doubts at all.

"We should intervene with all our forces," he said. "I am a colonel in the Swedish army, I know our situation. If Finland goes Sweden goes too. We should be in there now. Four hundred thousand Swedes and three hundred thousand Finns make seven hundred thousand men. It is a simple sum of arithmetic. But three hundred thousand Finns or four hundred thousands Swedes, standing separately—that is only half the strength.

"We have a great military tradition in Sweden—do not forget that. But we have had no experience for over a hundred years. But the Finns have had experience, both the last generation, and now. Their experience and our resources would make an unbeatable army. Believe me, there is not an officer of importance in the

Swedish army who does not believe we should be in there with all our might."

He paused to curse the Socialist politicians who had let the army's strength drop during the post-war years. I asked him about volunteers for Finland in the ranks of the serving Swedish forces. "Whole regiments have volunteered," he said. "But only a limited number are allowed to go."

The next morning Mack and I climbed out for breakfast in a station restaurant. We sat at a table with three young soldiers. One of them leant forward and said in English, "Finland?" I nodded, but this time decided I was going to get in first. "Journalist," I said. He paused, then grinned knowingly. "Yes," he said, "I understand. We see a lot of foreign 'journalists' going along this line to the recruiting depôt at Haparanda. Well, good luck."

Back on the train Mack got into a violent argument with a young N.C.O., who started out as a great champion of the Finns, and then revealed himself as a Number One rank Nazi. The Jews were really at fault for everything, and as for Churchill, well, who could believe Churchill? "Where is the *Ark Royal*?" he said, grinning as if he had made an original remark. We tried to tie him down about why he disliked the Jews. "Well," he said, "when I lodged at Gothenburg I had a Jewish landlady whom I saw tear the wings off a fly. That shows you that Jews are brutal, like the Russians."

At a wayside station half-way up the long coast he and a group of others got off. "We may see you in Finland," he said. "We are getting off here for a special machine-gun course." I discovered later that this was a training point for volunteers for Finland.

I gave up talking and typed out my expenses. It was dark when we got out at the railway station at Boden, the chief Swedish fortress city in the north, and junction for both Haparanda and the Kiruna ore mines. We prowled about asking for the Haparanda train. A tall man came up to us. "English," he said. We agreed that this was so. "On your way to Haparanda?" Right again. "Come along then, I've been told about you," he said. He led us to a room where a military telephone and a pile of maps and papers stood on a table, and a heap of mattresses in one corner. A man wearing the uniform of a Swedish army captain, but with the collar unbuttoned, came in and said in German, "You go on by the first train in the morning. Dump your rucksacks there. You can get something to eat in the dining-room. You'll find there are half a dozen others going on with you. One of you can sleep in the bathroom upstairs. But we've no ordinary rooms. The hotel is full of officers."

It did not need all this to make clear to us that this must be the volunteers "forwarding office" in Boden. So I came out with, once again, the fact that we were journalists and that, thank you, we would just as soon go on to another hotel. "Journalists, not volunteers," I repeated.

The captain nodded knowingly. Funny how some people stick to their alibis, even right up here, his expression seemed to say. Two other men who had come into the room smiled. I called in Mack's assistance. "If you can't make this fellow understand who we are you'll find us marching over the bridge at Tornio with rifles on our shoulders to-morrow," I said. "It's certainly the press-gang method," he said. So he started in too, flinging the word journalist around, but with no result. Finally we got hold of the big man who had met us on the station. He understood at once. "Of course, I know you are only journalists. The secret police rang me from Stockholm about you. That's why we fixed you up for the night here," he said. "I'll explain to the captain."

I was still puzzled why the secret police should have such intimate knowledge, or such great interest, in our movements. Then my eye fell on a notice on the wall. Printed in five languages—Swedish, French, German, and English and Russian—(Russian was the last)—it forbade any visitor to Boden to go outside a certain area marked blue on a map alongside. The rest was forbidden fortress zone. So that was it. The police, knowing we would have to stay overnight in Boden, were taking care that we did not wander about along the new line of fortifications which were being hurried up here to strengthen old defences.

The dining-room was packed with engineer-officers, tall young Swedes making huge suppers of herring, hors d'œuvres and Vienna schnitzels. The Christmas tree still stood in a corner of the room. We shared a table with one young engineer. He assumed at once that we were volunteers, and told us that the Swedes ought all to be in Finland fighting. These fortifications they were building now were not strong enough to stop any real push. The concrete did not set properly in the cold. The hours of daylight were too short to get the job done before the spring. Their best defence line was the Finnish woods, he said.

Just before midnight Mack retired to his bathroom, which stank, and I settled down on a mattress underneath the table in the operations room. Half a dozen other men came in and stretched out in the room. Three were Finns who had lived in Sweden, on their way back to be mobilised into the army. Two others were Danish volunteers. Under a huge Swedish military coat that one lent me, I was warm and comfortable. It was just as I was dropping off to sleep that I heard midnight strike. Only then did I realise that this was New Year's Eve.

The next day the Haparanda train was late. We decided to do the fifty-odd miles there by car. By ten o'clock we were lurching over ice-bound roads through red-walled Swedish villages, northwards. Our driver was a young Swede who looked with great respect at our rucksacks. Before the words "volunteers for Finland" could form on his lips I cut in with "Journalisti"— this time at least there was going to be no misunderstanding. But when we stopped for coffee at a wayside farm, the radio was tuned in to the Finnish programme. In Swedish a New Year's fighting message was being given by a bishop. "Finland . . . good?" I said by way of conversation to the chauffeur. To my horror he leant over and patted Mack on the back proudly, and said, "Good man. Very good man to fight for Finland."

But worse was to come. At Haparanda we drove straight to the Station Hotel. A Swedish sentry at the door paused, seemed to be in two minds, then saluted hurriedly as the chauffeur said, "English volunteers." Two curious, interested spectators followed the British volunteers upstairs. The chauffeur dumped our bags in front of the porter's lodge and said, again proudly, "Two British volunteers." The porter rapped out, "Take them over to the town commander."

Then I told once again our old old story, that seemed so simple and yet so incredible, that we were journalists. To prove it I asked for a phone call to the Press Officer at Rovaniemi. But the chauffeur was not to be convinced. When we paid him off, he shook hands solemnly, then slapped us on the back and said

"Good Luck" with an expression of hero-worship that made me literally blush. As he rushed down the steps towards his car he looked as if he were going to rush home, throw up his job at once, and join up as a volunteer. "If those fellows can do it, I can," he seemed to be saying to himself.

We lunched in strange company. Two young Swedes, obviously student volunteers, talked gravely at the next table, listening to the radio news. Behind them another young man sat with one of the most beautiful girls I have ever seen. Excellently dressed, made up, she looked as if she were a week-ender at a fashionable resort, instead of someone in this narrow, odorous station restaurant. God knows what she was doing in Haparanda. I hoped that at least she was going to turn out to be a spy.

By two o'clock we had at last got a car, and were safely through the customs. As we drove over the bridge into Finland, Mack and I agreed that probably the next day every Haparanda correspondent of the Stockholm papers would have a story about a great contingent of British volunteers passing through to Finland. If so, it was not our fault. We had done our best to disillusion them.

At the edge of the frozen river it was very still. The sun, sinking on the far side, made Finland a flushed, turgid red. There had been bombers over Tornio that morning, the frontier guards told us. They stamped our passes and wished us good luck. We drove over towards the sunset.

CHAPTER XVIII

THE BATTLE OF SUOMUSSALMI

On that New Year's Eve that I had slept on the floor of the Station Hotel at Boden, there had been taking place, in the forests of Central Finland, the most spectacular battle of this war in the north. For the fight of the Suomussalmi forests had reached its peak. It was the Finns' greatest victory. It showed their undoubted superiority in the warfare in the woods, where speed, marksmanship and individual training could count, and

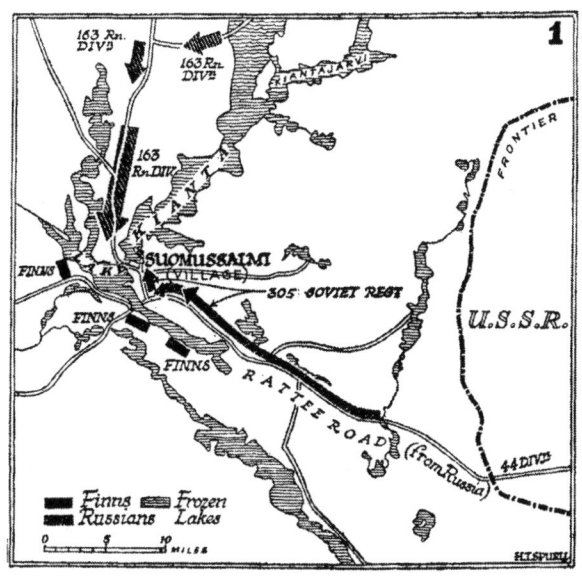
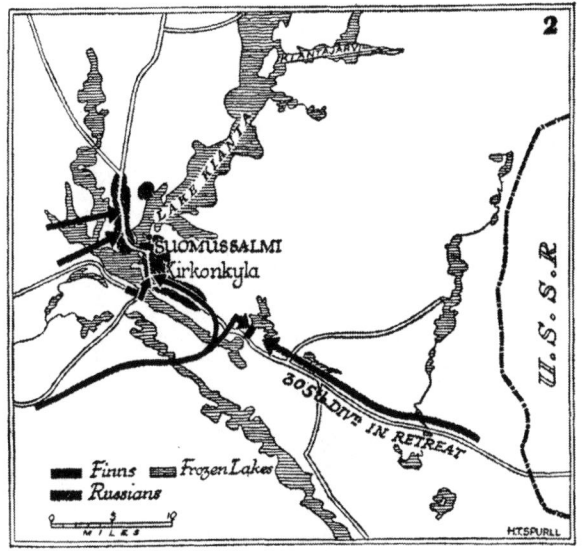

THE BATTLE OF SUOMUSSALMI

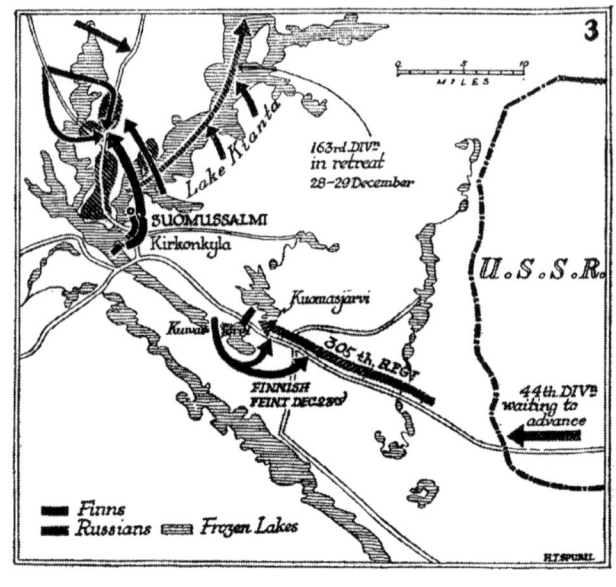
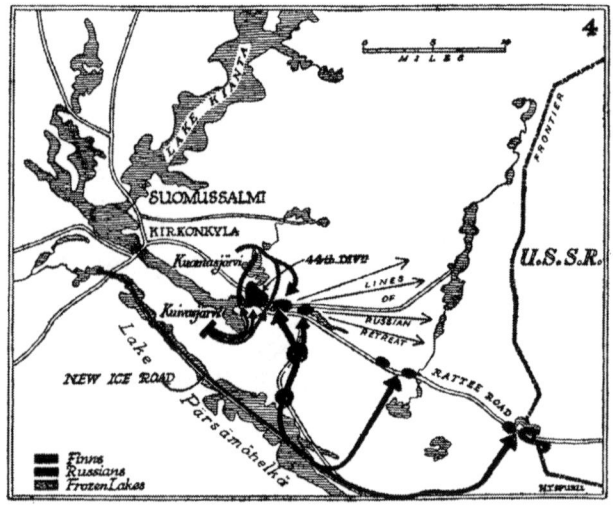

THE BATTLE OF SUOMUSSALMI

THE BATTLE OF SUOMUSSALMI

where material did not primarily matter. It was, it is true, a side-show. It did no more than check a Russian side-thrust and could not affect the ultimate Russian offensive on the Mannerheim Line. But it secured the Finnish army a sure place in military history. It gave them enormous added confidence for the battles in the south and it gave them valuable supplies of war-materials, particularly of artillery.

It had, too, another influence on the war which was not expected immediately. It made the Finns, if anything, a little too confident about their ultimate chances of success and less anxious for foreign aid. It also made such a scar on the Soviet military prestige that Voroshiloff had an additional motive for pouring in men and material regardless of cost to break the Mannerheim Line. Suomussalmi meant that there could be no compromise in the Finnish war. After that the Russians had to have an out-and-out victory before they could make peace.

The Battle of Suomussalmi developed out of the main Soviet "waist-line" offensive, which I had seen starting when I first went to Kuhmo. Under this, attacks were made at a series of points directed towards the town of Kajaani, and the road to Oulu and the Gulf of Bothnia. Had it succeeded Finland would have been cut in half at its narrowest point. The thrust towards Suomussalmi was the most dangerous of these attacks. Suomussalmi, a village on Lake Kianta, was a favourite spot for fishing holidays in peace-time, and was important because five roads centred there. These roads, laid down to develop the tourist traffic, were now essential lines of communication. Along them the Russians could move north, west or south, and paralyse one of the main Finnish road systems. There were, too, good routes in from Russia. One direct road, the Rattee Road, led from Suomussalmi village to the Russian frontier. Another road had been built secretly by the Soviet during the past six months through the forest farther north. This led right up to the frontier, from which there was only a short distance to the top of the lake. The lake itself, once frozen, was a great white boulevard along which Russian tanks could move as if on parade in the Red Square.

The Russian attack began with two big forces moving along these roads, one on each. In the north, over the secret highway came the 163rd Division. In the south, one full regiment, the

305th Regiment of the crack 44th Division, began to move along the Rattee Road straight for Suomussalmi village. There it was to link up with the 163rd, and form a base for the next move inland.

At first this advance went according to plan. The Finns, knowing that the Murmansk railway lay well back on the frontier opposite Suomussalmi, and having only the vaguest reports of the secret road in the north, did not believe that any attack would be made here. They had only one battalion watching the Rattee Road, and sixty men watching the area north of the lake. Both these Finnish forces fell back fighting rear-guard actions. But their blows were no more than pin-pricks against the might of the Soviet divisions. By December 9, both Soviet forces had completed their manœuvre. Their pincers closed and met amid the ruins of Suomussalmi village, which the Finns had destroyed.

Down in Kajaani, General Tuompo, the Commander of this region, had put in charge of the Suomussalmi sector a tough Swedish-Finn, a Colonel Siilasvou. He was one of the seven Fascist M.P.s in the Finnish parliament. With the one battalion at his disposal, he could do no more now than mask Suomussalmi village from the south and check any immediate advance southwards. The Russians, meanwhile, at once set about consolidating their position. The 163rd Division, with its transport spread along the road which ran on the west side of Lake Kianta, began to make dug-outs and gun positions twelve miles north of the lake-head and along the lakeside road. This was to protect their right flank against any hit from the north and enable them to concentrate on the next move towards Kajaani. Half-way along the road, between this fortified position and Suomussalmi village, they had their main supply train. They had with it over fifty tanks and full divisional artillery. The position to the north was held by one battalion and some artillery.

Siilasvou by December 10 had received more troops, so that his forces now numbered at least 2,500 men. With these he decided to punch at the junction of the two Russian forces, at Suomussalmi village. This formed an elbow, just as Sedan was to lie in the spring at the elbow of the French forces on the Maginot Line. His troops in their white snow capes, working in small battle patrols, went into action. The Soviet, harried day and night by these patrols, found the open ground of the village untenable and after three days of fighting they withdrew. At the same time, a section of the Finnish force attacked just east of the village and cut the Rattee Road. This meant that the communications with Russia, of the troops in the village, were severed. The 305th Regiment therefore withdrew towards the Soviet frontier to a point about five miles along the Rattee Road, and began to dig itself in behind a line of barbed wire. The left wing of the 163rd Division withdrew across the ice at the lower end of the lake. The Finns had now two separate forces to attack instead of one main massed force.

This fighting had taken place in some of the wildest country in Finland. Suomussalmi is a region of thick pine forests with an open cleared space of several square miles round the village. For the rest it is a jungle of pine trees, with only narrow forest roads, all snow-covered, and the lake. This made it literally a war in the dark for any side which had not good ski patrols. Aeroplanes were not enough for reconnaissance. Troops could always be easily hidden in the woods away from them. The Finns had ski patrols, the Russians had not. That is the essential fact of the fight around Suomussalmi. The Russians were to a great extent in the position of an expedition moving up some waterway in a jungle region in South America, fighting against highly-skilled local Indians. The Indians can move invisibly through the forest, watching every move on the waterways, knowing exactly where the enemy is. For the enemy is ignorant of the country and, by lack of jungle skill, must keep to the rivers. And that Finnish Indian has, too, not bows and arrows but modern machine-guns. So the Finns moved through the forests, spying on the Russians, who, weighted down with their tanks and supply column of stores, were kept to the roads. Their men, unable to ski, could not make any speed at all in the deep snow in the woods. At no time were any Russian patrols found by the Finns more than three kilometres away from the roadway. The Russian troops were, too, quite unused to forests. They were mostly men from the steppes and deserts of Central Asia. They had, one of their chief officers said later, an almost superstitious dread of trees.

By the 15th December the battle was about to enter on its second stage. More Finnish reinforcements had come up. Tuompo knew that he must move quickly now, for he could not always hope to keep the Russians split. Sooner or later they would drive through and link up at Suomussalmi. He decided that the only strategy to adopt was that of Tannenberg. He must turn on one unit and try to destroy it first; then on the other. He decided to begin with the stronger, the 163rd.

By Christmas Eve he had enough men to start the attack. How strong his forces were I never could discover for certain, but my estimate is that he could not have had more than 7,000 to 9,000 men at the very most. Against him he had to reckon, in the 163rd Division alone, with 18,000 men, of whom at least 12,000 were actual fighting men. The rest, lorry drivers, cooks, barbers, etc., could be counted as virtually non-combatant. He took, as his headquarters for that attack, the town of Ylinaljanka, thirty miles due west from the centre of Lake Kianta. As he steadily moved his troops into position, his advance patrols harried the lakeside road where the Russians were encamped. They fired on lorries and sentries and kept the enemies' nerves continually on edge. On December 20 in this fighting the Finns managed to cut the lakeside road, and split the division into two. After this success Tuompo decided to attack the whole division by this sector system, cutting the Russian line into a series of disconnected units, and destroying each separately by continual attack by forest patrols.

The Russians themselves precipitated the actual battle. Siilasvou had planned to make his main attack on New Year's Day, but on December 23 his scouts who were watching the 305th Regiment encamped along the Rattee Road came back with alarming news. The regiment was packing up, preparing apparently to advance towards Suomussalmi, to close the gap. Siilasvou at once went into action. He had two companies watching the Rattee Road. He ordered them to move up through the forest and make a feint attack on the head of the Russian column, before it got into movement.

This manœuvre worked. Firing from the woods, the Finnish machine-gun patrols at night attacked the head of the 305th Regiment and killed about 200 horses and several score of men. The horses, tied to supply sledges, reared and panicked. In the darkness the column was flung into confusion. Afraid that this was the first move in a major attack, the Russian commander ordered his men to dig themselves in along the roadside while he wirelessed back for instructions. His corps commander told him to stand up until the remainder of the division, the 44th, came up to join him. They were already massed on the frontier and were due to be at Suomussalmi in three days' time. But those three days, which the Finns had gained by their audacity, were to be decisive.

On December 26, at half a dozen points along the lakeside road, Siilasvou launched his main offensive against the 163rd Division. To the north, one Finnish battalion advanced southwards and, after hard fighting, captured the artillery positions and the fortified posts that had been set up to protect the Russian right flank. Another unit steadily rolled up the southern end of the road from Suomussalmi northwards. But the main attack came from the woods and straight at the Russian supply centre half-way up the lake. Here Russian troops sleeping by the roadside were suddenly attacked by fire from fifty different points. It was the same story as at Kemi River. The Finns, invisible, were sheltered by trees; the Russians were on the open road. Other Finnish patrols had moved across the lake and were hitting the Russians in the rear. Everything that moved along the road was attacked. Lorries could not get through to the troops. Field kitchens could not work. The route leading across the lake and the road in the north to Russia were already cut by Finnish patrols. No more food was coming up.

Then General Winter took his place on the Finnish side. The temperature tumbled catastrophically. On Boxing night it was thirty-five degrees centigrade below zero, the coldest night this region had known for over twenty years. The average temperature for the five days of battle was thirty degrees below, far lower than is normal. The Russian equipment and clothing, good enough for normal times, was useless. The better-equipped Finns had every advantage. They had even hot food during the battle, brought up by sledges from the rear. The Russians depended for their food supplies on services organised by truck up and down the road where the food was handed out to the troops. But the trucks were frequently frozen up, and could not move. Patrols and men were sent from different infantry units to collect supplies from the central depot half-way up the lake. But they had no speed and could make no distance on foot in the snow. For four days the Russians fought bravely, but for four days they froze and starved. At last the commander of the 163rd saw it was a hopeless fight. He asked to be allowed to withdraw and was told to do so.

His retreat was well carried out. He formed up on the edge of the lake a column of lorries and sledges, in the midst of which his infantry marched. On either side he put his tanks, about twenty in all. Carefully up the centre of the lake the column moved. The Finns, who were working along the lake shore, attacked with their machine-guns, but the range was too great. They sent over the three Bristol Blenheim bombers they had stationed at Kajaani, but the Soviet sent up chasers which held them off. By New Year the column was back over the Russian frontier. As a fighting unit it was finished. Its losses were huge. The Finns buried over 1,500 dead along the road in the woods nearby. Thousands of others lay frozen to death in the woods, undiscovered until the snows melted in the spring. Hundreds of prisoners were taken. On the road scores of lorries, masses of material and guns were captured. Enough chloroform, ether and morphine were taken to last the entire Finnish army for three months. A great quantity of surgical instruments, still unpacked from their cases, was also captured.

The cold continued to kill even after the guns were silent. Russian fugitives, maddened by the frost at night, used to creep back during the whole of the next week into a schoolhouse that had been fitted up as an emergency Soviet field hospital, and sleep there, amidst the corpses which covered the floor. This hospital was one of the most macabre sights of the war. Ebbi Munck, the Arctic explorer who worked in the North as correspondent to the Danish paper, saw it on New Year's Eve. Here is what he said of it: "We went over the school building in the dark. Two Finnish soldiers were sent with us. They went ahead into every room, revolver in hand, flinging open the door and flashing round their torches to see if there were any Russians hiding there.

"One room had been fitted as an operation theatre. On the table lay a corpse frozen, his stomach hastily sewn up with string. Blood had oozed out all over the table, so that it looked like a butcher's shop. One wounded man, his arm hacked off as if with a chopper, had been left to die in the corner. Beside the table was a bag of surgical instruments, all first class and still packed. There was a big jar of frozen human blood with which the Soviet had been experimenting for transfusions. The surgeons had clearly been told to go at a moment's notice. In the schoolyard were a number of wooden shelters where children in peacetime left their bicycles or ponies. These were filled with wounded who had frozen to death in their beds after the Russians had gone. A playshed was stacked high with naked bodies, white, like planks of wood. Their uniforms had been stripped off. A farmhouse nearby, used as headquarters by Russian officers, had been left, also in a great hurry. A smashed tank stood in the yard. On a table inside were the remains of a meal—bread, cheese, sausage—lying amongst the gas masks, maps and steel helmets."

On the roads, exhausted Russians for days afterwards staggered forward and gave themselves up as prisoners. One group, completely worn out, were being taken to the rear in a lorry which, as Finnish lorries so often did, skidded into the ditch. The prisoners were thrown out into the snow. They lay there, too weak even to stand. When I drove over the road a week later I picked up maps of the district, and, significantly enough, a proclamation in Finnish telling the people to give up their arms within forty-eight hours to the Soviet commander. There were great masses of propaganda material and red flags lying everywhere. Here, too, it seemed that the Russians expected an occupation and not a battle.

The 163rd had been completely defeated. Siilasvou could feel that half the battle at least was won. But only by a hair's breadth. For already, on December 27, he had heard that the Russian reinforcements were moving on the Rattee Road. The bulk of the 44th Division was coming up to support the 305th Regiment. It was for him a time of great anxiety. For he had concentrated against the 163rd all but two companies of his men. Masking the 305th Regiment in the woods east of Suomussalmi during the time of all this fighting were only these 200 Finns. They kept up a continual sniping and patrol activity to give the impression of being a greater number, but one attack would inevitably have broken their line. But that attack never came. The 305th Regiment during the whole of the battle on Boxing Day and the days after had not stirred a yard. For they were blinded by their lack of patrols, and could not have any idea how many troops were lying in front of them. They waited for the whole division to come up before making a move, on the flank of the Finns. But they had left it too late.

By the night of December 31, when the 163rd were finally in flight, Siilasvou allowed his men three hours' sleep after the five days of battle. Then they were marched over to concentrate on the attack on the 44th.

The Rattee Road runs through thick forest and over undulating country for all its twenty-eight miles from the Soviet border to Suomussalmi village. Two feet of frozen snow lay on it and throughout the surrounding woods. The head of the two regiments of the 44th which were coming to join the third regiment crossed the frontier late on December 27, and moved steadily forward. Their orders were to attack on January 1 or 2. By the night of the 31st, the full division was in position, with the 305th Regiment still as their spearhead. Their commander, Colonel Vinagradov, had in all three infantry regiments, the 305th, 146th and 25th; two artillery regiments, one regiment of engineers, one regiment of patrol troops, and a communications regiment. It was a first-class division famous for its fighting in the civil war, and the war of intervention after 1918. Its parade march was one of the best-known Soviet tunes. (After the defeat of Suomussalmi, the tune was banned in Russia.) Its popular name was "The Blue Division". It was a regular army unit, but the divisional papers captured by the Finns showed that its strength had been considerably increased since October 7 by reservists. The men had been elaborately trained in open warfare, but they were found to be scary in these dark northern forests. The bulk of the troops were peasants from Ukraine, but there were many other nationalities. Of 461 prisoners later taken in one area, 363 were Ukrainians, the others included a Sudeten German, some Poles, two Turks, a White Russian, Carelians, Jews, Greeks, Georgians, Turkestans, Baskirs, Usbecks, Murmans. Most of them spoke only Ukrainian and no Russian. One Finnish-speaking man was attached to each battalion.

The division with their tanks and guns now occupied a stretch of over five miles of road. Their advance-guard was opposite the barbed-wire entanglements that had been run across the road five miles west of Suomussalmi village.

Colonel Siilasvou decided to use the same tactics that he had employed against the 163rd—cutting the Russian lines of communication and hitting them in the flank from the woods. To move his troops more quickly he had had built, during the last ten days, a road through the snow along the frozen line of Lake Parsamonselka, which ran thirty miles south of the Rattee Road, roughly parallel. The Finns then divided their forces into four groups. One company was sent right through the woods to cut the Rattee Road at the Soviet border. A second small force was sent to harry the road half-way along from the frontier and to watch a bridge which crossed a fifteen-foot gully there. The third main force was sent through the woods from the south to strike at the left flank of the head of the Soviet column where it lay on the road. Another smaller force worked round to hit at the same time from the north. Guarding the road in front were only three companies, some 300 men. Had the Russians tried to advance they could have pushed these men aside at any time. But Siilasvou, just as Wallenius did at Kemi River, gambled on the Russians not moving forward.

At midnight on New Year's Eve, the company sent to the frontier cut the road by felling some trees across it, and took up their position in ambush at the side. From that moment onwards not a single Soviet supply lorry and not a scrap of food reached the 44th from Russia. When they crossed the frontier on the 28th, the Red Army men had carried two days' supply of food with them. This would soon be gone; only limited quantities of reserve food was carried with the division. Its leaders had counted on a steady flow of supplies from the frontier.

On the night of January 1 the Finns launched their first main attack. They examined the ground carefully and hit at the three regimental headquarters and at the divisional headquarters along the road. Their men crept in the darkness within a hundred yards of the road, and opened fire with light and heavy machine-guns, rifles and light mortars. Sections ski-ed up in the forest, hurled grenades towards the road and ski-ed away. They started a battle which was to last for four days, almost without a break. When I later went over the road I could pick out the spots where the fighting had been heaviest, for the trees were blasted and splintered by bullets and mortar shells.

The Russians in answering this attack were faced with a double task. They had to try to hold their main front on this road, a strip of territory five miles long and at the most a quarter of a mile to half a mile wide. This "salient" was thrust out into a forest where their enemy had perfect cover and freedom of movement. At the same time they had to launch counter-attacks along the road to their rear to try to break the block at the frontier and get their food supplies in. Both jobs they did with fatalistic courage, but in both cases without success.

The best account of the battle comes not from any Finnish sources, but from a Russian major who was captured wounded, and later talked in detail in his prison camp to a group of journalists. He had been in the Red Army twenty-two years. He was a former Tsarist officer who, as a young lieutenant, had deserted from Kolchak's White Army and joined the Red Army. He had only recently been attached to the 44th Division. He said that all the men in it were well-trained, and the only reservists were barbers, cooks and other extra men. He himself had crossed the frontier with the last of the bulk of the division on December 30. The plan was that the main attack would be launched on the 1st or 2nd as soon as the regular food supplies came up. No extra fodder for the horses was carried. They had only been settled in position a few hours before the Finns launched their first main attack. The major said: "They went first for the centre of the column where the 146th Regiment was stationed. We suffered severely. Their machine-gun fire, backed by some artillery fire, took great toll of the men.

"At the same time one Finnish plane flew over dropping propaganda leaflets promising our men free return to Russia if they surrendered.

"By the evening of January 2—the Tuesday—most of the officers could see that the situation was very serious. At mess at divisional headquarters that night we urged Vinagradov to give the order to retreat. But he refused. Instead he sent, the next day, two companies of the 146th Regiment—the only two of that regiment in any real shape to fight on—and one battalion of the 25th to force a way to the frontier and let the supplies come through.

"But they were held up by Finnish fire from the woods and could not do the job. At the same time another Finnish flank attack was launched. We then sent more men to try to force open that stranglehold on our communications, and kept on doing so throughout three days. But each time we lost heavily—about seventy per cent of the effectives who went.

"All this time, our men were suffering terribly from cold and hunger. On the 4th three Russian planes of the V2 scouting type tried to drop some food, but much of it fell in the woods. So we went on through the 5th, still fighting back attacks. By the 6th the men were panicky and so weak that they were unable to move.

"At 5 p.m. Vinagradov at last got the order by radio to retreat. He was told to go at nine-thirty that night. This order must have come either from Meklis, the commissar-in-chief of the corps, or from General Duhinen, the corps commander, himself. At nine o'clock Vinagradov told me to take over command of the remnants of the 146th and fight a rear-guard action. He then got into a tank and drove off. We were then near the head of the position, twenty-two miles from the frontier. He went off in a column with seven other tanks. They got three miles farther on, then were held up.

"At nine-thirty, with three officers and two hundred men who were all that were left of the regiment, we began to march back. I was wounded in the arm and was finding it difficult to walk owing to loss of blood. Two men helped me. We were sniped all the time. Once one of the men with me was shot dead by a bullet in the back.

"Eleven miles from the frontier, worn out, we left the road and strayed into the woods. There in the morning we were found asleep by a Finnish ski patrol and taken prisoner."

The Finnish officers later told me that they intercepted, either by listening in to the phone, or by tapping the wireless messages, Vinagradov's appeals for help. The first reply that the High Command sent was: "You have troops enough. Fight on." Later two companies of frontier guards and a company of sappers and ultimately a company of G.P.U. guards were sent up to lever loose the Finnish grasp on the road to the frontier. But they never got past the Finn ambushes.

The final rout of the retreating Russian column was largely the work of the Finnish patrol sent to watch the bridge over the gully. They blew it up the moment they saw the retreat was beginning. One tank on the bridge was hurled thirty yards into a ravine nearby. At the same time land-mines they had laid in the snow on the roadway blew the tracks off another tank leading the retreat. Behind it the long column of the Soviet division, tanks, guns, lorries and tractors, were jammed up together, unable to turn or to manœuvre in the snow-covered ditches on either side. At that moment the main Finnish forces from the woods closed in with their grenades and machine-guns. The Russians, starved and frozen, suddenly broke. They clambered from their tanks and lorries and rushed for the woods, trying to get away from this torrent of fire and make for the Russian frontier. That finished the battle. From then on it was simply a question of mopping-up operations.

CHAPTER XIX

THE RATTEE ROAD

MOPPING UP WAS still going on when we reached the battlefield late on the afternoon of Tuesday, January 9. We had driven down in a white military bus from Rovaniemi in an atmosphere which was either intolerably hot—for the bus had an elaborate heating system—or freezing cold if we opened the door to try to get a little air. After fourteen hours of swaying over the frozen roads we came to the outskirts of the battle, on the western road along the lake-side where the 163rd had been defeated. The debris of the battle was still there. It was Kemi River all over again, but here fresh snow veiled the land. The carcasses of two Russian bombers brought down either by the snow or by anti-aircraft fire were being hauled by Finnish troops along forest tracks to the roadside. Already looking ancient under their snow-coating, like the ruins of some battle of prehistoric times, were the lorries and gear scattered along the road near the cross-roads, where the main column had been hit. Over fifty Soviet wagons and sledges were parked around the farm-house there. Bodies of Russian dead were still crumpled in the ditches. Derelict lorries marked, like signposts, the road to the lake-edge of Suomussalmi village.

At the very foot of the lake, a Finnish plane on skis and a biplane fighter were camouflaged under the trees. Along the road which had once been the street of Suomussalmi, we found an officer, bespectacled, riding a pony whose shaggy coat was covered with hoar-frost. At the most, only two or three houses in the village were standing. The rest were only blackened beams and the gaunt smoke-begrimed chimney stacks. We passed the ruins of the little hotel famous among fishermen. In the yard troops were unscrewing the cap of a dud bomb. A mile down the village was the vital road junction of Suomussalmi for which the battle had been fought. Snow covered the one signpost, making it look like a great monument. Beyond, under the trees, Finnish artillerymen were standing by two batteries of 75's. From the Kajaani road a long column of troops on skis and on sledges was winding towards an avenue-like road that ran westwards between the tall pines—the Rattee Road.

It was dusk, the hour of troop movement. The road, swinging in majestic curves over rolling ground, from which we could glimpse the pine forests of Russia, was crowded with a macabre cavalcade of war. Coming towards us in one long stream were the men who had fought the battle, returning to rest; moving up with us were the fresh troops. It was the sight I remember most vividly of all in the Finnish war. For the men from the front came on skis, on foot, piled four or five on sledges pulled by ponies. Some led strings of captured Russian horses. "Molotovi," they called, pointing to them and laughing. Others rode on lorries. Their snow capes were stained yellow, grimy. Their rifles were slung on their backs. Their faces were the faces of men who had seen terrible things and looked on death for many days. Many had cheeks and foreheads blackened with fire of the machine-guns. Almost all had dark, staring, exhausted eyes. They were unshaven, bronzed. Some had the lined look of old men; others had round open peasant faces which under white snow capes looked sometimes like the faces of women. Others again were mere boys in their teens. Some rode on their sledges proudly pointing to the Russian steel helmets they carried, or swords, or rifles. Others stared fixedly ahead, or plodded on on their skis, their faces set. On the other side of the road went the fresh troops, ski-ing swiftly, dragging machine-guns on little boat-like sledges, driving sleighs packed with boxes of supplies and ammunition.

They stared eagerly at the troops coming back. Sometimes a man would break out to talk to a friend in the column, then begin a jerky, duck-like run on his skis to regain his place. Both lines, almost in single file, kept to the right side of the road. On, on, along this white road in the dusk with the grey clouds low overhead, went these two streams, men going to kill and men returning from the kill.

Then we saw the barbed-wire entanglements where the 44th had dug themselves in, and just beyond that the shambles of the first fighting. The Russian field-guns under the trees were caught amongst massed tree-trunks and over-turned lorries. This was the head of the column where the Finns had contained the Russians for the two critical weeks. Here the 305th Regiment had stayed, waiting while the 163rd Division was attacked. Ahead, one mass of destruction led to another. I had expected to see the Kemi River scene again. I saw it tenfold. For this had been a far greater battle; the losses had been heavier; the material captured much greater. This was like a scene from a painting of Napoleon's retreat from Moscow, a picture of death in the snow. For over three miles in the growing dusk I walked along a road which was choked with Russian material. At first it was chiefly captured smashed supply-wagons drawn off the roads under trees splintered with shelling. In one place the tree-trunks had been gnawed by the horses, maddened through lack of fodder.

Farther on in an open space nine Russian field-guns were surrounded by great heaps of empty shell-cases. Smashed trees opposite showed that they must have fired almost point-blank at the woods southwards where the Finns had attacked. Below them, under a group of young trees, were Russian dugouts. They were filled with dead men. The fighting here must have been very heavy, for many of the men had the smashed faces of men hit by hand grenades. I noticed again and again Russian dead lying with bare hands. They must have taken off their gloves to fire. Probably the gloves were too thick to let them grip the trigger properly.

Then came the bulk of the column. It was a long line of tanks and lorries and staff cars and gun carriers, packed on to the narrow road in one fantastic traffic jam. They had clearly stopped suddenly on the move. Lorries had run into the rear of tanks.

One armoured car had run on over an anti-tank gun being dragged by a tractor. Heavy machine-guns on sledges had been run almost under a lorry on which was mounted one of the series of quadruple Vickers anti-aircraft machine-guns. Some of the tanks had their guns slewed round to face the woods at the south. Others looked as if they had been left by their crews without a fight.

I went on, winding in and out beside this jam, while all the time beside us the Finnish relief troops went forward on their skis and in their sledges. The troops bent over to look inside captured tanks, or picked up pocket-books of the dead, searching for money and souvenirs. From the woods at the side came the occasional crack of a rifle, the occasional smash of a grenade. In there, thousands of Russians were still being rounded up, or hunted down.

At one point a file of Russian prisoners, haggard and terrified, stumbled out of a forest ride on to the main snow road. Beside them moved three Finns on skis. Exhausted, cold—few of them still had overcoats—the Russians' faces were ghastly under their peaked caps. The Finnish troops moving up, regarded them for the greater part in silence. But one man, I noticed, broke out of line and skied back alongside the line of prisoners, shouting jeeringly, menacingly, "Now go to Helsinki. That's where you wanted to go, isn't it?" The Russians stumbled on. One of them started to grin. It was the grimace of a man who, terrified, tries to placate his captors. It was the most horrible expression that I have ever seen.

At one point a piece of cardboard, tied to a string, marked a break in the road: "Danger, mines." We and the troops made a detour through the woods on the side for a chain or so. The mines were Finnish, laid during the first part of the fighting. At last we came to the head of the column, the heavy twenty-ton tank with its caterpillars blown off by a land-mine, and beyond it the bridge that had been blown up. In a clearing just before it, six Bofors anti-aircraft guns pointed their barrels skywards. The Finnish artillery officer told us that these had been built for the Poles, and probably captured by the Russians in Poland. Behind them were trailers from field-guns, packed with ammunition. Much of the ammunition was charred and burnt. Breech locks had been taken from the guns. The Finnish officers with whom we went over the whole line insisted that the Russians had fought with the greatest bravery. They said that the artillery had had little effect on the Finns in the woods. Starvation and cold had been, above all, the decisive factors. It was still terribly cold on the road that night, twenty-eight degrees below, we were told.

I tried to check up, in the dusk there, the figures of the Finnish communiqué which had announced the victory, two days before. When I first read this communiqué I thought that it was an exaggeration, or at least the Finns must have added for the second time the material captured with the 163rd. Now, hurriedly, I counted 45 tanks, over 80 field-guns, anti-aircraft guns and anti-tank guns, at least 20 heavy machine-guns and masses of rifles, light machine-guns and 4 armoured cars and carts and lorries running into hundreds. The official figures later announced were that 112 guns in all were taken. These included 44 anti-tank guns, 20 howitzers, 45 field-guns, 3 mountain guns and a quantity of anti-aircraft guns. As well there were 106 heavy machine-guns, 191 sub-machine-guns, 16 quadruple anti-aircraft machine-guns, 5,000 rifles, 66 tanks, 6 armoured cars, 31 armoured tractors, 420 lorries and cars, 75 field kitchens, 1,400 live horses and over 2,000 dead horses, 1,900,000 rounds of ammunition, 19,000 field-gun shells, 16,000 hand grenades, 1,110 land-mines, 16 trench mortars and 8 Bofors anti-aircraft guns.

I asked the officers what they put the Russian losses in manpower at. Most agreed that close on 4,000 to 5,000 men had been killed in the fighting (the 5,000 rifles came chiefly from the dead), and thousands more were being hunted down or were freezing in the forests. "Our patrols are shooting them in batches all the time," one officer told me. "It is almost too easy. You see, they have no skis, and we have only to follow their footsteps in the snow. Our men can always catch up with them. Then they just wipe them out with machine-gun fire, or they wait till the Russians, driven desperate with the cold, light a fire. One group of ten of our men accounted for over a hundred Russians huddled round one fire last night."

This slaughter was even then going on in the woods. As we walked forward we heard, again and again, the crack of rifles and the smash of hand grenades as the Finnish patrols moved through, combing the woods. No one can say how many Russians ever got past the lines of the patrols which the Finns had flung along the frontier immediately after the battle. But it cannot have been many. The 44th Unit as a fighting division was destroyed. I think it is no unfair estimate to say that at least two-thirds of its men were dead, killed, frozen or taken prisoners. Its commanders had disappeared. No one ever found the body of Colonel Vinagradov after he took to the woods. He may have got back to Russia. The Soviet radio indignantly repudiated the suggestion, made in our despatches, that he had died. "He is in the district of the 44th Division," the announcer cried back. "We tell those journalists that, which is the truth." Which, of course, means nothing. Dead in the forest, he could still be said to be in the district of the 44th Division.

I found in Suomussalmi that, as I walked along that road, I did not pay much attention to the dead. I had seen all I wanted of these frozen figures at Kemi River. The fact of the battle, the material captured seemed to be of far more importance this time than the human spectacle of these men everywhere frozen in their death agonies. So I concentrated on counting, at least roughly, the materials. I am glad I did this, for the disaster of Suomussalmi has already been surrounded by violent controversy. I personally met dozens of people who believed that these defeats never happened in the north. I only wish some of the writers who later poured sarcasm on our reports of Suomussalmi could have walked along the road. There, sculpted by the hand of frost, was evidence enough of this disaster. That telephone operator, dead with the wire still in his hand, bending over to make a repair; that man running with a plate of soup along the road, sniped as he went; that other, with his foot still on the step of a lorry, so natural you would think he was living; that man killed in the photo van where, against the back-drop, the Red Army men had had themselves photographed; those hundreds crumpled everywhere in their last agony; they could not be brought to life by any propaganda, by any writer in London or New York pouring scorn on our stories.

Among the gear lying by the roadside were ski manuals which symbolised much of the faulty Russian preparation for this attack. I picked up one of them, where it had fallen from a lorry. Around it were bundles of skis still untied, their bindings either not in place, or made up of elaborate mechanical catches too complicated for easy use. It was dark when we got back finally to the barbed-wire entanglements at the Finnish end of the road. The head-lamps of the Finnish lorries made the scene more macabre than ever. I realised what the word "shambles" meant.

We drove back to Colonel Siilasvou's headquarters at Hyrynsalmi. Here we had herrings and potatoes and bread, and listened while he told us details of the story of the battle. I still have copies of the four maps which he had prepared for us there. On the wall hung, side by side with the fortress of Mannerheim, a huge, beautifully-executed, tinted portrait of Stalin, smiling benignantly. It came from a lorry which had been found packed with propaganda portraits of Stalin. In one corner of the lorry was found a bundle of notepaper headed in Polish "Ministry of Foreign Affairs, Warsaw". Beside this portrait of Stalin hung one of the flags of the regiment of the 44th. Over the elaborate hammer-and-sickle design, Stalin's face, worked in embroidery, smiled down again. One of the Finns pointed to it and said, "Even Hitler does not have his portrait embroidered on his armies' flags. He is shrewder than that".

We cross-questioned the Colonel at length. He was particularly scornful about the Russian officers.

"The ones we have made prisoner are laughable. Why, if I took them on show in a circus round Europe, they would be the laughing-stock of the Continent. They are not soldiers, they are exhibits. Vinagradov had been merely a sergeant in the old Tsarist army. They were badly trained and lacked experience."

I think his pro-Fascist feelings carried him away here, for several of the officers taken prisoner were alert and highly intelligent. Most of them we saw in the nearby barracks of a prison camp. In the darkness, our bus stopped in a yard surrounded on three sides by low wooden barrack buildings. It was, like the prison near Oulu, an alcoholic's prison, dating from the days of Prohibition. A boy, hardly seventeen, with a rifle and bayonet, in the uniform of the Civil Guards, was the only guard in the centre of the yard. The Finns had clearly not much fear that the Russians were going to try to get back to the horrors of the woods.

In the rooms, crowded so that they covered every bunk, every shelf, every inch of the floor, was an exhausted mass of Russian prisoners. The room stank. Wounded men moaned; others, their eyes dark with an agony of exhaustion, stirred and looked up at us, too weary even to wonder if we were an execution squad. I talked through an interpreter with a young, keen-looking officer. His uniform, I noted, was warm and new. All this division had, incidentally, good, fairly new uniforms. They were, mostly, peasants from the Ukraine, tall, well-built men, some standing over six feet.

I offered the officer a cigarette. "It's good of you to give me a smoke before they take me out and shoot me," he said.

"They don't plan to shoot you," I said. "So far as I know, the Finns have never shot any prisoners."

He shrugged his shoulders. "Don't try to make it easier for me. I'm not afraid to die."

At that moment, from the back of the room, a plump, dark-haired figure arose and picked his way across the bodies of his comrades towards us. Even in this uniform, with his hair completely cropped, he was unmistakably Jewish. Put him in a pale-grey suit, and sit him at a table in a Corner House on Saturday night, and he might have come out of Bethnal Green. He spoke to the interpreter, asked if we were journalists and then asked if we could get him some better treatment for his leg. The Finns did not seem to bother about it, he complained.

Amidst this tragedy there was something comic and yet slightly magnificent about this Jewish capacity for survival. He alone, of all this roomful of wounded men, had the nerve and the initiative to ask for special attention. Here he was, wounded, lying in a barracks, in the middle of a Finnish forest, and yet he was up and on the job at once. We told him we would do what we could.

Among the prisoners taken was a girl of twenty-two, married, with two children. She lived in Leningrad, where she worked in an office. She had been mobilised as a nurse. She said that when the first attack came she and the other nurses had been listening to a lecture on dysentery by a doctor in a field ambulance. In the prison camp she wept almost continuously, and no one could console her.

CHAPTER XX

KUHMO FRONT

SUOMUSSALMI FINISHED THE fighting round Kianta Lake. The Russians retired to the frontier and simply kept enough troops there to protect the aerodromes they operated on the lakes over the border. From then on till the end of the war there was only intermittent patrol fighting on the frontier, with some shelling and grenade-throwing from the Russian side. The Soviet waist-line thrust was broken.

On the other two fronts of this central region, Lieksa and Kuhmo, where I had been in early December, the situation for the Finns was already safe. The attack from Lieksa had been beaten back in the first months of the war. Finnish patrols from the forest broke up Russian columns on three roads, even though these had had only twenty-two miles to advance to get to the main east Finnish railway. But the Finns had been well-prepared here. Elaborate defence lines had been built. Against these the Russian attack broke and by Christmas Eve the Finnish communiqué was able to announce, "We are fighting on Russian soil". Finnish advance patrols were across the frontier, past the blue-and-white striped Finnish frontier posts and the red Russian posts. Strategically, of course, it did not much matter which side of the border the patrols were in this particular area, for the Finns could not hope to advance deep into Russia. But psychologically, and from a propaganda point of view, it was invaluable for Finland.

Farther north, round Kuhmo, the warfare had developed into the motti type which was to become the general technique of the forest regions for the rest of the war. Motti is the Finnish word for a cord of wood. The Finns used it to describe the sectional defensive positions which the Russians took up when their lines were cut and the Finns closed in from the woods. The Finnish tactic was to cut the main Russian communication artery, then chop up the Soviet troops into a number of mottis, and settle down to besiege them. The Russians replied by digging substantial defensive positions, usually circles of gun-pits and trenches with tanks half buried at the corners as pillboxes. In these stockades they waited, being fed by supplies dropped from the air, and sometimes by columns that forced their way through. The Finns, flitting through the trees around them, sniped them continuously and made small attacks by night to wear them down.

The 54th Soviet Division, which had advanced on Kuhmo at the start of the war, had its communications finally cut late in December. It built then four mottis, spread along the thirty miles of road over which it had advanced from the frontier. Here they were to hold out alone till mid-February, when the Soviet command sent in a brigade of Siberian ski troops to relieve them. This force, numbering some 2,000 men, was formed of fully-trained skiers, well equipped, and with light artillery. They were ambushed by the Finns near Kesseli, twenty-four miles in from the border, and virtually wiped out. Towards the end of February a battalion of tanks and a regiment of heavy artillery were sent in to open the road. The guns, which ranged from .76 to 1.522 mm. in calibre, were put into position to shell the line the Finns had taken up across the road at Loytovaara, between the mottis and the frontier. They hammered away day after day, and at intervals attacks were launched by troops from the Soviet 33rd Infantry Division, who had been brought up to the frontier. Light Russian fighter planes machine-gunned the Finnish lines, but by the time peace came in mid-March both Finns and Russians were holding their positions virtually unchanged. The Russians had not broken the Loytovaara Line; the Finns had not forced the four main mottis.

The Soviet attacks here cannot, however, be regarded as a complete failure. They had drawn away thousands of men from the Mannerheim Line, men who were to be badly needed during the vital month of February. But with the defeat of Suomussalmi all offensive sting had gone out of the Russian waist-line offensive. It marked the end of an era in the war. After Suomussalmi the "war of occupation" which had been launched to put Kuusinen into power was over; the war of the great Red Army offensive, aimed at smashing completely the Finnish military machine, was about to begin.

CHAPTER XXI

WHY RUSSIA FAILED IN THE NORTH

THE FINNISH WAR was really two wars. That is, I think, the fundamental fact about it. It explains why the Red Army was at first defeated, and then why it was so spectacularly victorious. The Finns won the first war; the Russians the second. The Russians, believing that Finland was either internally ready for Sovietisation, or at least that it was sufficiently divided to be militarily weak, sent in at first what was really an army of occupation. This was intended, it seems, to move in and take over the country, co-operating with Finnish peasant and working masses who would rise to greet it. At the worst the Red troops would have to fight only short actions against White Guard elements, actions which would give them valuable military experience. Only when this plan proved to be based on such false assumptions that it led to disaster was the real Red Army sent in to break the Mannerheim Line. Then the weapons were changed. Fire power and air power were adopted instead of political propaganda.

There is ample evidence that the first forces sent in were mainly reserve divisions in which the men had had comparatively little training, and were not prepared as in any way a shock force. In a prison camp near Oulu on December 13 I spoke, through an interpreter, with eleven men. Nine of these were reservists, chiefly farm labourers from the Tula military district near Moscow, who had had only three months' military training. An officer, Alexei Samoiloff, was thirty-seven years old, and was an assistant in a Moscow bookstall. He had seen nothing of warfare since the civil war days, and had been recalled only for short refresher courses of a fortnight at a time until he was hastily mobilised in September. Prisoners whom I saw at Rovaniemi had never even learnt to fire a rifle before they were sent in. At Kouvola a tank officer stated that in his unit—a specialised one—half the men were conscripts, half reservists who lacked any refresher training. On the Isthmus, too, in the first fighting the Finns often found themselves being attacked by companies made up entirely of officer cadets from the Leningrad Military Academy—a sign that no great opposition had been expected, and that these youths were being sent in to get experience. They bought it dearly.

The equipment of the troops, particularly in the north, also spoke of a war of occupation rather than of combat. For the Russian High Command later showed itself to be anything but foolish and anything but lacking in material. But all the same the armies in the north had inadequate clothes and bad boots. The photos of rotted Soviet coats and gaping boots did not lie. Why? Because no one in the Soviet Command expected the men to have to spend weeks in freezing forests, fighting. They were going to move in in lorries, sleep in requisitioned houses in the villages where the peasants would welcome them. The great masses of propaganda material, too, carried in lorries which could have better served for extra food or ammunition, all pointed to this.

The very tactics were affected by this refusal to believe there was going to be heavy opposition. When I first heard of the Russians pouring on to Kianta Lake, or along the Salla roads in great masses, in steam-roller fashion, I doubted the reports. But they became so frequent as to be undoubtedly true. The Soviet High Command that had developed tank tactics to a high degree, that had invented the parachute troops, could surely not just blunder on in the old Tsarist way, wasting men right and left. In actual fact what happened was that the troops came in masses because they never expected opposition. They marched ahead, expecting friends instead of preparing to fight ahead, expecting enemies. This is far nearer the truth than the view that Stalin launched a blitzkrieg that failed because the Red Army was no good anyway. There never was a blitzkrieg against Finland at any time. There was a steady push at the start which did not succeed because the structure was not, as the Russians expected, rotten; after that there was an elaborately prepared and magnificently sustained heavy offensive which succeeded by sheer weight of men and material, not by surprises or suddenness.

One Soviet aviator who was taken prisoner confirmed this view openly when he was cross-questioned in mid-January in the prison camp at Kouvola. He said that many of the planes employed till then were old second-class machines. He had himself been flying a biplane bomber and had blown the tail off his own machine by dropping his bombs when flying too low. He said straight out, "You haven't seen the Red Army yet". Two planes which were captured by the Finns at Suomussalmi were old-fashioned fighters armed with only four machine-guns.

This view explains, too, two of the mysteries in the early stages of the war. It is the most reasonable explanation as to why Helsinki was bombed and why no mass air attacks were made on the lines of communication in the Finnish rear during the critical early days of the war. The bombs on Helsinki, to my mind, were meant as a blow at the rotted social structure that, given a push, the Russians believed, would collapse. The masses, seeing that the Soviet meant business, and that their leaders had led them into war, were expected to throw up a Government which in any case was expected to flee. This, as the Russians learnt, did not happen.

But more significant still was the lack of air attack on the Finnish rear in the first three weeks of the war. In all December the Soviet made no real attempt to bomb the Finnish communications system. I travelled up and down over hundreds of miles of Finnish railway in that month, but never once had to leave the train because of an air raid. None of the big junctions like Riihimäki, or Oulu, or Mikele, which were later to be pulverised, were then really attacked. The Finnish reserves which won the battles of Suomussalmi and Kemi River were moved into place without a hitch along railways where, for instance, at Rovaniemi, a bomb on a vital bridge could have caused infinite delay. After the first air raid on Helsinki the main attacks were on the ports like Hango and Abo, to which war materials from abroad could be brought in, and on strategic centres like Viipuri behind the Mannerheim Line. The Russians, it seemed, did not want to damage the country they expected to capture easily.

In all the first thirty days of the war, 203 places were bombed, an average of just over six a day. This is a tiny figure for a blitzkrieg if one remembers that the raids included support for military operations. Just over 200 people were killed. In this month the Russians lost 160 planes, chiefly through anti-aircraft fire and weather conditions.

GENERAL WALLENIUS

KEMI RIVER SUPPLY COLUMN

FEW HAD GLOVES

SWEDISH HELP CAME – BUT NEVER ENOUGH

MOSTLY PEASANT TYPES

IT WAS LIKE A SCENE FROM NAPOLEON'S RETREAT FROM MOSCOW

IN TIME ROVANIEMI HOSPITAL TOO WAS HIT

GHOST PATROL

At the end of December it was clear that not only were the Finns fighting toughly but that the Red Army's prestige was badly damaged. Of all the six main offensives launched since the first day of the war, only one, at Petsamo, a place strategically of little value, remote and hardly defended, had succeeded. Every capitalist newspaper in the world was shouting more or less intensely that the Red Army was rotten. It had been "unmasked", "debunked", "revealed in all its inefficiencies" and so on and so on. Cartoons poured out showing little Finland punching big Russia through the ropes. Not only at Salla, Suomussalmi, and Lieksa had the Russians been beaten back. Their forces north of Ladoga had met with one great defeat at Tolvajärvi and were being checked on the four other roads that they had attacked on. Their direct attack on the Mannerheim Line had also been unavailing. The first round had gone unmistakably to Finland.

CHAPTER XXII

TOLVAJÄRVI BATTLE

TOLVAJÄRVI RANKS WITH Kemi River and Suomussalmi as the greatest Finnish success of this early period of the war. It was actually the first Finnish victory, for it started on December 10 and finished on the 13th. But no reporters were near the spot, and no details of it got out till Christmas-time. Like the action at Kemi River, the Soviet defeat here knocked the keystone out of an elaborate strategic scheme, a scheme which at Tolvajärvi was aimed at bringing Russian forces around the north of the great inland sea of Lake Ladoga, and using them to take the Mannerheim Line in the rear.

Tolvajärvi is a Finnish tourist resort fifty miles north of Lake Ladoga. It stands deep in pine forests which provide the best timber in Finland. Its outstanding natural feature is a narrow tongue of peninsula nowhere more than 200 yards wide, which runs from the east side of the lake almost across to the other side. There a bridge links it to the mainland, so that in effect it cuts the lake into two, like the figure eight. On the peninsula stood a tourist hotel. These tongues are a feature of the lake formation in this area.

The Battle of Tolvajärvi was fought on this peninsula, for across it ran one of the four main roads from the Russian border. The Soviet, with incredible confidence, packed a division on to this narrow strip of land around which the lake was not yet quite frozen and marched them straight across. On the shore on either side was a supporting regiment, given the task of working their way round the edge of the lake and preventing any flank attack. These forces fought the right wing of the series of columns thrusting into the north Ladoga area to outflank the Mannerheim Line. South and north of Tolvajärvi, other invading columns had already been halted.

At Tolvajärvi the Finns had a force under Colonel P. Talvela who was to emerge as one of the best officers of the war. In civilian life he was a business man in the pulp industry. As the Russians approached the lake he decided to let them advance right across the peninsula to the bridge. Then he counter-attacked. In the dark of December 12, Finnish troops forced the bridge-head, which was in Russian hands, with heavy losses both to themselves and the Russians. At the same time they ambushed and forced back the supporting forces on the shores of the lake. Patrols then harried the bottle-neck line of communication of the Russians right where the peninsula joined the mainland. At the same time Finnish forces crept across the ice at night and hit the Russians along the whole length of the peninsula. There were three days of fearful fighting, in which the tourist hotel at Tolvajärvi was contested room by room, just as the University City buildings were fought for in Spain. Dead were heaped high in every room, and the staircases dripped blood which froze there in black icicles. By December 15 it was over. The Russians were retreating. They retired and on December 23 took up positions at Ägläjärvi, twenty miles farther back, from which they never advanced again. Talvela was made a General.

South and north of Tolvajärvi, the other invading columns had already halted before Ilomantsi, Loimola and Syskyjärvi, and a period of bitter fighting against their positions started. Below, right on the edge of Lake Ladoga, the Russian attack met with an unexpected obstacle. The Mantsin Island, a strip of flat land

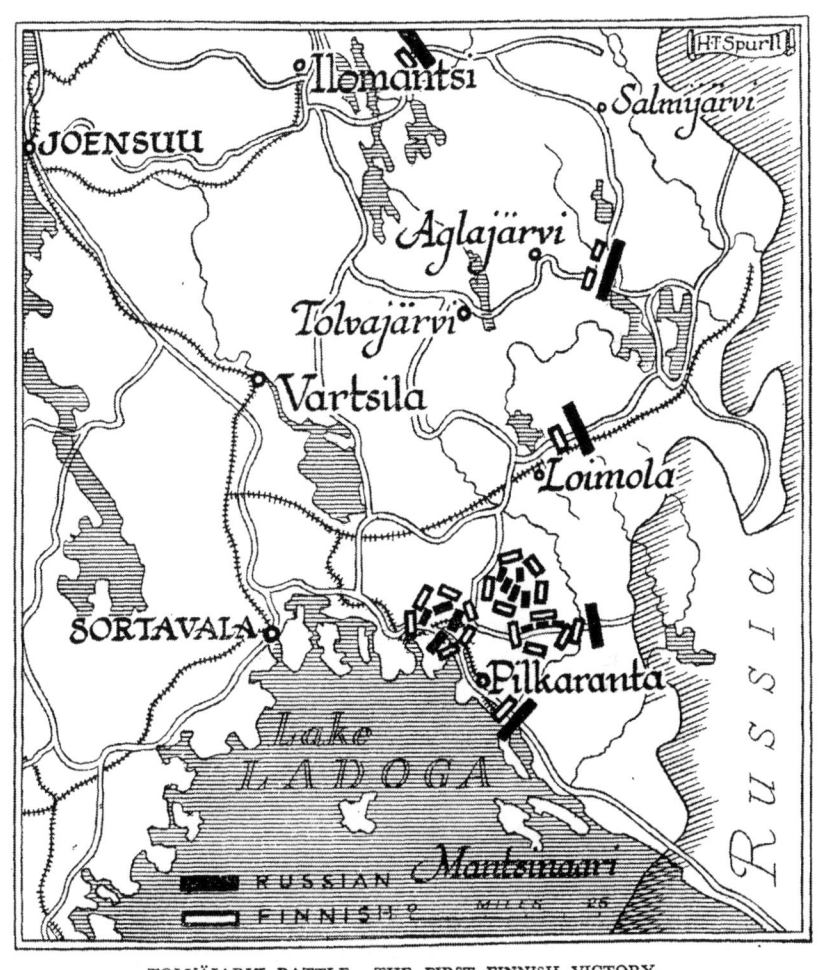

TOLVÄJARVI BATTLE—THE FIRST FINNISH VICTORY

lying just off the coast and just inside the Finnish waters of the lake, had been secretly fortified by the Finns in the last days before the war. Batteries of field-guns with a range great enough to command the coast road had been installed. The Russians as they advanced found themselves suddenly under fire. They halted and, on the fifth day of the war, assembled an armada to attack the island. Three tugs, fitted with 75 mm. guns, set out towing a string of barges filled with troops. The Finns held their fire for the tugs to come within range. Then they fired, sank all three tugs, and then sank the barges at their leisure. The next week the water froze round the island. This made the problem of supply easier, for the ski patrols could now cross the ice at night, but it made attack easier for the Russians too. From that time on hardly a night passed without the Russians trying to attack across the ice, against Mantsin and the outlying fringe of tiny islands closer to the shore. But to the end it remained in Finnish hands. The peasantry remained there straight on throughout the war, supplying the garrison with vegetables and fresh milk.

While these spectacular actions were taking place, in the frontier forests up and down the 500 miles of northern border, the first attacks had been launched on the defences on the Karelian Isthmus called the Mannerheim Line, after the seventy-two-year-old General who had been called back to take command of the Finnish armies.

CHAPTER XXIII

MANNERHEIM

THE MAN WHO strode through the doors of the Societetshuset Hotel in Helsinki on the night of Sunday, December 3, looked like a Prussian staff officer. Tall, stiffly upright, with gold leaf on his peaked cap, and in grey uniform, he walked with the curt stride and flung open his grey cloak with the brisk movement of a trained military man. Around his throat I could see a white cross hanging below his high buttoned collar. I recognised it as the cross of the White Rose of Finland. His face was set, determined, hard. He strode on stiffly into the hall. I thought it must be the German Military Attaché. Then I noticed every officer in the hall stand stiffly upright at attention. Behind me Kenney, the British Press Attaché whispered: "It's Mannerheim."

It was Field-Marshal Mannerheim, in Helsinki for the last time before taking over his command at the front.

The Field-Marshal remained to newspapermen at least a figure almost as remote as a war god. He rigorously avoided any personal contact with the foreign Press. During the whole of that campaign, apart from this chance encounter, no correspondents were even to catch a glimpse of him, except a group who were called in at Christmas-time to hear him read a curt declaration. At that time he strode into the room, briskly read out a few words in French, and strode out again. The only interview he gave was to the correspondent of *Match*. (The proprietor of *Match* was, incidentally, Monsieur Provost, later to be Minister of Information in the Bordeaux Government and one of the men who supported most enthusiastically the capitulation of France.) Mannerheim had no time for the Press. They were annoying people who had spent a great deal of their time criticising him, and who interfered with wars which were the business of soldiers, and soldiers only.

Yet Mannerheim was undoubtedly the most significant and interesting figure in Finland at war with Russia. I did all I could to learn at second-hand something of his true character. It was not easy. For he was one of those men who has always been painted completely black or completely white. He was either "Butcher Mannerheim", the man who had massacred the workers in Finland in 1918 and was now hurling them into another fight with the Soviet Union, or he was the "White Knight" who had checked the spread of Bolshevism at the end of the last war, and was checking it again now. The truth, I think, is simply that Mannerheim was a White Russian General and remained a White Russian General. In that lie the clues to his character. He is both White Russian and therefore bitterly and deeply anti-Bolshevik, and he is a General, a military expert. He is not primarily a politician nor is he by race a Finn, though the cause of Finnish Nationalism, and the independence of capitalist Finland, is intimately associated with his name.

By race he is actually Swedish, a descendant of one of the branches of the Swedish nobility who settled in Finland in the eighteenth century, where they formed an aristocracy over the Finnish peasantry. He comes from the Aaland Islands, where his family settled towards the end of the eighteenth century. One of his brothers is a Swedish subject. From this background of Finno-Swedish landed aristocracy, young Mannerheim went to a cadet school in Finland, Frederikstrand. Then he went on to the cavalry school in St. Petersburg, falling naturally as the young aristocrat into the system of Russian rule then dominant in Finland. He passed into the Tsarist cavalry. The Tsar personally took an interest in this tall, lithe, good-looking young man. At the Tsar's coronation he was one of the two army officers who escorted the Tsar and the Tsarina to the altar. By thirty he was a General, the youngest in the Russian army. He fought in the Russo-Japanese war.

During the first outbreak of the Finnish independence movement, at the time of the Russian Revolution of 1905, he made no attempt to support it. He remained in the Tsar's service. He travelled widely in Central Asia, partly because he was interested in archæology, and partly because he was carrying out military observations for the Russians. At the age of forty-eight he held the rank of Lieutenant-General. When the Great War broke out he was stationed at Warsaw. He served first in Poland and then became commander of the 6th Cavalry Corps on the Galician front. There he achieved distinction by consistently disregarding the stupid instructions of the Russian General Staff, and waging his own campaign on the spot. When revolution came in 1917 he stood by his old masters. But he saw that inside Russia there was nothing that could be done to preserve the Tsarist régime. He decided to return to Finland.

Two stories are told of his journey back there. They are contradictory, but both may be true. One is that he travelled from Rumania to Moscow in a train wearing openly his uniform as a General and with his breast ablaze with decorations. No one harmed him. For there is no doubt that Mannerheim is a brave man. But his sister told a different story of the last stage of the journey. Apparently, to get from Petrograd to Helsinki he had to disguise himself as a railway porter. He arrived in Helsinki late in 1917, carrying in a bundle under his arm the blue-and-white flag of the St. Petersburg Yacht Club. This club, of which he was a devoted member, had been one of the centres of Tsarist society.

The flag he carried with him he was later to get adopted as the Finnish national emblem.

Back in his family at length, Mannerheim discovered that revolution had spread to Finland, too. So he took on the task of forming and leading the Finnish White armies. He was inevitably chosen for this because he was by far the most outstanding soldier available and because the Jaeger Battalion of Finns, who had been training in Germany since the start of the war, was still away. None of them was available for the task. Mannerheim began his campaign in the "Kulak" peasant province of Ostro-Bothnia around Oulu. The White forces that he gathered there gradually advanced towards Tampere in the south. At this point in March 1918 the German division under Von der Goltz landed at Hango, and stabbed in the back the Finnish Red armies struggling round Helsinki. Mannerheim's attitude towards German intervention has never quite been cleared up. He told Sir Walter Citrine, who visited him in January 1940 at his headquarters behind the Mannerheim Line, that he had been against German intervention. "On my way to Tampere from Vaasa I heard that the Government had decided to call in the Germans to help them. That was the first I had heard of their decision, Sir Walter, I give you my word. I was very angry about it. I thought it quite unnecessary." Yet Hampden Jackson, that cautious writer, in his book on Finland, states: "On March 20 (1918) Mannerheim, now in a position outside Tampere, telegraphed via Stockholm to Berlin 'I consider it an urgent duty to hasten the arrival of the German expedition. Delay fatal'."

Mannerheim must bear too, before history, his full share of responsibility for the White Terror that followed the capture of Helsinki in 1918 by the White armies. For he was Commander-in-Chief at this time when, according to Mr. Josiah C. Wedgwood, in a speech in the British Parliament on May 29, 1919, "between 15,000 and 20,000 Red prisoners were shot out of hand early in May, many being mown down in batches with machine-guns". Even the official Finnish encyclopædia admits that 10,000 people died in concentration camps later of hunger and disease and of lack of water.

When the civil war was over, Mannerheim was not, as he expected, elected Regent of Finland. From that time on he played no official political rôle inside the country, though his indirect influence was very great. He resigned his post as Commander of the Finnish army at the end of May 1918. Rudolf Holsti, Finnish representative of the Allied capitals, suggested in the first draft of his Memoirs that the General resigned under German pressure, because he had formed a plan to occupy the Soviet province of eastern Karelia and join in conjunction with the British forces at Murmansk in a march on St. Petersburg. The Germans, still at war with us, did not want this.

Yet for all that, it is a great mistake to attach loosely to Mannerheim the label "Fascist". There was nothing of that bullying mixture of politics, militarism and demagogy which makes up the personality of men like Mussolini or Hitler, or the real Finnish Fascists like Wallenius. He was prepared to remain in the background as the soldier during much of the political troubles of the twenties and thirties. In 1931, when Wallenius and the Lapua movement were pushing Finland towards Fascism, Mannerheim kept clear of the whole business. He did nothing to help it and a certain amount behind the scenes to check it. From then on till the war, though the indirect power he exercised from his villa in Helsinki was great, he restricted his public activities to being head of the Supreme Defence Council. When war came he stepped into the post which had always been kept warm for him, that of Commander-in-Chief. Throughout the war he was virtual dictator of the country, but once it finished he stepped back out of the limelight. A half-hearted attempt was made by one Helsinki newspaper to work up a campaign for him as a peace-time dictator, but it was soon dropped. Mannerheim knew his limitations and was prepared to leave politics to the politicians. He gave people the impression that it was too dirty a job for a soldier. Mannerheim has been called "The uncrowned King of Finland". It is in a way true—but he acted as a constitutional king. He kept himself aloof in the background so that he avoided the attacks and abuse of day-to-day politics. People—the upper-class Finns anyway—referred to him as similar people might refer to the King of England, as a figure to be accepted or rejected, not criticised or attacked. There was always a slight awe about him in Finnish bourgeois circles, so that to criticise him was like criticising the British royal family in a middle-class London home. When official receptions were given at Helsinki, his presence was a slight embarrassment to officials, for protocols demanded that precedence be given to the President, but instinctively people tended to give it to Mannerheim.

Some attempt was made during the Finnish war to build up some of the "Führer" atmosphere around him. His portrait, usually a somewhat unfortunate photograph in which he had a faintly arrogant smile, rather like a film villain, was on the wall of every army officer's tent or dugout, in most shop windows, and on the covers of magazines. But I never saw any evidence that this had any great effect. People felt a respect for him because he was leading them well in a fight at a moment when good leadership was vital, but little more. Outside certain army circles there was no tendency to regard him as a Führer, no intention to hand over to him the country's fate indefinitely any more than such a feeling towards Churchill exists among the British people in 1941.

Everyone who knew Mannerheim spoke of his great personal charm. He had something of the capacity for making people feel at ease that was found so attractive about the Duke of Windsor. His character followed, in fact, the lines of a certain definite ruling-class type—a man charming in his private life, courageous and efficient, yet prepared to be absolutely intolerant and ruthless towards anything smacking of the Left. He unconsciously assumed that there were rulers and the ruled, and was prepared to crush out anything "Red" where it cropped up. Mannerheim was, in fact, a pukka sahib, with all that that phrase has come to mean. His tastes were even those of a British Empire builder of the older type. He shot tigers in India, hunted, visited England regularly to get his suits cut in Savile Row, and passed a short holiday every year in Paris. There was about him none of the Fascist impatience with the old aristocracy. He belonged to the race of the Von Papens, the Hindenburgs and the Curzons, rather than of the Hitlers and Mussolinis. He was strongly pro-French in his feelings and later pro-British. He spoke excellent French. One of his daughters, the Baroness Sophie Mannerheim, lived in Paris. He showed his gentlemanly attitude to propaganda war by refusing to allow any atrocity stories to be published about the Russians. All atrocity incidents were censored from the Press, and filed away for the official Finnish war archives.

Mannerheim is undoubtedly an excellent soldier. The ski

tactics of the Finnish army were, I am told, his own adaptation of Cossack cavalry methods. He was also intensely interested in the works of T. E. Lawrence and it may be that Lawrence's desert tactics influenced the Finnish ski methods. His conduct of the White army campaign in 1918 was itself first-class and the Finnish war of 1939-40 will leave his name high among great Generals. I do not know how far he personally devised the strategy of the Finnish war. But if it was the work of his staff, he will at least get the credit for giving them the opportunity to carry it out.

But the war must have been a terrific physical strain for him. He worked intensely and for long hours and slept very often in his car on his way to the fronts. He was seventy-two years old, but the photographs of him released throughout the war hid this fact. They showed a man in the early sixties. When peace came a photograph on the front page of the *Soumen Kuvalehti* showed a man whose lined face was almost puffy with weariness and strain. It is possible that he took too much of the duties of war on to himself. All questions of Press facilities and propaganda were, for instance, concentrated in his hands. The list of correspondents being sent to any front had to be submitted to him. When one correspondent got into trouble for suggesting that the Russians were not bombing civilian populations, the question of whether he should be expelled or not was referred to Mannerheim. He was expelled.

The strain on Mannerheim must have been immense. The Finnish war was hard enough, God knows, even on people like correspondents. Towards the end, in the critical days when Viipuri was being held by the Finnish army which was almost dying of exhaustion, Mannerheim caught influenza. He must have made many of his final decisions from a sick bed. Yet I do not think this can have been a factor in his decision to make peace. For his antagonism to Russia was so strong that he would have fought on if there had been any reasonable prospect of success. He knew all along that it was a hopeless fight, unless the Finns could get allies. He had urged settlement in the autumn, anything to gain time, till Finland would be sure of allies. For he knew that the Finnish army could never fight Russia alone. He made no secret of the fact that his hatred of present-day Russia was not an expression of the old Finnish national hatred of Russians, but was the hatred of the aristocrat for Bolshevism.

He published (on November 2, 1919) in *Husvudstadsbladet*, the Helsinki Swedish newspaper, this statement: "Finland should go to the help of Yudenich immediately." It was at the moment when General Yudenich was attacking Leningrad and was in great difficulties. He had appealed to Mannerheim to launch an attack on the outskirts of the city from the Karelian Isthmus. He was prepared to risk the fate of the young Finnish republic at this time for this purpose. Yet he knew clearly that a White Russian victory at the Paris Peace Conference would endanger greatly the whole movement for Finn'sh independence. For the White Russians were definitely in favour of re-incorporating Finland in Russia for strategic purposes, or at least of taking all the naval bases which the Soviet later claimed.

It is of interest, incidentally, to see how great a rôle the Finns of Swedish stock have played in events since 1918. Wallenius is a Swedish Finn; so is Siilasvou, the commander at Suomussalmi, he had had his Swedish name Finnicised after the Great War, so were a number of other Generals who had played a prominent part in the conduct of the war.

Your final opinion of Mannerheim must depend ultimately on your own political views. For the light they throw illuminates in completely different proportions different aspects of his character. If you believe that Bolshevism is a great evil or that the road to a decent life lies only in some form of authoritarian disciplined society, based ultimately on private property, Mannerheim is quite truthfully the White Knight who flinched from nothing that was necessary to achieve that goal. He fought for the old order consistently, courageously and, where necessary, ruthlessly. If, on the other hand, you see the Left as a source of real progress, if—despite the excesses into which Russia has been driven by her fears and her isolated position—you believe that there can be no progress until private property is done away with, and the work of the community lies in the hands of people who can be reliable trustees of it, then Mannerheim is a reactionary, even though a thoroughly gentlemanly reactionary. His place in history is undoubtedly alongside the General Francos and the Von Hindenburgs, who, at a decisive moment in the history of their country, flung their weight against the movements of the Left at a time when those movements represented the instinctive passionate struggle of people for a better and fuller life. That was undoubtedly the situation in Finland in 1918. It is a fact which must be placed side by side with the courageous, determined, and above all clear-headed leadership which he gave to the Finnish people in this war which was thrust on them in the winter of 1939-40.

Whatever his personality, one thing is undeniable about the position of Mannerheim in this Finnish-Soviet war. He had, in the struggle, the mass of the Finnish people behind him as solidly as Churchill had the mass of British people behind him in the summer of 1940. Many who did not agree with him politically accepted him willingly as a leader, following him confidently both into this hard war and the hard peace which followed it.

CHAPTER XXIV

THE MANNERHEIM LINE

A MANNERHEIM LINE in the sense of a Maginot or a Siegfried Line never existed in Finland. There was never a belt of modern field fortresses, with elaborate underground chambers, ammunition lifts, supported by a mass of smaller forts and machine-gun posts, such as lined both sides of the Saar frontier between France and Germany. There was, however, a series of strong field-works—trenches, dugouts, machine-gun nests, tank barriers and tank traps, stretching in a sixty-mile curve across the Karelian Isthmus between Viipuri and Leningrad. Only in one area, around Summa, were there any real concrete fortifications. Here a series of small forts, twenty-five feet wide at the front and thirty-five feet wide at the back, built of reinforced concrete four feet thick, were placed at intervals of approximately 200 yards to cover the country with fire from their guns. They were half sunk into the ground, and armed each with one 75 mm. field-gun and two heavy machine-guns. They were fitted with armoured periscopes for observing fire, and the stores and gun crews were in the part below ground level. Each fort was equipped with charts showing the exact range of every road and village.

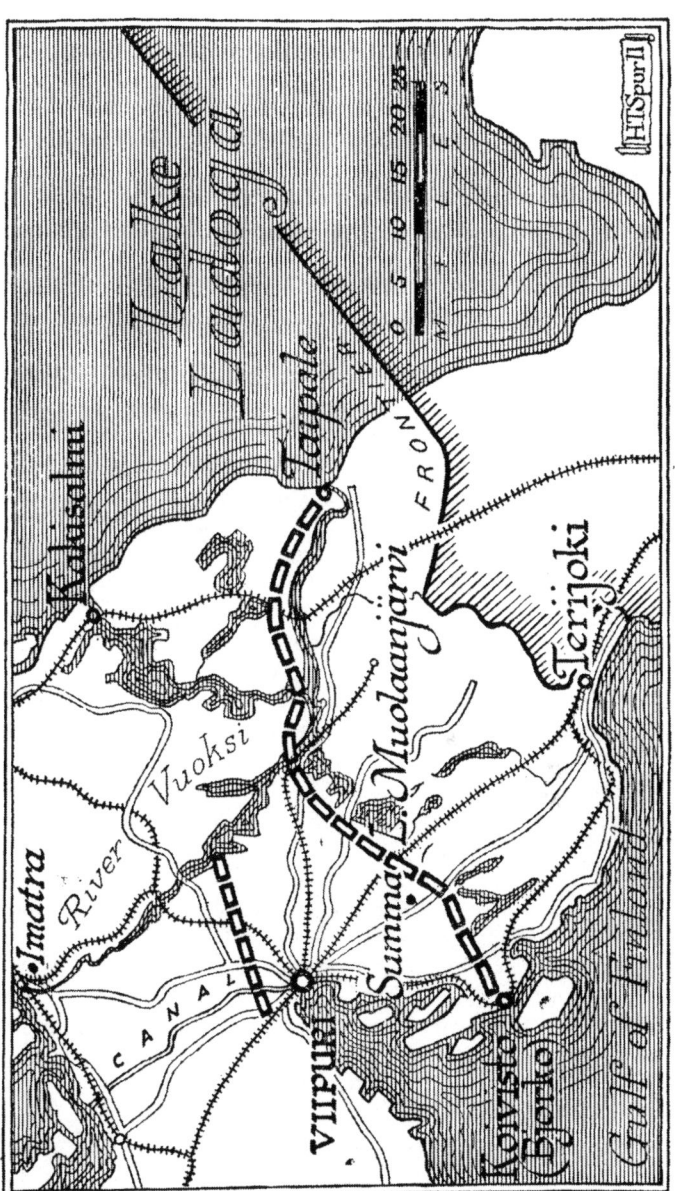

THE MANNERHEIM LINE

In front of these forts were series of anti-tank barriers, formed of triple lines of the native granite blocks of the region sunk three feet into the ground. Eight belts in all of these tank teeth ran across the Isthmus in the Mannerheim Line region. They linked with wide belts of anti-tank minefields and tank traps. These were partly ditches half a chain wide, and twenty feet deep, partly marshy areas. In the forested stretches there were wide defence belts where the trees had been lopped off about three to five feet from the ground, and the stumps left standing, over an area from a quarter to half a mile wide. Barbed wire was strung among the tree trunks and mines placed along the paths and roadways through the belt.

In some areas, however, the Line was made up only of belts of trenches and dugouts along the edge of frozen lakes. The chief defence of the Line was, in fact, water. Two-thirds of it ran along rivers or lakes. It ran in a curve with the convex area pointing inland towards Finland roughly from east to west, from Taipale at the mouth of Vuoksi River on the shore of Lake Ladoga, to the Baltic just below the great coastal fort of Koivisto. The wide swift Vuoksi River formed one-third of the Line. This was linked by a series of land defences to Lake Ayranaan: then on to Lake Muolaan: but then came the weak part, the open Summa sector, strengthened by the concrete forts. It was an area of undulating forest country twenty-five miles wide. Then came Lake Kuolema and finally the coast, with Koivisto's guns commanding the flank. A strategic railway served the area behind the Vuoksi River: five other lines and a network of roads ran down to the sector between the Vuoksi and the sea, just out of Viipuri. In the open area, particularly just before Viipuri, there were marshy tracts and flat areas that could be flooded. It was on this water defence that the Finns relied and which, when the frosts continued excessively late in March, let them down. What should have been, by late February, soggy marsh, forming perfect anti-tank barriers, was to remain frozen, hard as a paved road.

Not that the Line was not strong. It was in an area naturally suited for defence. The Karelian Isthmus has been, throughout history, one of those natural barriers to conquest such as the Sudeten Mountains.

The great squat bulk of Viipuri Castle which, with its edges crusted with snow, towered above the wooden houses and modern buildings of the city, was the remnant of the Mannerheim Line of other years. Viipuri had always been the main point of Finnish resistance against Russian invasion. When I went to Viipuri, I stayed at an hotel called the Knut Posse. It was named after a Finn, who, in his time, had held out in Viipuri Castle during a great siege by the Russians. The flat land that ran along the coast shore to Terijoki was the natural road from Leningrad towards Scandinavia—or, as Stalin was never tired of pointing out, from Scandinavia and Germany to Leningrad. The modern Finns remembered, too, that around Viipuri the last battles of the civil war of 1918 had been fought, and that on the Isthmus the last Red troops had made their stand, before retreating into Leningrad. The Finnish High Command had always trained the bulk of their army there. Ski battalions in the winter, cyclists' battalions in the summer had held their manœuvres on the Isthmus. The 34,000 men of the Finnish standing army in peacetime were stationed mainly around Viipuri. Since the first days of the Republic, in 1918, defence positions had been prepared there. But it was not until the summer of 1938 that the real defence line was started.

At that time the Finnish General Staff smelt war in the air, even if Mr. Chamberlain was still marching, head up, towards peace in our time. They secured substantial credits for the Line. At the same time, through the student associations and the Civil Guard, they organised volunteer labour gangs to work on the Line. On Sundays special trains ran to Viipuri from Helsinki and other cities, taking the volunteers to dig anti-tank canals and trenches and dug-outs. All over Finland, on the walls of hotels and barracks, one came across a coloured photograph showing the men at work, on one of those Sundays. It showed hundreds of Finns, stripped to the waist, working on a long anti-tank ditch. In the foreground a burly Finn with a magnificent stomach, the acquirement of which must have taken years of schnapps drinking, was wheeling a wheelbarrow across a plank, while others chopped trees and wove bushwood hurdles to line the ditch.

To get money, even fruit machines were pressed into service. Gambling machines—in which you had to try to " hole out " one-mark pieces—were put into restaurants and hotels. I reckoned that, by the time I left Finland, at least the price of one small bunker had been extracted from me by this method. Walter

Kerr, of the *New York Herald Tribune*, however, found an excellent way of beating the bank, by stacking up coins in the empty spaces so that you had only the high-priced holes left. Surrounded by hosts of admiring small boys, he used to clean out machine after machine in restaurants and railway stations.

Foreign experts assisted in the building of the Mannerheim Line. It was designed, on German advice (for the whole Finnish army maintained the closest ties with Germany), on the same principle of defence in depth adopted to defeat the infiltration tactics used towards the end of the last war. A Belgian, General Badoux, designed the granite anti-tank barriers. Sir Walter Kirke, head of the Territorial Army, and an old friend of Mannerheim, visited it and rather over-enthusiastically, according to most Finnish officers, described it as "As strong as the Maginot Line". The Finns guarded its secrets jealously. The Press never got more than a vague glimpse of the concrete defences at any time. The Finnish Generals were, in fact, always rather annoyed about the label "Mannerheim Line". This was an invention of a foreign journalist and they resented it. To them, it spoke of stronger defences than they had in actuality. They were also aware that the Line had not been constructed directly by Field-Marshal Mannerheim, but by the General Staff during the time when he was still merely head of the Defence Council. In the Finnish communiqués the term "Mannerheim Line" was never used, and I saw it used only very rarely in Finnish newspapers. The official statements spoke always of "Fighting on the Karelian Isthmus".

Against the Isthmus the Russians concentrated, at the start of the war, their Seventh Army under the command of General Mereskov. Based on Leningrad, it was formed of three army corps. It operated in three sectors, in each of which there were four divisions, ranging over a front of twenty kilometres deep. At the same time four brigades of heavy tanks and three corps of light tanks were attached for the attack.

During the first week of the war the Russians advanced over the frontier at half a dozen different points and moved steadily on towards the Line, skirmishing with the Finnish outposts. By the end of the first week, their artillery was in contact with the Finns at the mouth of the Vuoksi River on the shores of Lake Ladoga and the first attacks were being launched against the

THE MANNERHEIM LINE

Line near Lake Muolaan and in the Summa sector. The first Russian tanks reached the anti-tank barriers of the Line on Thursday, December 6. From then on, till the end of the year, the Russians launched a series of frontal attacks at many points. They waited only to get up their artillery and for the ice to freeze across the rivers. Their attacks showed little originality in method or tactics. It was orthodox fighting following a monotonous pattern. The Russian guns would pound away at the Finnish lines, usually about three in the afternoon just before dusk. This barrage would continue for about half an hour. Then almost exactly twenty minutes after this lifted the Russians would come over, mostly in wedge-shaped formation with tanks at their head. They seldom employed a rolling barrage. On the wedge the best men were on the flanks, and patrols went ahead with long poles trying to explode land-mines. These attacks were beaten back with complete regularity, and every time the Russian losses were heavy.

The Russians had apparently expected their tanks to be able to force the Finnish positions with a good deal of ease, for they made little attempt to use surprise or vary their tactics throughout this first month. Yet their light and medium tanks could not stand up to the land-mines or the Finnish artillery, or even to the Finnish patrols working with grenades from the woods. On December 14 the Finns claimed to have destroyed fifteen medium tanks. This failure of the light tank units was the dominant factor in the first month of the war. By the beginning of January the Finns claimed to have destroyed 200 tanks on the Mannerheim Line alone. One regiment on Lake Muolaan had knocked out thirty-seven tanks itself.

The Russians then made their first change in tactics. They began to attack with masses of infantry, in advance, and with the tanks in support, brought up as a mobile force, ready to be pushed into any gap that the infantry might find. They began to attack, too, more at night. But the Finns installed batteries of searchlights and switched these on across the lakes as the Russians advanced. Again and again the Russians were mown down by machine-gun fire. These lakes and rivers, now solidly frozen, provided the Finns with admirable fields of fire in front of their positions. They were flat and open for stretches of anything up to three and four miles or more. At night the

Finnish patrols would move over the frozen Vuoksi, or through the forests, and attack Russian outposts, capture prisoners and harry the Russian lines. Against these men the Russians could never put out any adequate counter-patrol. Their men were still without white snow capes; they had no ski-troops; and their men were unused to this warfare in the cold.

So it went on, throughout December, and into the early days of January, this steady, grim trench-warfare that cost the Russians heavily in men and materials, but never even dented the Mannerheim Line. The Finns were amazed themselves at the courage of the Red troops, which carried out again and again these repeated costly manœuvres, but they scorned the "blundering tactics" of commanders who sent over men to face certain death. Then, abruptly, the attacks began to dry up. They slackened after Christmas, and from early January everything but artillery and patrol activity stopped against the Line. An "all quiet" period set in on this front. But behind the front the Russians were frantically busy. They were massing men and supplies for their great February offensive. The second stage of the war was about to begin. In the air it had begun already.

CHAPTER XXV

AIR WAR: STAGE TWO

On the mid-morning of January 3 I stood in a wood by the roadside outside Rovaniemi and watched fourteen Soviet bombers, high in the pale-blue sky, droning their way southwards. That night we heard that Kemi Junction and Oulu had been bombed. Within the next week every day brought stories of heavy raids by massed bomber formations on Abo, Tampere, Viipuri, and a dozen other centres. The second stage of the Russian attack had begun.

This stage was characterised by heavy air acton against Finnish manufacturing centres, communications and, to some extent, against civilian centres. At the same time, on the fronts, a thorough reorganisation of the Red Army forces was being carried out, and stores and troops accumulated for the third phase, the push against the Mannerheim Line. Only north of Lake Ladoga, in the jungle-like area which was to become for the Russians a Passchendaele, was there any heavy fighting.

Wailing sirens; people rushing through the snow to the log-topped trenches which were the main shelters; wooden buildings blazing; icicles coating the blackened beams around the gaunt brick chimneys; these were the characteristics of this month to people throughout the length of Finland. In Rovaniemi we had an alarm almost every day, though no bombs were dropped till the very end of January. From other centres came reports of heavier and heavier raids. On January 14 thirty-five different towns and villages were bombed, and at least 1,500 bombs dropped. Fifty-six buildings were smashed. On January 20 forty-five different localities were attacked, and about 2,550 bombs dropped. On this day the Finns estimated that at least 500 bombers were over Finland. By the end of January the Finns announced that there had been 643 different air raids, and that 207 different towns or villages had been attacked. Over 20,000 bombs had been dropped. The official figures do not make it clear if incendiary bombs were in this total, but it appears that they were not. In these raids the Russians used high explosive bombs ranging from 50 kilograms to 500 kilograms. Fragments of bomb cases up to 30 millimetres thick were found. Shrapnel or splinter-type bombs were used in weights from 12 to 50 kilos. These contained, in addition to the explosive, iron balls and pieces of jagged angle iron. Even artillery shells were dropped from aircraft behind the Mannerheim Line. Incendiary bombs (thermite) ranged from 0.2 kilograms to 10 kilograms. Many of them were hurled out in "Molotov Breadbaskets"—torpedoes over six feet long and about a foot in diameter, which spun open as they dropped and hurled out 125 2-kg. thermite bombs. The Russians had also a 50-kg. naphtha bomb with an explosive charge, and bombs containing both a thermite mixture and naphtha. On wooden Finnish houses these were very effective.

Casualties in these raids on towns in the rear were surprisingly low. From the beginning of the war till the end of January only 377 civilians had been killed in air raids and 323 seriously wounded, 585 slightly wounded. How were these figures kept so low?

There are three explanations. One is that the Finns, an admirably disciplined people, organised an excellent A.R.P. system. At first they had tried to meet air attack by dispersion, by evacuating the big cities and scattering the people round the country. But that was not successful. Small villages as well as big towns were bombed. So they set to work and dug trench shelters, usually ten feet deep with a five feet thickness of logs and earth above. Into these shelters they went almost unfailingly, even in cities like Helsinki where alarm followed alarm without any bombs being dropped. They felt no lack of dignity in running for an air-raid shelter. That was part of the war; it was an order —and to a Finn, orders are very definitely orders. Again and again, when we much preferred to stay, we were turned out of the hotel at Rovaniemi, to go into the cold stuffy trench. And of course one day there came a real raid that blew in every window. Dozens of people would have been injured if not killed, had they not all been safely in the shelter.

The shelters were, of course, no protection against a direct hit. In Vaasa fifteen people were killed when a bomb struck a trench shelter. In Rovaniemi two nurses were burnt to death when an incendiary bomb dropped into the hospital shelter. Yet there were cases to balance this. In one place a 250-kilo bomb fell right beside a shelter. The explosion left most of the shelter dangling over the crater, yet not one of the sixteen people in the shelter was injured. The value of even a rudimentary shelter was shown by the fact that over a quarter of all the people killed in the first two months of raids, and over forty per cent of the seriously wounded, were people hit in the first three days of the war, before any proper A.R.P. was in force.

The second thing which saved the Finns many lives was the nature of their country. Most Finnish towns are built of one-storied wooden houses widely spaced out along broad streets. The actual target was dispersed and hard to hit. What is more, the women and children in places that were heavily raided, such as Vaasa, frequently trekked out and spent all the hours of daylight in the woods which were always near. In towns which might be bombed, shops were allowed to open only after three in the afternoon, when dusk was already descending.

We must remember, too, that the Russians were flying in

Arctic conditions, and had comparatively few hours of daylight to attack in.

The third explanation is that the Russians, in these raids, gave few signs that they were out to kill civilians. Their attacks were, with certain exceptions, primarily against military objectives, but with the secondary object of cracking morale as well. They undoubtedly wanted, when they raided a town, not merely, for instance, to smash up the railway station but to weary and exhaust the people as well. Main railway junctions, such as Riihimäki, Kemi and Tampere were raided repeatedly. At the same time manufacturing centres like Lahti and Tampere were hit in their factory areas. But smaller towns were also attacked. Oulu, for instance, and Vaasa were both the targets for raids at least once a week in the early part of January. These raids achieved little damage of military value. Vaasa was a port, but was already ice-bound. Lorries were actually coming in every night across the frozen Gulf of Bothnia, but there were no clearing centres in the town which were worth hitting. The Russian raid there was, in fact, typical. A line of bombs was dropped right across the small wooden town, starting from the railway station, and a circle put down round the station itself. Burnt houses lay in a singed strip across the town. When I flew over the city a month later I could see them, a black band against the snow. After two or three raids of this type the town authorities stopped all work and sent the workers to the shelters or out into the woods. This meant a huge loss of working time. At the same time it wore down people's nerves. The repeated wail of sirens, the climbing into coats and rushing out to spend hours in a freezing wood brought endless strain. A strangely active night life grew up in these places, which by nine o'clock were usually dead with echoing streets. In Viipuri the town was practically closed up till five o'clock, even though only 6,000 of its 70,000 people remained during the first two months of the war.

Hospitals, in the Russian view, appeared to be certainly regarded as bombing objectives in this war, where their main object was to exhaust the Finns' small reserves of man-power. They were bombed repeatedly. Between mid-December and January twelve hospitals were attacked, three of them hit badly, and one sanatorium destroyed by incendiary bombs.

On January 23, when I was in Viipuri visiting the Mannerheim

Line, a military hospital just behind the Line was bombed and destroyed by fire. I did not see this myself, because I was at the front at the time, but a dozen other journalists were on the spot within half an hour. Three planes had swooped out of low clouds and hit with explosive and incendiary bombs a manor house converted into a hospital. Four nurses and Lottas and seventeen patients were burnt to death. Only six of the wounded men managed to crawl to safety. Two men, terribly crippled, had to clamber out of one room leaving a third burning in his bed. The hospital had had a Red Cross painted on the roof, though this may have been covered with snow. Again, in early March the hospital at Mikele was bombed severely. Giles Romilly, who was in the town as *Daily Express* correspondent, watched the flames and smoke mounting up around the great Red Cross flag that was flying from the roof. Here, however, it is possible that part of the army intelligence staff was working in a wing of the hospital. Romilly said that a suspicious number of typewriters and papers were hurled out of the upper windows, as well as medical gear and bedding.

But the Soviet cannot escape the charge of having made raids against what were primarily civilian centres. Porvoo, a small town on the coast between Helsinki and Viipuri, known chiefly because it was the home of the national poet Runeberg, was bombed on Christmas Day. The attack centred on the school, probably because schools were widely used as billeting places for recruits. Two bombs killed an old school-teacher and injured a number of people in a shelter nearby. The people of the village had already subscribed eight hundred pounds to buy an anti-aircraft gun, but they had not been able to get it yet. Hango town was repeatedly attacked, long after the port had frozen up, though the forts on the islands off the coast were seldom raided. Trains were also machine-gunned. Richard Busvine, a British journalist working for the *Chicago Times*, was in the Abo train on December 18 when it was machine-gunned outside Helsinki. People were recommended to take white cloaks with them when they travelled, so that they could jump from the train and hide in the snow.

Behind the fronts both Viipuri and Soilavda, the chief base towns for the Isthmus and the Mannerheim Line, suffered terribly in the later stages of the war. Viipuri, at the end, came near to being a Guernica—a mass of blackened, smashed buildings. Yet the railway station, which would have been the most obvious military target, was hardly touched.

Rovaniemi, which was my home for the greater part of January, finally got its share of attack. (By the end of the war every Finnish town had been bombed at least once.) This raid was typical; it sums up better than any figures the Russian methods and results. After weeks of alarms that brought no bombs the raid came with terrible suddenness, on January 29, just after nine o'clock in the morning. The planes were overhead before the sirens had stopped wailing. Nine planes, flying at about 7,000 feet, came steadily down, following the line of the river. They dropped their bombs almost simultaneously, bomb after bomb thudding down on the frozen earth like a series of earthquakes. They went for the hospital, the main railway bridge, the hotel, which was serving as a hospital, the General Staff headquarters and the office of the local government chief. Their espionage work had clearly been good. Two bombs passed through the steel-work of the bridge and exploded on the ice below, but did little damage. One wing of the hospital was badly damaged, and seven people, including two pregnant women, were killed. An incendiary bomb fell at the entrance to a trench shelter, outside the hospital, where the nurses were sheltering, and seven people were burnt to death. A bomb killed the wife and daughter of the chemist, next door to the local authorities' offices. Shops near the centre of the town were hit, and all the windows of the hotel blown in. Our old haunt, the sauna, was completely smashed.

Half an hour later the second raid came. Four bombs struck the centre of the town. People fleeing over the ice of the river were machine-gunned, and bombs dropped on the iced roads. A British photographer, Eric Calcraft, who was crossing the river at the time, had to lie hidden, and half frozen, for nearly half an hour among the great blocks of ice that had been cut and stacked close to the river bank.

Two days later came another raid. This time the bridge was hit and damaged, but not severely. Shops and banks at the main cross-roads were smashed and burnt, and three people were killed. The baby bear also fell a victim. He was hit by a splinter and bled to death.

The technique of raiding a second time within a short period was almost invariably used by the Russians. The moral effect was very great. The first raid gave a considerable shock. The second gave a feeling that this agony would go on repeatedly, inevitably. One might have been a chance raid, but a second and third convinced you that every day the planes were certain to come again. The people suffered almost the same strain even when the planes did not come as when they did. This effect was particularly intensified if the raids were made at the same hour. In Rovaniemi at nine o'clock in the morning the hotel offices, shops, and workshops closed and the whole town crossed the river to the woods of Ousnawara, and waited there till three in the afternoon. The hotel issued sandwiches; you could brew coffee in the hut or tents of the local shooting range. On skis, dragging sledges, carrying bundles, Rovaniemi set out wearily on this trek. Even in the Arctic Circle, total war had become a reality.

CHAPTER XXVI

PETSAMO: FORGOTTEN FRONT

LATE IN JANUARY I went north from Rovaniemi to visit Finland's forgotten front, around Petsamo, on the Arctic Ocean. Here, two hundred and fifty miles away from any other battle-field, and five hundred miles north of Helsinki, a singular, separate war had been going on ever since the end of November. It was like a colonial campaign, something distinct from all the other attacks. It was, in fact, almost a private war of the local inhabitants of Petsamo and the International Nickel Company against the Soviet Union.

I heard the story of it from Major Roinen, the Finnish frontier guard officer who, in a forester's hut in the woods eighty miles south of Petsamo, was holding this front with a force of certainly no more than five or seven hundred men against two Russian divisions. We had made the long journey over the Arctic Highway, which runs straight as a Roman road from Rovaniemi northwards, in our lurching white bus. Eight hours' driving, with a stop for a

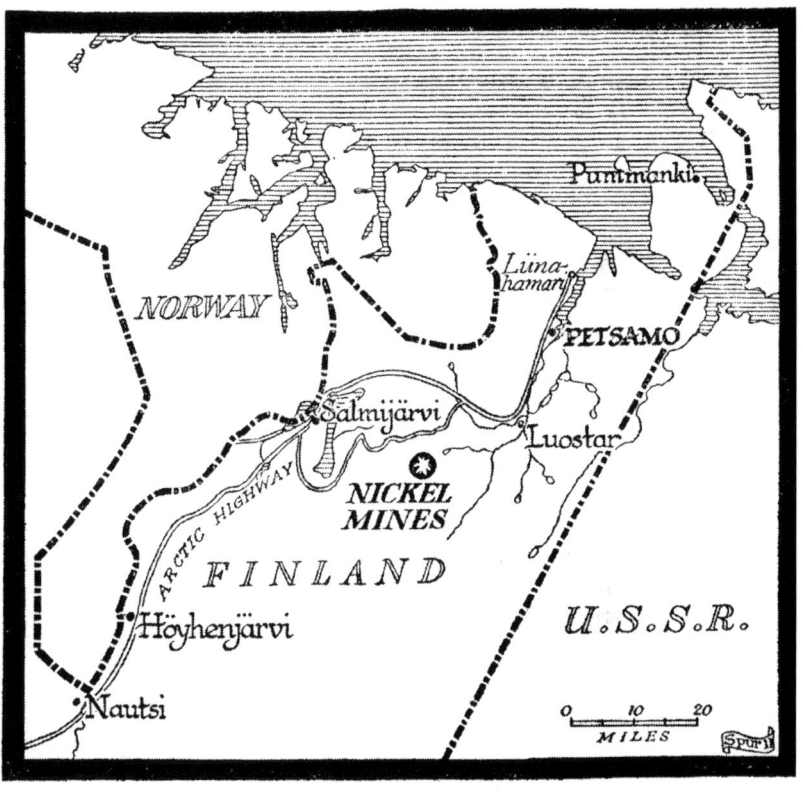

THE PETSAMO CORRIDOR

great breakfast of sausage and herring and coffee and cheese at Sodankyler village—it means the village of war—brought us to Ivalo, where at the cross-roads stood a soldier in bright-blue Lapp leggings bound with yellow and red cord, and with high reindeer-skin boots. Children in gay Lapp clothes ran along the frosted roads. It was all very romantic—till, at the inn at the cross-roads, they showed us, first of all, their air-raid shelter, deep down in the river bank.

In all over six hundred bombs had been dropped in Ivalo. They had done very little damage. Two buildings in the centre of the village were smashed, the roof of a school was burnt; one dud had gone right through the roof of the chief bank, a small wooden building. The others had ploughed up the fields. It seemed a sheer waste of ammunition, for Ivalo was one of the most widely dispersed places I have ever seen in my life—just a number of scattered houses and buildings spread amidst woods and fields. It was the main base, however, for the Petsamo front, and there was always a chance of getting a building full of troops or a petrol or munitions dump.

Three Finnish soldiers produced for us, with pride, a large black Soviet bomb that had failed to go off, and dumped it in the courtyard of the inn. We began to argue about its weight. Was it a fifty or hundred kilo? They decided they would soon settle that. They carried it inside, set it down in the corner of the dining-room, and produced a huge pair of grain scales, which they hung from a beam. It turned out to be just under fifty kilos. After that they suddenly got out a spanner and started to unscrew the detonators. No one seemed at all concerned. The drinkers from the main bar poured in to watch, and we, to maintain face, had to continue eating our lunch as calmly as we could, while the whole infernal machine was stripped.

In the early afternoon we set off on the last ninety-mile stretch to the front. We climbed into the hilliest country I had seen in Finland—wild rolling forest hills that were a wonderful natural fortification. We lurched past lorries taking up supplies and munitions, past an occasional peasant in a sledge.

Through these hills five defensive positions had been built, or rather cut—bands of lopped-off trees, trenches, tank pits. They were some of the most formidable lines I had seen in the whole of Finland. Any army that could fight its way through them would lose enormously in men and material. It did not look to me as if the Russians were likely to try any direct drive south on this road, at least in winter. They must have had too, from their aerial reconnaissance, full knowledge of this system.

We swung down to a wide river-bed, with a few huts on the edge of the ice—Nautsi, the old frontier post between Finland, Norway and Russia in pre-Great War days, before the Petsamo corridor was handed to Finland. Four miles farther on we found the headquarters—with the major, a small neat man with the green boar's head of the frontier guards on his uniform lapel, the inevitable portrait of Mannerheim on the wall, and a fine series of bullet holes in the log roof and walls, the visiting cards of Soviet planes.

He turned to the map on the wall. The Petsamo corridor, a strip of wild, bleak fells, runs, from forty to twenty miles in width, eighty miles north from Nautsi to Petsamo Sound on the Atlantic Ocean. There is no railway, and only the one Arctic roadway. Strategically it is important because Petsamo harbour, washed by the Gulf Stream, is ice-free all the year round; economically its value lies in the vein of nickel which was discovered in 1922 on the edge of the great Petsamo Tuntura, the Petsamo fells, twenty miles inland from the harbour head. The Petsamo Nickel Corporation, a subsidiary of the British Mond Nickel Corporation, and part of the International Nickel group, was developing this. They had constructed a power-house near the mine at Rauiatuntuki and were driving a tunnel in towards the nickel vein.

It could not have taken the Soviet General Staff much effort to work out what to do in the Petsamo region. The obvious course was to occupy it with a strong force, in order to seal the harbour against any possible relief expeditions, seize the nickel mines as a pawn at any peace conference, and—perhaps—weaken the Finns on the distant Salla front by drawing away men. The Finns for their part knew that there was no hope of their holding the harbour against any such invasion. The nearby Russian base of Murmansk was too close. So they stationed here only fifty men of the frontier guards, with the plan that they should, if necessary, fight a delaying action, and trust to the cold and the distance to protect Ivalo and the lower stretches of the Arctic Highway. But events changed this. The fishermen of

Petsamo and the men from the nickel mines put up such a fight that it was possible to form a solid front just north of Nautsi, and hold it all winter, and to inflict heavy losses on the Russians as well.

Petsamo was the point at which the first Russian attack of the whole war was launched. It took place on November 29, before the bombing of Helsinki, and was one of the actions which were thought at the time to have been just one more frontier incident. It began on the Fisherman's Peninsula, a great double peninsula which was half Russian and half Finnish territory, sticking out into the Arctic north-east of Petsamo Sound. Russian troops advanced towards a Finnish frontier post held only by ten men. The Finns called on them to halt, then fired. The Russians, two hundred strong, swept on. A Lapp woman, Uurasmaa, managed to escape, and ran to warn the other troops, and the people at Petsamo. She was later killed in a bombardment and received a posthumous decoration from Mannerheim. The next day the remainder of the garrison on the peninsula managed to escape.

But that next day, too, November 30, the main Russian attack was launched. From the sea, by boats from the head of the Fisherman's Peninsula, and straight across the neck of the narrow corridor towards Luostari, and the head of Petsamo Sound, at least a full Russian regiment was sent forward. The frontier guard commander dropped back to Luostari village to organise some sort of line across the Arctic Highway. Around Petsamo Sound the fishermen—the place had never been evacuated—fought bitterly, practically from house to house, while lorries were rushed up from the nickel mines to evacuate the women and children, the dozen monks from the Petsamo monastery, and half a tribe of Skolte Lapps, the oldest race in Europe. Koskivirta, the local pastor, and Rauta Vesi, a forty-year-old fisherman, took command of the forty men who had assembled to fight in Petsamo proper. All that Thursday and Friday they harried the Russians there and they gained valuable time. For back in the nickel mines an army was being organised.

The fifteen hundred men in the mines had been grouped for many months as a local section of the Civil Guard, and had rifles and ammunition with which they trained. Engineers of the company were their officers. When word of the invasion came the Guard paraded, were issued with their arms, and rushed up in lorries to meet Major Roinen. By the Friday night the first patrols of them, on skis, were already taking the counter-offensive. They moved up the side of the road in the forest right to the head of the sound, attacked a Russian encampment, and captured some ammunition.

After that there was nearly a fortnight's quiet, broken only by Finnish patrol action. But on December 13 scouts ski-ed back from their posts on the hills overlooking the sound to say that three Soviet boats—a transport and two armoured trawlers, and a submarine—were in the sound. Out of the transport came not only men and guns but something the Arctic had never seen before—tanks. With these on December 14 the Russians launched their first main attack down the Arctic Highway.

Against the tanks—all light models of the nine-and-a-half ton size—the Finns had nothing but rifles, light machine-guns, and one old 75 mm. gun. They decided to set this up, well camouflaged, at a bend in the road and try for at least one tank. When the tank column finally approached they let the Russians get within six hundred yards and then fired the gun over open sights. The first shell hit the front tank and blew it to bits. From then on till the end of December it was a story of a steady Soviet advance, of a great tide of men and machines—at least one full division was landed at Petsamo—against at the most one Finnish battalion. The Russians came on with full equipment. Their field-guns shelled the woods where the Finns lay; their tanks, preceded by a new anti-mine roller which blew up land mines, moved on looking for Finnish machine-gun posts; their infantry came after; then they laid a light railway of German Montania diesel trucks to bring up supplies. Every day, too, their bombers were over, working from Murmansk.

By December 18 they had the nickel mines. The Finns, at the request of the British parent company, did not destroy them. It would have been of little use to do so, for the exact position of the vein was a close-guarded secret known only to four men—the mine manager, Mr. I. J. Simcox, and three engineers. The shaft was still at least half a mile from the vein, and it would have taken the Russians six months of prospecting to find where the vein lay. Only sheds that could have been used for shelter at the shaft-head were burnt. Blue-prints of the workings and the vein were taken, the day of the invasion, at once southwards to

Helsinki and on to London by the manager. Two of the engineers in the secret, both Finns, stayed on to fight as officers. Their commanders were always worried that they might be caught and forced to give up their knowledge, but they never were.

This fighting went on in terrible cold, with the temperature ranging from thirty-six to forty degrees centigrade below zero and with winds from the Arctic sweeping across the open fells. The Russians, who had no proper Arctic tents with them, must have lost hundreds of men from cold. The battle went steadily on, along the Norwegian border by Salmijärvi down through the forest towards Nautsi. Thirty Finns, cut off at Salmijärvi, were forced over into Norway. Always, moving through the forests on the edge of the battle, were the Norwegian frontier troops, watching their country's neutrality.

This advance down the frontier provided an eye-witness story by a Norwegian journalist which was later used to prove the success of the Red Army in the north. It described this great Red Army tide moving in, and how the Finns were helpless against it, and spoke of the great victory of Salmijärvi. In itself true, its implication was utterly false—the implication that this was the true account of what was happening on all fronts in the north, and that reports of Russian defeats were nonsense. In fact Petsamo was strategically an unimportant front, always in Russia's grasp any time she liked to reach out from Murmansk, and very lightly held by the Finns. And in the end this tide of the Russian Murmansk army was to stay put eighty miles south of Petsamo and remain there till the end of the war.

The advance went on until the end of December. By this time the Russians had reached the ruins of Hüyhenjärvi, a village ten miles north of Nautsi. Here they halted. Ahead of them was the first of the great Finnish defence belts, fitted with artillery positions, machine-gun nests, anti-tank traps. Four miles before it the Russian outposts halted, and except for tank and patrol raids made no further attacks during the war.

We walked up to the Finnish line that night in the brilliant moonlight with the officers of the Finnish defending unit. The trenches and gun positions were cut in the bank of a frozen river. Ahead, like some petrified forest in a dead continent, stretched the half-mile-wide belt of cleared forest, tree stumps and barbed-wire. Beyond were the woods where the Russians were. In the middle of the belt a sauna building still stood, and men's voices, laughing, came from it. Lottas—this was the one front where women served right in the lines—were handing out hot food from a sledge kitchen to orderlies.

Suddenly, silently, a line of men in white ski-ed down the slope past the black iron plates that had been thrust up in the roadway to mark the line. Their leader could not have been more than twenty-one. Over his shoulder was slung a Suomi machine-pistol. The others carried rifles, grenades, food. The man at the end was smoking a cigar. He grinned as he passed us, threw it away, and pushed on to catch up with the others. In a few minutes they were swallowed up in the greenish-white waste of the belt.

"A reconnaissance patrol?" I asked one of the officers. He grinned. "Hardly that. More of a battle patrol. I think they are going out to make some trouble for someone. The Russians are building some new barracks behind their lines, and we are going to burn them down."

An hour later, as we stood by the roadside waiting to start homewards, we heard suddenly a blaze of machine-gun and rifle fire, and then the crash of grenades, very distant. The patrol was in action.

We went back to the black tents where the reserves waited. They were sitting round eating their porridge suppers and listening to the Finnish propaganda broadcast from Moscow. They laughed at the speaker, mostly, though some listened carefully. One boy's face—he could not have more been than eighteen—stood out from the others. He had the merry, dark-eyed expression of someone who was finding life terrific fun. All these men, in fact, definitely gave the impression that they were enjoying this war. For now it was purely patrol warfare in which they were definitely on top. They had none of the horrors of heavy shelling or dive bombers which make war a neurotic hell for most men. They were fighting a struggle in which skill, marksmanship, physique, swiftness, courage all counted, and they found it good. One of them was a champion ski jumper, who the night before had surprised, on patrol, a Russian ammunition lorry and a tank five miles behind the Soviet lines. The driver of the lorry, unwilling to sleep alone in his truck, had left it and gone to sleep in the tank. The Finns set the ammunition alight, then knocked on the side of the tank. Believing they were in safety the

Russians opened the manhole. The Finns hurled in a grenade and ski-ed away. They could see flames from the burning tank as they went through the woods.

"They hold the road; we hold everything else," said the major to us.

Every night at least one reconnaissance patrol set out on a fortnightly journey right round the Russian lines, up to the edge of the Sound. It took them three weeks. Every move the Russians made was known in detail to the Finnish commanders.

Another Finn, a mere boy, had been surprised when out on patrol and had to run off leaving his skis, which he had kicked off for the moment, behind him. Skis were valuable on this lone front, and his officer said, "You will have to go back and get them." The next night, alone, he went back and returned not only with his own skis but two pairs of Russian skis as well.

The Soviet troops here too were mostly from the Volga and Ukraine. They knew nothing of snow warfare. Their patrols were frequently surprised carrying their unwieldy skis on their shoulders. They had had heavy losses in lonely farm-houses as they came south, for the Finns mined every building that they did not burn.

One Finnish patrol, retreating from Haukila village, burnt every building except the sauna, which they mined. They then hid in the woods and waited. The Russians came on, opened the sauna door, and as soon as the mines exploded rushed for the most obvious cover nearby, a gravel pit. But this too had been mined, and blew up with a roar as the Russians jumped into it. Next day the Finns found a notice pinned on a tree in the woods saying: "That is not fair warfare. If you do that again we will kill every Finnish prisoner we take."

Both Finns and Russians left pamphlets and messages for each other in the woods on their patrols. Every night the Finns came back with yet another bundle of leaflets urging them to give up the fight.

It was almost all night fighting. When the war first began there were only two and a half hours of light a day, and this really only a grey twilight. It was literally a war in the dark. Soviet planes repeatedly machine-gunned and bombed this Finnish position south of Höyhenjärvi. Nautsi had been plastered, the day before we got there, in one of the most mysterious bombings the

Russians have ever carried out. The eighteen houses and huts and the bridge had had 688 bombs rained on them. Three huts had been hit, but nothing had hit the bridge. Even if the bridge had been smashed it would have meant nothing, for the ice was there as a perfect natural roadway. It was either stupidity, sabotage, or just that the Russians had enormous bomb supplies that could be wasted.

No Finnish planes ever appeared on the Petsamo front. We kept hearing tales of a fleet of Bristol Blenheim bombers which were the private property of the Mond Nickel Corporation, and which were bombing Murmansk from bases just over the Norwegian frontier. I went into this carefully and I could never find one scrap of evidence for it. Five Russian planes were brought down on the Petsamo front by machine-gun fire during the war. The Finns claimed as well to have knocked out thirty Russian tanks.

By the end of January the Russians had at least two full divisions stationed in this Petsamo territory. They were part of the 40th Army Corps based on Murmansk. Field-guns had been set up commanding Petsamo Sound, and minelayers stood by ready to close it. In all 142 tanks were landed there, the Finns claimed. These precautions were clearly not against the Finns but against any attempt by the French or us to force a way in through Petsamo. Sir Hubert Gough, on December 11, had advocated that we should send a fleet to Petsamo. At that time it might have been a feasible proposition, but only just, for any force landed would have always had the Russians from Murmansk on their flank. And later, when *Le Temps* in Paris was calling for an expedition to open the Arctic Highway for Allied arms and troops, it would have been sheer mid-winter madness. Even if the harbour had been recaptured there existed no proper port facilities for landing supplies, and everything landed would have had a 300-mile journey over open, snow-bound roads at the mercy of Soviet bombers, before they got near any front where they could be of any value. We were well out of Petsamo—as experience was to show that we were well out of Finland altogether.

CHAPTER XXVII

GHOST PATROLS

The vast Finn in the corner of the tent took out his bayonet and showed us the blood caked on it. "Colonel," he grinned, tapping it. "Russian colonel. Got him on the road behind Salla three days ago."

Laboriously I wrote down the Finn's name—Wilhelm Valkypaa. The next day I talked with his platoon commander. I wanted to nail down the truth of these many stories of unbelievable exploits of Finnish patrols. The commander confirmed it all. Valkypaa had turned up with a strip of ribbons cut from the breast of a Soviet colonel, and with the papers and badges of two other officers, a captain and a lieutenant. He brought also a bundle of papers showing that the colonel had been the divisional artillery commander. In them were details of the whole Soviet artillery dispositions on the south Salla front. Valkypaa, ski-ing on a reconnaissance patrol behind the lines, had seen a lone car coming down the road towards him. He got into the ditch, and with his first shot killed the driver. The car slewed over and fell on its side. Two officers clambered out—the captain and the lieutenant. Valkypaa shot them both. Then he saw the colonel struggling to get clear on the under-side of the car. Deliberately he bayoneted him. "It's not often you get a chance to use a bayonet, you know," he told us, smiling rather ruefully.

Valkypaa was a killer, a killer of Russians, down to the last hair on his reindeer-hide boots. I should hate to have to face a man like that in a forest fight. He was typical of tens of thousands of Finns who formed the most effective weapon the Finns had —the ghost patrols. These patrols, in their white "lummi puukus" with their automatic rifles and machine pistols, waged an unceasing silent fight against the Russians, hitting at their nerves, their supplies, their outposts. They both reconnoitred and fought. They were Finland's best substitute for her virtually non-existent air force.

One of their best leaders, Aarne Valkama, who was a sergeant patrol leader, and who was brought in wounded to Rovaniemi hospital, told me of their methods and organisation. He had been world champion of ski-shooting in 1930. This was a sport in which men, going at full speed on their skis, shot at floating toy balloons or tiny fixed targets. It was one of the many ways in which, through their sports, the Finns had been trained for this war with Russia which their leaders believed to be inevitable, both from their side and the Soviet.

"For shooting at speed from skis we had a leather thong bound round our left arm. We thrust the rifle through this and raised it to fire. This gave us one hand free for ski sticks. But in forest warfare the country was almost always too rough for shooting at any speed. What we do is to kick off our skis, fire from a firm position, and then slip them on again. This is particularly necessary for throwing a grenade. It's very difficult to throw a grenade accurately from skis.

"We work in patrols of three, six or twelve men usually, thought a battle patrol may have fifteen or more. The same men work together all the time. We try to get a balanced patrol—one man, for instance, with an excellent sense of country; one first-class shot, one man with outstanding hearing, or especially good stamina.

"Patrols are of two types—battle and reconnaissance. A reconnaissance patrol never fires unless it has to. Its job is to get information about enemy positions or lines. For a short job the patrol usually goes out at dusk, travels all night, and gets back just before daybreak. In that time they will cover about twenty-five miles. Once I did that every night for twelve nights in succession. Often after we get back with information we fight in the battle which is launched because of that information. Other reconnaissance patrols go out for longer stretches of three days, or even a week or three weeks."

On the Salla front Finnish patrols completely circled the Soviet positions every night, bringing back a constant stream of information to their commanders. Others would lie throughout the darkness close to the Russian lines, watching trench digging, and spotting where headquarters were being placed and stores dumped.

Valkama told me that at this time—mid-January—no Russians on patrol in the north had even worn white snow-clothing.

The Finns always had this. They carried special iron rations, amongst them quantities of sugar, which they found gave immediate energy to a tired man.

The battle patrols were sent out to do a specific job, such as blowing up a bridge or cutting a road or harrying a supply route. They were always armed with at least one Suomi machine-pistol per patrol. They frequently dragged a light machine-gun and ammunition in a small wooden snow-boat. On the Isthmus and all fronts they waged a continual night war in the forests that formed No Man's Land, and in the Russian rear. Their favourite tactic was to place land-mines under the snow on a busy road, lie in wait to fire on men thrown out of tanks or lorries by the explosion, and then ski off. It was one of these battle patrols which attacked the Murmansk railway behind the Salla front, at least thirty miles inside Soviet territory. They had travelled through the forests for ten days till they came up against a siding packed with trucks of war materials. They waited till dark, hurled grenades into the trucks, set fire to a great pile of skis nearby, and bolted on their skis for the woods. The whole raid was over in two minutes, but they saw the sky blazing behind them. There never was any real dynamiting of the railway that I could discover, though stories of it were the commonplace in every Helsinki hotel lounge. It was simply impracticable, for there were no bridges of any size worth destroying and to blow up a stretch of flat track that could be easily replaced was not worth while.

The light machine-gun and the ski (with the puukko, used for knifing sentries) were the weapons which gave these patrols their great striking strength. Officers on the Salla front vouched to me the truth of a story that one Finnish soldier, angry at being kept on communications work, took a light machine-gun one night, skied off behind the Russian positions, and fired into a company of Russians drawn up for orders behind a hill. Black against the snow, they were an easy mark. He came back with a wooden sledge full of rifles and the shoulder badges of over fifty men.

The great value of this patrol work was that it kept up offensive spirit among an army necessarily on the defensive throughout the war. Every day these Finnish patrols were attacking; every day they could report some fresh success, even when the main tide of battle was against them. They represented in its most spectacular form the truth that two of the greatest military weapons are speed and surprise. They were like T. E. Lawrence's Arab cavalry in another element and they proved themselves every bit as good.

CHAPTER XXVIII

SALLA FRONT

ON THE AFTERNOON of January 18 I stood once again on a battlefield strewn with Russian dead. This time it was on the shores of Joutsijärvi, a lake fifteen miles east of Kemijärvi, on the Salla front. Here, during the previous week-end, the Russian force, which had advanced in early December on the southern road from Salla under orders to attack Kemijärvi, had been struck in the flank and thrown back by Wallenius's men.

This force found itself fighting a difficult battle the moment its right wing, caught at Pelkosenniemi, had been smashed. Immediately the Kemi River battle was finished on December 18 Wallenius, after detaching two companies to chase the retreating Russians back up the northern road, had swung his main force down to cover the southern approach to Kemijärvi. Here the Russians had reached, with the bulk of their forces, the small frozen lake of Joutsijärvi. The western shore of this was defended by Finnish machine-gun posts and trenches, covering the road across the ice and the bridge. To advance the Russians had either to work round the sides, through thick woods, or to try a direct offensive across the ice. They did both. On their right wing they sent a full battalion on a night march and managed to get them through the woods and into position on a hillside commanding the road five miles behind the Finnish lines. They were even in full sight of the farm-house which Wallenius was using as headquarters. Here they dug themselves in, and began to get mortars into position.

They were discovered by an astonished Finnish patrol. Wallenius again acted with promptitude. He detached a full battalion—practically all the reserves he had—and made a dawn attack on the Russians. Ugly fighting ensued, but the Finns, with skis and superior cover, gradually got the upper hand. After twenty-four hours the Russians broke and surrendered or fled, leaving over four hundred dead on the field. But the very audacity of their manœuvre, even though it failed, gave the Finns a new respect for their enemies.

At the same time came the direct Russian attack across the ice. From positions in the hills which overlooked the lake from the Russian side, their field-guns pounded at the farm-houses and trenches where the Finns lay. Bombers circled over daily dropping their loads. And every day, usually at dusk, but often again in the night, the peak-capped Soviet infantry poured out onto the ice to cover the half-mile of white dead level space that separated them from the other shore. Every night the Finns replied with rifle and machine-gun fire, and held them off.

Checked on the north and centre the Russians now tried to work round the south side of the lake. Here they took up positions in a farm-house on their shore of the lake and sent out patrols into the woods south, but it was terribly thick, difficult country, and the intense cold made it worse still for them. And here, too, they suddenly came up against a flank counter-attack that Wallenius had prepared. It was his old tactic—leave as few men as possible directly in front of the enemy; bring as many as possible to the rear, or the flank. So he concentrated all but three hundred men on his right flank. In the night they advanced across the bottom of the lake, and crept round the woods from the south side. They surprised the Russian post in the farm-house, and drove back the Russians there through the woods till they were retreating onto the main road where the bulk of their column lay. Then the Finns hit at the road itself just half a kilometre behind the lake. The Russian command was not going to have any second Suomussalmi. The colonel in charge of the division was told to take out his artillery and other material and move it back to the safer position of Märkäjärvi, twenty-eight miles nearer the Soviet frontier. This was done, and the strongly fortified lines which the Russians had built opposite Joutsijärvi, with deep dug-outs, trenches, gun-pits, and the long line of troop shelters and huts behind, were abandoned without a struggle. Kemijärvi was now completely saved, and the Russians were on the defensive around the natural stronghold of Salla Mountain.

We trudged across the lake ourselves on skis, past sheds on the western shore smashed by Russian shells. Then we came on the dead. They lay in the snow and the outhouses around the lakeside farm; in the farm itself they lay, their faces smashed with hand grenades, one man with both his feet blown off, great blond men from the Ukraine dead in this wild corner of Finland. From the wall a portrait photograph of a man in Finnish soldier's uniform stared down at them. Outside in the woods a trail of bodies, lines of bodies, showed where the Finns had advanced. Men were dead, crouching to fire, huddling together under trees, in the tracks where they had been running. I felt I had been seeing dead Russians all my life.

Back at the centre of the lake, where the road crossed it, the farm-houses that had stood amid the Finnish trenches were smashed by shell-fire. Children's dolls, a mangle, straw mattresses lay on the floor of the rooms. On the other side we went over the Russian lines—solidly built dug-outs, well constructed, with warm shelters. It had a look of solidity and efficiency.

In a farmyard five miles farther on, where the divisional headquarters had apparently been, we found, amid abandoned army wagons, two simple wooden posts, newly erected. On each the side had been smoothed with an axe, and on it written in indelible pencil, in Russian, inscriptions to the men buried there. One man had died "fighting the Finnish White Guards and bandits"; the other had died "for a free Finland". Both were officers. One had, at the end of the inscription, the words, "he was a good soldier". I looked round this farmyard, bleak now in the grey afternoon with the wind tearing at our faces. Nearby lay the carcass of a dead horse, a great steak cut from its rump. Flakes of snow began to fall. Two Finnish soldiers, who had had the inscriptions translated for them, stared at the posts curiously. Did they feel that those words were true? I could not believe it. They had grinned when they were spelt out. They were peasants who, however "white guard" might be their leadership, felt that in this war right was on their side. So, too, did the bulk of the factory workers of Tampere whom I had seen in their billets back at Kemijärvi. No men who felt that freedom and a fuller life lay in a Russian victory in this war could have fought as these individual Finns did, day after day, night after night, on these lonely patrols, these grim cold forest struggles.

We drove on. Out of a side road came a sledge; on it was a stiff white shape that I thought at first was a log of wood. We stopped. The shape was the body of a Finn, shot through the side of the head, and stripped of everything except his vest and underpants and identification disk. The stripping must have been carried out almost immediately after his death, for his body had frozen into this position, with arms outflung after the jacket had been torn off. It was a magnificent body, the long-limbed smooth-muscled body of an athlete. Now it was stiff as if carved of wood, with the arms out like a man crucified. The Finns with us watched our faces almost angrily, as if they hated showing us this sudden glimpse of one of their men in his death. If anyone felt in Finland that those words "for a free Finland" were right, it was certainly not this group of Finnish soldiers on this front, with their dead comrade.

Twenty-eight miles from Joutsijärvi the front had stabilised again just west of Märkäjärvi. Here the Russians, holding the village, had dug in and formed a solid fortified position. From it they shelled steadily the road and woods on the Finnish side, and made steady tank attacks. In the darkness that night shells hurtled over towards the Finnish machine-gun posts, splintering trees, throwing up the snow. Two smashed Soviet tanks, hit by shells from anti-tank guns captured from the Soviet, lay by the roadside at the top of the ridge. Small bodies of Finns moved in open order just behind the shelled positions. In one gun-pit a man had been hit by shrapnel and badly wounded. His companions went back to get a stretcher. Thinking he was being left alone to face the Russians, that a retreat was ordered, he shrieked in a voice that rose above the gunfire, "Don't leave me, boys, don't leave me." Then the shells came again, drowning everything.

The line was stabilised on that ridge till the end of the war. The Finns were later withdrawn, and the Swedish volunteers under General Linder took it over, and Wallenius was sent south. The Russians brought up better troops, who learnt to ski well, and who fought well on patrol. But as an active fighting front of importance Salla was finished.

On the northern Salla road, where the Russians had retreated, there was little fighting from January 1 onwards. Two Finnish companies, commanded by a black-bearded, dark-eyed captain who had fought throughout the Finnish civil war, held the Russians by repeated patrol attacks and by nibbling at their communications. The Russians shelled back, usually exactly at eleven o'clock, and bombed them at intervals. It should have been a dull front, but I will remember it always for the scene of almost unbelievable beauty we saw on the moonlight night when we visited it.

We had driven up past the smashed farm-houses at Kemi River, and along the road that showed now no signs of fighting except some broken gear in the ditches, and here and there a snow-covered shape under the trees; I was amazed to see how rapidly every sign of battle can fade away. But if ever a place is entitled to have ghosts, those grey woods around Kemi River should surely have them.

Then we came out on a frozen river, just east of Saija. In the cloudless sky, greenish in the full moon, the Northern Lights, yellow, red, and gold, writhed and turned like streams of molten metal. To the north two great yellow arcs stood like single coloured rainbows. From a round black hole in the ice beside us a pony was drinking. We climbed into sledges and, lying back, were swept up the slope towards the road. As we reached the top two white-caped figures, like Arabs, appeared on horseback. They were our escort. They trotted ahead, watching the woods for the Russian patrols. Onto the seat by our driver jumped another man, who fitted a circular magazine to his sub-machine-gun and pointed it cheerfully at shadows among the trees, grinning back at us as if to say, "You should see me when I sight a Russian".

We drove on, with the wind biting the tiny slit of my face around my eyes that was not covered. Frost formed on my eyelashes. By the road a white-coated patrol skied silently forwards, dragging sledges filled with red bread boxes.

So we went on, to meet a young officer who apologised with a smile for not being able to get orders to carry out a local counter-attack that very night so that we could see it. "We have to do it some time and I'd like to show you what we can do, but the higher-ups won't let me," he said; we talked with young workers from Tampere, stretched out now on their beds after nearly twenty-four hours continuously on patrol; we ate reindeer stew with bacon—dry but tasty—and frozen Dutch cheese and hot coffee; we learnt that this company had fought five battles in one week when they chased back the Russians after the Kemi River battle; we found that their cook was a Lapp, and the commander cursed him because he was newly married and wrote long letters every day that took endless censoring. They had just taken, too, some Russian prisoners. I asked the commander if they had had lice. The commander grinned, "Their reply was—we used to have but the frost killed them." We watched a patrol ski back and report that they had found the tent headquarters of the Russian patrol commander, attacked and burnt it, and killed three men there; and we motored back over a road that was mined by a Russian patrol an hour later, blowing up the next car that came along. We talked till late in the night with a young officer who spoke again and again of the student Paris he had left to come back to this war, of the Dome and the Coupole and the Boul' Mich'; we talked of where we could go fishing after the war in this Salla region; and we dragged out among all this, detail after detail of the campaigns of Kemi River and the other Salla battles, details I have used in a dozen different places in this book. And all the time, overhead, the lights turned and moved in their beauty above these forests where men stalked each other to kill.

CHAPTER XXIX

THE VOLUNTEERS

ON THE SNOW-COVERED lake outside Oulu a line of men, all in civilian clothes, moved their legs stiffly and clumsily on their skis as the order came "Right turn". It came in English first, then in Finnish, and was given by a lean man in a khaki coat, whose accent was definitely Canadian. The first British and American volunteers for the Finnish army were in Finland and were being trained at their base camp.

It was mid-January. For days past the three-quarter-length white coats and the white fur caps of Swedish troops had become more and more common in the streets of Rovaniemi. Swedish officers, in their own army uniforms, with only the buttons changed to the Finnish lion, but with their rank marks unaltered, appeared at meal times in the Pohjanhovi. Swedish aviators came in there to sip orangeade or one per cent beer between taking their Swedish army planes up on patrol or reconnaissance. It was clear that the army of volunteers on Finnish soil was growing steadily.

Walter Kerr, of the *Herald Tribune*, had learnt, from a chance acquaintance in a train, that the main volunteer training centre was at Oulu. So one Saturday afternoon we escaped from our Press officer guides by saying we planned to go back to Helsinki—the only trip one could make unaccompanied—and set off for Oulu. For I remembered from Spain that the International Column was one of the greatest stories of the war, as well as being one of the dominant military factors. Perhaps we would find the same here.

It was not a difficult search. At Kemi junction the ravintola was full of men who were clearly volunteers. Swedes in their long coats leant over the counter flirting with the girl who served there; a party of Danes, under a young officer, waited with us for the Oulu train; at our table we found two Dutchmen and a Czech Jew, all bound for training camps.

We travelled down with the Danes, much to the anxiety of the secret police officer attached to the train. He kept coming and going, asking to see our papers, sitting down to listen in to our conversation. But there were few military secrets to be given away. These men had, like all the volunteers, been brought over the frontier at Tornio in lorries at night, and sent on from there. They had been equipped with uniforms on the Swedish side, with rifles in Finland. They had Swedish army rifles of the old pattern that had just been replaced, and had short Swedish bayonets. And they were annoyed. They found that they got less pay than the Swedes, and they distrusted their officers deeply. "They're just a bunch of young stuck-up Danish army regular officers who know nothing about war. Can't you write something that will get us transferred to Finnish commands?"

We questioned nine of these men closely. Not one of them

said he was coming to fight because he disliked Bolshevism or Communism. They were coming because they wanted to help a small country that they considered had been unfairly attacked; to keep the Russians out of Scandinavia; for adventure. The only ones who talked of a crusade against Communism were two Danish Nazis in another group, and they seemed personally unpopular with their fellows. They had been recruited quite openly in Denmark. When they applied to the Finnish Legation they were directed to a house in a suburb of Copenhagen. Here they were interviewed by four officers of the Danish regular army, and their political views tested as well as their military records. From Denmark no one could go who had fought in Republican Spain. They were suspected of being Communist spies. The recruits were then given train tickets through to Haparanda, in northern Sweden, after signing a six-months' or one-year's contract of service. This contract bound them to obey Finnish army discipline; at the end of one year they could resign on giving one month's notice; in return the Finns paid the passage from and to their homes; Finnish army pay (five marks a day, about one shilling); compensation at Finnish army rates for wounds, and at 30 per cent more than Finnish army rates to their wives if they were killed.

For the Swedes conditions were slightly different. They received Swedish army rates of pay (100 Swedish crowns a month), the difference being made up by the Swedish volunteer organisations. All the contracts, so far as I could discover, were underwritten by the Swedish Government, which guaranteed to pay the volunteers if the Finns could not.

At Oulu we found, billeted in a school, nineteen Canadians and some thirty-four Americans. They were almost all of Finnish origin, and their story almost always the same. They had heard of the danger to their old fatherland, and had come back to fight for it. One officer had served in the Canadian army in the last war; he had been given "sick leave" from it this time to come to Finland. Almost all had given up good jobs to come. One was a painter who had heard over the radio at eight in the morning that the Russians had invaded and bombed Helsinki, and by 9 a.m. had left his job, his family, and volunteered. He was an ex-U.S. marine, a great tough man who would make an admirable soldier. Another was a university student, an American whose family had been fifty years in the States. He had been on holiday in Helsinki when war broke out, and had seen the first bombing. He had allowed himself to be evacuated to Stockholm with the rest of the American colony, and then, he told me, "I felt it was, after all, my country and my war, so I had to come back". Some had fought in the Finnish civil war, and gone to America later. Others had had Finnish army training after the civil war. One squad of these men, all American citizens, was put into action as early as late December, and fought north of Ladoga. But the bulk were kept back for two months' military training.

Only one or two of these men talked fiercely about any campaign against Communism. In fact the only real ideologist among them was a rather slick "drugstore cowboy" type who had fought in Franco Spain, or rather served in Franco Spain, for, as far as I could judge, he had seen little action. The others were animated by a type of old-fashioned patriotism, by the peasant instinctive sense of defending their homes.

I found them, in fact, slightly dull. I groped in my mind for the reason, for I remembered the richness of experience and character I had found among the first International Column men who came to Madrid. The reason was not hard to find. These men were fighting for the simple motive of defending their country, a motive that is very admirable but much less interesting to the observer than that of a man who has formed a faith in his mind by bitter struggle. The first volunteers in Spain were almost all men who, at one time in their lives, had been through some deep and often terrible experience which had made them anti-Fascist. There were men from the French army who were cashiered for refusing to charge German workers in the Ruhr; Germans who had escaped from concentration camps; Italians who had struggled for years against Mussolini. They had been through that period of soul-searching which every genuine man on the Left must experience before he adopts a creed against which he knows all the weight of modern society is flung. Few of these volunteers in Finland had had this experience. It did not make them worse men or soldiers, but it made them less interesting to the observer.

This volunteer force was, in fact, not so much an international column as a Scandinavian army, formed chiefly of Swedes, with

Danes and Norwegians and a handful of other nationalities thrown in, to defend Scandinavia against an expanding Russia. Swedes outnumbered the others by at least twenty to one. Their badge, the four hands clasped to represent the unity of the four Scandinavian countries, symbolised their attitude. When they ultimately moved up to the front, to take over the Salla sector, they went virtually as a part division of the Swedish army going to fight on Finnish soil. Their commander was a Swede, General Linder; the bulk of their officers were Swedes; they wore Swedish uniforms. There were one or two colourful characters—Prince Ferdinand von Lichtenstein, who served for a short time, and then hurriedly left the country, perhaps because he was a little too obviously in contact with certain German businessmen in Oulu. A charming man, Prince Ferdinand. The description he gave me later of the happy days in the late twenties, when he and Princess Stephanie von Hohenloe and Lord Rothermere were all co-operating, on plans to reshape Europe, was one of the most interesting things I have ever heard. It was, of course, strange to find him in Finland. Later I found him staying on in the dull Grand Hotel at Stockholm. "I wish to God everyone wouldn't assume I'm in the Gestapo, it's so silly," he used to say with a laugh to Giles Romilly and me.

No final figures of the strength of the volunteers in Finland have been given out, but I do not believe they were ever as high as ten thousand. At the time of peace, they formed, the Finns stated, two over-strength battalions. They fought confidently and bravely on the Salla front and did valuable work in releasing Finnish troops for service on the Isthmus. But as a real military factor affecting the result of the war, they were too few to be of importance. Finland's war was fought by the Finns themselves. It was not for nothing that their ancestors had had inscribed on tablets in the island fortress of Soumenlinana, that guarded Helsinki, "Posterity, take your stand here on your own ground and do not rely on the help of strangers".

CHAPTER XXX

LOTTAS

LOTTA SVARD WAS a camp follower who became a Finnish national heroine. Her name has been given to the national women's movement. This movement, the Lotta Svard Organisation, 100,000 strong, was Finland's A.T.S., F.A.N.Y. and everything else rolled into one. Formed during the time of the 1918 civil war, it had grown up side by side with the Civil Guard, and had gone on steadily training its members to meet the strain and work of war. That training was so well done that when war came the outside world heard almost as much of the Lottas as they did of the ski troops.

Lotta Svard may actually have never existed in real life. But she exists very vividly in the poems of Runeberg, the Finnish national poet, and that has given her as much existence as reality could have done. In the poem she is a young beauty who marches off to the front to accompany her husband when he goes to fight the Russians.

> "When the drum called Svard as a patriot
> She followed it at his side,
> For a pearl on the pathways of war was she
> And a pearl all genuine too.
> Though sometimes laughable she might be
> More oft was honour her due."

But one-third of her beauty fades in the winter cold; another third goes in the summer heat; and the third

> "She let it drown in her tear-drop flood,
> When he fell in the conflict, Svard."

After that she became a vivandière, who followed the regiment with her store of schnapps and brandies, setting up her little stall right behind the battle line, and selling tots to the brave as they went forward, and the weary and wounded as they went back.

In this new war with Russia the Lottas, in their grey uniforms, and with their blue and white swastika badges (adopted by the Finnish whites when Adolf Hitler was still a lance-corporal running messages behind Verdun), carried out the same dangerous work, though they now handed out coffee and milk instead of schnapps, and wore their puritanical uniforms. Again and again, close behind the lines I saw Lottas working field kitchens, nursing in advanced dressing stations, keeping watch for planes, running canteens, organising concerts. Many, in their sombre uniforms, were plain; but many others were extraordinarily good-looking. Often, in some remote village or town in North Finland, we would go into a ravintola for coffee, to find behind the counter a girl looking like a film star. Their war work was of enormous value, far more, proportionately, than women can do in other countries where there is ample man-power. For the Finns had not a man to waste; they had no slack of unemployed to take up, and when the men were mobilised, the women took over a huge part of the work at the rear. They became postwomen, shopkeepers, teachers, postmistresses, factory workers. And they did it all with a grave simplicity. There was little lipstick or nail varnish about the Finnish women in war, and little jazz or excitement. War for them was a grim business, to be taken grimly. Dancing was stopped throughout the country during the war, except for one or two places in Helsinki. Modern Finland went to battle in the same calvinistic spirit that it had gone to battle in the preceding centuries.

I remember deeply shocking a Finn in Rovaniemi by asking jokingly, during a concert for the troops, when the cabaret part would begin. For, far from having any Gracie Fields or Jack Warner tone about it, this concert had been serious throughout. But it provided me with another unforgettable glimpse of this strange country and its strange, hard people who asked that no one should love them, but everyone respect them. It was held in the hall of the hotel at Rovaniemi. The only light came from the flames leaping from two big birch logs in the grate. The troops and wounded men sat in rows on chairs, or on benches around the wall. Three girl students, in peasant costumes rather Hungarian in colouring, sang slow, sad peasant songs. On the kautele, a type of zither, a man sang verses from the *Kalevella*, the national epic. The tunes too, had a hint of Hungary about them—Hungary without its paprika. Then came the comic turn. An artist joked about the Russian radio, imitating its propaganda. The men laughed here and there, but there were no real bursts of laughter. War and religion, I felt on this occasion, were closely linked in the Finnish mind. Their national life had been forged in this series of wars in their forests, and deep in themselves they knew it. Neither they nor their womenfolk were prepared to take it as anything but a grim necessity, the price of holding the dark forest and the lakes where their homes stood.

CHAPTER XXXI

ON THE ISTHMUS

ALL DAY LONG the guns had been going crunch, boom, boom crunch in the woods close to Summa. All day long there had been the drone of Russian planes in the shining blue sky above the pines, and the sentry outside headquarters had been winding his hand siren till no one could tell which was the danger signal and which was the All Clear. Up in the trenches which formed the front line just west of the great ice space of Lake Muolaan the sentries peered through their loopholes towards the barbed wire that marked the Russian positions, and the gun crews stayed close by their machine-guns. But there was no firing beyond the occasional crack of a sniper's rifle or a burst from a patrol somewhere distant in the woods. It was quiet here on the Mannerheim Line in these last days of January, except for their planes and the intermittent artillery fire—Russian guns pounding Finnish railheads, Finnish guns hitting back on the roads where the Russians were massing their supplies. But everyone knew here that it was a false quiet. The men resting in dugouts behind the lines, the working parties setting up more granite teeth in the anti-tank barriers, could sense the attack as if it were something carried by the wind that swept up the Isthmus from the direction of Leningrad.

I had come up to the Isthmus on the Viipuri train, a train that, God knows, has seen its full share of human emotion, as all leave trains must. It left Helsinki at eight at night, pulling out in the darkness that hid the faces of women who turned away quickly as their men with them, the great, grim-faced Finnish men, clambered aboard with their equipment, going back to the Line. There were no sleep cars; everyone packed into the carriages, sitting on seats or kitbags or coats. All Finnish trains, except crack expresses, are run on wood, and during the night, as the train moved on its slow, jogging way, the soldiers sang their slow unhappy peasant songs, and joked, and drank beer and schnapps. And in the morning it rumbled over the bridge into the granite station of Viipuri, where the lorries waited to take the men up towards the Line.

Viipuri at this time had been bombed thirty-one times, but had suffered no great damage. Many wooden houses had been hit, and here and there one of the big buildings had been struck. But the real attacks were not to come until the offensive was launched on the Line. In the Hotel Knut Posse, the correspondents slept calmly in bed at night, though in time it was to be bombed to the ground. There were still seven thousand people in the town, and in the modern restaurant that opened at six you could get an ample Finnish meal served by pert, pretty girls who drew every young soldier to their tables.

Three miles outside, on the road leading towards Summa, gangs of workmen were placing granite anti-tank blocks in position to form yet another line—the line on which the fighting was ultimately to halt. We drove on through deserted woods, hiding from time to time under the trees as squadrons of planes went over, till we left our car close to headquarters because the roads were unsafe. The Russians had observation balloons up that reported every movement to their guns.

This sector, just to the north of Summa, was commanded by General T. Laatikainen. He was a burly, genial figure whom we met strolling alone down the road, without a single staff officer or even an orderly with him, to inspect some bomb craters made the night before. He had been a schoolmaster who had joined the Jaeger battalion in Germany and come back to fight in the civil war. Our conducting officer told us he was popular with his men, and I can believe it. He had a genial, fatherly air, and a sense of efficiency with it all. When the officer with us stood at the salute as he talked, the General put his hand up and with his little finger tugged down the saluting fingers. It was a gesture that was friendly and yet dignified, evidence of confidence and informality without endangering discipline. He later let the photographer of *Match* snap him stretched asleep in his clothes on his bed. Yet I can believe that to anyone whom he felt to be his enemy he could be as hard as Wallenius.

He was confident that this Mannerheim Line front could not be broken. Every Russian attack till then had been beaten back. "The others will be, too, even though the Finns have few men. Tell your generals to send us out some of their men; they have plenty," he said to us as we left.

I found the same confidence felt by the colonel commanding the front-line sector. I sat with him for over half an hour in his dugout, which was hung with maps, and where a phone rang from time to time as the observation posts gave in their reports. He, too, was an old Jaeger officer. "We will hold, for the Line is strong, and our men are getting more rest now. But if only we had bombers we could be sure. We could smash the railways and roads on which they are bringing up troops every minute of the day and night. Why, our reconnaissance planes have photographed Russian bombers standing wing tip to wing tip crowding their landing fields on the Isthmus. We could smash them by the hundreds if we had the machines."

A young staff captain, black bearded, with bright dark eyes, came in to report. He rode off through the woods on a shaggy brown pony to another post. Galloping past, in the snow, his face flushed, he looked magnificent. He had been, he told us, a student of music. He had sung with a Finnish choir at Budapest the summer before. "I'll go there again this summer, when we've won the war," he grinned.

A week later in this sector the storm was to burst. For throughout the later part of December, and all January, the Russians had been reorganising their forces and massing eighteen full divisions of first-class troops—eighteen divisions of the real Red Army—for their offensive. General Stern, according to the Finnish information, had visited the front and discussed with Mereskov, who commanded the Seventh Army, a wholesale scheme of reorganisation. Material of every type had been massed.

Even electrical trench-digging machines were brought up. White snow capes were issued to the advance troops for the first time. Great dumps of ammunition were formed.

Details of the Red Army reorganisation were naturally very difficult to get on the Finnish side. The most reliable information I could get came, by an indirect route, from the Italian military attaché, who in turn had got it from the Germans. The German Legation was, militarily, by far the best informed of all in Helsinki, for, despite Germany's new orientation, their long-standing personal contacts with the Finnish Officer Corps still held. I never found in Finland at all during the war any real anti-German feeling, though Hitler alone had given Stalin a free hand in the Baltic. The Germans stated that at the start of the war three army corps, each of four divisions, had been grouped on the Isthmus under Mereskov. Each held a sector approximately twenty miles wide. The four brigades of heavy tanks worked directly under the Army staff; the three corps of light tanks worked directly under the corps command with the infantry. The light tanks were Vickers, Christie, Renault and Ford models, with one 47 mm. gun and two machine-guns. The heavy tanks, particularly the 33-ton model, were a Russian adaptation of a Vickers model. These tanks carried a 75 mm. gun, two 47 mm. guns and three machine-guns.

The chief reorganisation made by the Russians was significant. It contained a lesson for the western war, which Hitler had himself learnt in Poland and in the Saar. The light tanks had proved ineffective. They were easily blown up by land mines or knocked out by heavy grenades or anti-tank fire. The Russians for the big offensive therefore dissolved the units of light tanks, but kept the heavy and medium tanks. These were grouped in brigades, formed of three batteries each of thirty-two heavy or medium tanks, and with fifteen light tanks as scouts. In all Mereskov had 981 tanks under him.

At the same time heavier artillery was assembled. Batteries of 105s which could outrange the Finnish 75s were brought up. Five batteries, each of two 240 mm. guns, were also moved up.

In December and early January the Russians had also used a 200 mm. railway gun, which bombarded Viipuri with aerodynamic shells pointed at both ends. In all, over seventy shells were fired into Viipuri, but they did little damage. Further, automatic rifles were issued to the infantry, and divisions which had been using the older rifles, a Great War pattern adapted for modern use, with the old type of long French bayonet, were now issued with the 1939 Soviet rifle, which is first-class.

That, in any case, was the report of the Germans and Italians. They expected the big attack to come at the end of January, and, so far as I could judge, they expected the Finns to be broken by it. But I could find few other military attachés or military experts in Helsinki who at this stage believed the Mannerheim Line could be broken. Their view was that the Russians could not, in winter conditions, hope to mass enough men for the sustained offensive necessary to break the Mannerheim Line in the one month of cold weather which they were sure to get. For normally it would snow most of February, and their planes would be of little value; it would start to thaw in March and the country around Viipuri would be a bog, and the tanks of little value. The Finnish High Command shared their view. Material, above all bombers, and not troops was what they wanted. Thirty thousand troops in May would be enough, Mannerheim told the Allied commands. It was to prove a miscalculation as dangerous as the French General Staff's miscalculations on the Meuse.

CHAPTER XXXII

LADOGA AND THE 34TH TANK BRIGADE

I CAME BACK FROM the Line at dusk and in the post bus drove out of Viipuri next morning on the ten-hour ride back to Helsinki. We crossed the low wooden bridge and skirted the great bay where the last decisive battle of the war was to be fought in the early days of March. Thirty-five miles farther back men were working in the snow building yet another line to protect Helsinki if Viipuri fell. Here again granite tank blocks studded the fields, and the frozen ground was blasted to make dug-outs. Then the sun came out, sweeping the mist from the blue sky, and with the sun came the Soviet planes. Outside Kotka we waited half an hour in a wood while nine machines circled over and bombed.

In Kotka itself we passed half an hour in a cellar, and again in Porvoo, where I drank coffee in Runeberg's old house while we waited for the All Clear. In every town police inspected not only my passes, but the papers of everyone on the bus, and nine times on the road we were halted by police patrols. For this was a parachutist area, or at least a parachutist rumour area. Everyone was seeing and denouncing saboteurs and spies dropped by the Russians by parachute, though there had really been comparatively few cases of this type so far to the rear. In the first days of the war a former Finnish Communist, dropped by parachute just behind Viipuri, had been shot by a peasant, and was to linger on in Viipuri hospital until the end of January. Others were dropped in small numbers later. And on one occasion cars coming from the Ladoga front to Viipuri were fired on from an ambush that could only have been parachutists or Fifth Columnists inside the country. But that was all.

Back in Helsinki in the grey afternoon I found there was another story breaking. The fighting north of Ladoga, a confused, dark struggle in the thickest forests of Finland, was coming to a head. The Soviet 18th Division, surrounded now for over a month near Syskyjärvi and besieged in "mottis", was on the point of being finally knocked out. Within the next week practically every motti was to surrender or be stormed, and the bulk of the division, with its material, wiped out.

This fighting north of Ladoga was the most difficult to follow of the whole war. Yet it was very important, for the north Ladoga region was the only place where the Soviet, if they did not storm the Mannerheim Line, could carry out a large-scale invasion towards southern Finland. One American military observer told me that in his opinion it was the point where the U.S. Army would, in such a war, have launched its main attack. If the Russians could work round the northern shore of Ladoga they could cut the great north-south rail system that led from Viipuri to Kajaani, and thereafter outflank the Mannerheim Line and swoop down on Viipuri from the rear. This the Soviet never managed to achieve, but they did draw there thousands of Finnish troops who might otherwise have given decisive aid on the Isthmus.

Apart from the Isthmus in the month of February, Ladoga saw the most terrible blood-letting of the whole war. It became in truth a type of forest Passchendaele, into which division after division of Soviet troops were poured with huge casualties. Once again here, as in the north around Kajaani and Suomussalmi, the Russian plan of attack was of a direct advance on every available road. Once again the Finnish plan of defence was to allow them to advance some distance, then cut their supply routes and attack and harry them from the forests till they starved or froze or broke.

The battle of Tolvajärvi had been the centre of these actions. But it was in no way isolated. The Soviet column which had been thrown back while trying to cross the narrow tongue of land over Tolva Lake was just one of five columns which, the day war was declared, had been sent into the north Ladoga area.

To the very north one full division with tanks and artillery moved in from Liusvaara towards Ilomantsi, striking towards the railway centre of Joensuu. It did little of importance. Held up by a strongly prepared defence belt twenty miles before Ilomantsi, it dug itself in and remained there fighting a war of position, a deadlock war, till peace came.

South of it were the divisions which had moved in on the Tolvajärvi road. Hurled back to Äglajärvi, they, too, were held for the rest of the war along the river back at Suojärvi, where they never managed to break through the Finnish machine-gun screen.

But farther south the action was spectacular. Three columns, each formed of a full division, were launched along the three main roads leading round the bend of the lake towards Sortavala, the "paper city" of Finland. One came down the roadway and railway from the north-east; one—the 18th Division—came straight in by a small road from Tulemarjärvi; the third—the 168th—came round the lake shore.

The 18th came on, pushing back the Finnish troops, till it got to the cross-roads on the Syskyjärvi–Korronopa road, nineteen miles inside Finnish territory. Here it turned north, apparently intending to help the division advancing down the railway towards Loimola by driving at the rear of the Finns. But it met with disaster. Early in January, in the intense cold, its supply routes were cut, and the division itself completely surrounded. It settled down into mottis and prepared for a siege.

At the same time, the 168th, on the coast road to the south, were also in difficulties. Their drive towards Sortavala was halted suddenly just after they had passed Pitkäranta. Their communications were being steadily struck at by Finnish artillery on the Mantsinsaari Island. And they, too, in time were surrounded and endangered.

The Russian High Command, faced with the prospect of two more Suomussalmis, decided that this time they would not, as they had in the north, leave the divisions to fight their own way out. This time reinforcements would be sent. To the relief of the 18th Division they gathered a whole tank brigade, the 34th, under Colonel Kongratjev. To the relief of the 168th they moved up a further division.

Kongratjev was an impetuous leader. He had recently been decorated by Stalin with the Order of Hero of the Soviet Union, and he had confidence in his tanks, and some contempt for the Finns. Officers who had escaped from the 18th Division's imprisoned forces warned him that on these narrow roads it was a grave risk to take in more mechanised stuff. But he brushed such warnings aside, and early in January ordered the advance. The Finns waited till the whole brigade was across the Uuksun River, then flung their patrols into action across his supply routes. Every petrol lorry, every food truck coming up was attacked by grenades and machine-gun fire. Within ten days Kongratjev found he had nothing else to do but repeat the tactics of the 18th. He formed his tanks into stockades, sunk some of them half into the snow to make pill-boxes, and settled down for a siege. It was on January 6 that the Finnish patrols cut the Soviet communications. The last line of lorries reached the brigade on January 5. From then on for fifty-four days, till the night of February 29, they had no food supplies by land. Their rations were one biscuit and a plate of tinned soup a day. They had their last cooked meal on February 22. Soviet planes dropped food in bags to them. Some of this fell into the Finnish lines. Packets of Vitamin C were amongst the supplies.

The position of the 34th was finally stormed, at the end of February. Among the Russian dead were found thirty girls. They were either medical students or trained doctors or Red Cross workers. All were in uniform, three wearing the uniforms of officers. They all carried revolvers. The Finns said that many of them "fought like lions" till the end. When the cleaning-up operations were in progress, one girl and a Russian soldier and an officer held out in a machine-gun post till the end, when all three were killed.

Snow barricades had been built at the end of the road, as protection for the Soviet sharp-shooters. Petrol had been dropped to them by parachute from planes, in thirty-five gallon tins. But the men had obviously suffered terribly, not only from starvation but from cold. One of the corpses lying on the road was of a man who had lost his left boot; his frozen toes stuck out of the wrapping of flannel that he had worn instead.

At the same time, these victories had not been without heavy losses for the Finns. They were the result of terribly hard fighting carried out by small bodies of troops who became more and more exhausted as the winter wore on. For, once the Russian supply routes were cut, it was the Finns who were on the offensive. They had to make the attacks against the strong Russian positions, and they had to keep attacking the roads to make sure they remained closed. Ladoga not only took great toll of the Russians. Till the end of the war it was a sore which drained away much of the best of Finland's manhood, and exhaustion here, no less than on the Mannerheim Line, was to force the Finns to make peace.

CHAPTER XXXIII

INTERVENTION?

On FEBRUARY 1 I stepped into the Swedish Junkers air-liner, with the blue-and-gold Swedish flag on the wings, on the lake airfield at Vaasa, and started off over the frozen Gulf of Bothnia for England. Four days later I was on the deck of a channel steamer watching a destroyer potting mines off Dover, while a great convoy of fifty-six vessels wound slowly past the cliffs towards London.

When I returned to England people were talking of Finland on every side. How long could they hold out? How true were these reports of repeated Finnish successes? Was the Red Army as bad as it seemed? Were all these pictures of frozen tanks and captured lorries fakes, or just the same place photographed over and over again? I tried to answer those questions a dozen times a day. Then I found another question took their place, a question on which I realised that I would have to make up my mind. Should we go to Finland's aid?

My first taste of England's information about Finland had been a shock. I started talking with a man in the Folkestone train. He was interested to hear I had been in Finland, and mildly suspicious when I told him that things like Suomussalmi were true. "After all, you must admit," he said, "it is really as much a civil war as anything. You can't tell me the Finns are all on the side of fellows like Mannerheim. How many of them have deserted to fight with the Russians?"

In London I bought a copy of *Picture Post*. An indignant correspondent had written to ask why only photographs of Mannerheim's White Guards were shown; why were there none of Finland's People's Army, that was fighting side by side with the Red Army for freedom? I bought other papers. In many papers, particularly the intellectual weeklies, there were letters saying that the whole Finnish war was falsely reported, that Mannerheim was a butcher whom the Finnish people detested. I bought D. N. Pritt's Penguin, *Must the War Spread?* and took it down to the country to read. Parts of it left me gasping. I have just looked again at the passages I marked then. In his discussion about the responsibility for the war there is no mention of the fact that the Russians never presented any ultimatum, never gave the Finns any last-minute chance to give in without a fight: there was an assumption, without one bit of proof being produced to support it, that we had definitely urged the Finns not to give way; there was the statement, made as proof of Finland's sympathy with Kuusinen, that the Finnish army in retreat burnt all the villages and took the inhabitants along with them "as if they feared the results of the slightest contact between the population with either the Soviet army or the army of the new Finnish Republic". Now that last sentence, at that time, early February 1940, was sheer nonsense. The villages were burnt as a purely military measure, to leave the Russians no shelter. And no one who had seen what the Finnish troops, most of them peasants from these villages, had done to the Russians at Kemi

River and Suomussalmi could say that the Finnish High Command had any fears of the "slightest contact between the population with either the Soviet army or the army of the new Finnish Republic". The fears were far more on the side of Colonel Vinagradov, and Kongratjev—the other commanders now locked up and fighting for their lives in stockades surrounded by these apparently discontented Finnish peasants. And the army of the new Finnish Republic? Did anyone ever hear of it, see a single photograph of one soldier from it? Was that the army of the new Finnish Republic, those regiments of Ukrainians, Uzbecs, Turks, Mongolians, Georgians I had seen crowded into the prison camp at Suomussalmi?

This belief, which was being carefully and intensively spread, that Kuusinen had real backing inside Finland, was confined to sections of the Left. But far more widespread was a belief that the greater part of the Press reports from Finland were phoney, that the Finnish successes were greatly exaggerated, and that there was something wrong somewhere. Both Left and Right believed this, the Right because the failure of the Red Army seemed too good to be true, the Left because it seemed a logical impossibility that a nation of 3,500,000 should hold up a nation of 180,000,000. And when I looked through the Press files for December and January I am not surprised that this belief had grown.

Piled on the top of the reports of those of us who had been on the front, where we had an opportunity of checking in detail what was happening, were countless rumours and fake stories from Stockholm, Copenhagen and Oslo, untrue or greatly out of proportion. I will not go into this now, for it belongs to another wider question, that of the whole reporting of the Finnish campaign. But it was one of the main features that confused and worried British opinion at the time when the question in every newspaper editorial was, "Should we help Finland?"

Amid the mist and mud of the Chilterns that February I tried to work out my answer to this problem. I felt deeply that those Finnish troops slogging day after day into the battles of the frozen forests should be allowed to win the independence for which they felt they were sincerely fighting. I wanted to help those people in Rovaniemi so that they would no longer have to cower in their woods day after day from the bombers. I wanted to see that the bravery of people like those shop assistants in Helsinki during those first grim days should get as its reward the freedom they deserved. But how was this to be done? Would they be any better off if they were brought by our help into a greater war? Was there no way of getting this freedom to Finland without spreading the world war? For what the Finns wanted was not just victory. It was rather freedom and an honourable peace. Above all a right to settle their own internal affairs. The Finns claimed that if we could give them aid enough in material to hold the Mannerheim Line till spring, the Russians might offer a fair peace rather than fight on right through the summer.

But what were we to do if this intervention brought us into war with Russia? Were we to risk that? Were we to carry aid to Finland as far as war? Here I could only reply "No". However wrong the Soviet invasion of Finland might be, however much the Finns were entitled to their full independence, no good could come out of merging this wrong in the greater evil of a full-dress war between Britain and Russia. For that would only have handed all Europe over to Hitler. After what Hitler did to France in the spring of 1940 the mind recoils from what he might have done had we been already fighting Russia at that time. The Finns were entitled to their independence, but were we to try to save it in a war which would cost millions of British lives, and which would divert our power from the war against Hitler?

When I came to follow this "non-intervention" trail to its logical conclusion I found, too, that it led in ugly directions. For though many of the people anxious to help Finland were those who had struggled with the same sincerity to help Republican Spain, many others were the old pro-Fascist crowd who had done so much to prepare our present horrors for us by their support for Hitler in his early days, and for his friends Mussolini and Franco. They had no real interest in Finnish independence —at least not in the independence of the men I had seen slogging up at Suomussalmi and on the Isthmus. What they wanted was to strike at Russia, and this was their golden chance, because for the first time since 1918 public opinion was now roused against the Soviet. This desire to "switch the war" stuck out particularly in France. Stephan Lausanne, of the *Matin* (now the most pro-German paper in Paris, just as it had been pro-Hitler right up to the outbreak of war), gave this away plainly in the talk the B.B.C. allowed him to make when he visited England with a party of French editors at this time. He almost sobbed for the chance to fight the Bolsheviks—"the root of all evil"—as well as the Germans. In Paris I saw a French official propaganda film which by incredible shuffling purported to prove that Lenin was the spiritual father of Hitler, who had inherited the "Bolshevist mission to destroy the world". The Lavals and the Flandins, who had always been for Hitler and at heart anti-Soviet, were all in favour of intervention against the Soviet. When I read later Daladier's list of war material sent to Finland, including over 140 planes from the scanty French air force, I felt there is much truth in the accusation that if the chief powers in France had shown half as much eagerness to fight Hitler as they did to fight Stalin, we and the French would still be holding our original lines on the Continent to-day. The half million rifles the French sent could have armed the Paris population at least.

No, I did not like this "non-intervention" trail when I started to follow it out.

Was there then no alternative either to war with Russia or the destruction of Finland? There seemed to be none except the slippery-pole policy of gradual help that must not go as far as war, a policy which looked increasingly impracticable. Against this policy was ranged not only powerful forces on the Left, but at least one considerable voice on the Right. Lord Beaverbrook had thrown the whole weight of his papers against intervention in Finland. He presented the issue simply. We had already one war on our hands; we could not afford to risk getting into another. How wise this was did not appear at the time, but it showed itself only too clearly when the collapse of the expedition to Norway and the break-through in France demonstrated how much farther we had to arm to get on equal terms with Germany. Lord Beaverbrook has been considerably criticised for his "There will be no war" campaign after Munich. I think myself that his campaign was wrong there. But on this issue of Finland he showed himself unquestionably right and to him much is owing for the avoidance of what would probably have been a doubly-disastrous Norway adventure.

By mid-February his view was already being justified. For by then the whole military basis for "non-intervention" was crumbling. The cornerstone of it had been the theory that the Mannerheim Line could be held, and that even slight aid would be decisive. But the impregnability of the Mannerheim Line, in which so many military experts had now come to believe, existed no more. From February 15 onwards, when the Summa front cracked, there could be no longer any question of partial aid to the Finns. After that they could be helped only by full intervention, or, more bluntly, by open war.

CHAPTER XXXIV

THE SUMMA OFFENSIVE

THE GREAT SOVIET offensive against the Mannerheim Line which was to last forty-six days without a break, and which was to settle the war, began at midday on the morning of February 1. The massed Soviet batteries, standing virtually wheel to wheel right across the Isthmus, opened up on the Finnish positions along the Vuoksi River and near Muolaanjärvi. By February 3 the fire was intense all along the line, but was particularly concentrated at Taipale and in the Summa sector. At the same time 130 Soviet planes began a violent bombardment of the Finnish lines from the air. They rained down high explosives along the trenches and dug-outs, and around the concrete forts that covered the open ground in the Summa sector. They began to smash to bits Viipuri, Sortavala and every railway junction behind the lines. They attacked the Finnish rail-heads, supply depots, hospitals. They machine-gunned the roads, so that hardly a lorry could move in the daytime. They bombed the woods at night, so that the men could not sleep. They attacked the main junctions farther back, Riihimäki, Lahti, Kouvola. Steadily they began to close with a steel grip the veins that fed the troops from the Isthmus lines.

This heavy bombardment continued for ten days. The Finnish troops waited in their dug-outs while their few batteries replied and while the fortress guns of Koivisto smashed back at the Russians. "There goes the tram," the Finns would say in their trenches as one of the great naval shells from Koivisto screamed overhead. They were hopelessly outgunned. The Soviet artillery, particularly the 105s, could outrange anything the Finns had. They were safe from air bombardments because the Finns had so few planes, and the guns could fire from open positions on the hilltops, almost in full sight of their targets. Always, too, the Soviet reconnaissance planes could hover unharmed above the Finnish positions, checking every shell-burst.

The Soviet bombardments followed a definite rhythm. There would be two to three hours' continuous shelling, usually starting at dawn. At the height of the bombardment the Finns estimated that 300,000 shells a day were being put over by the Soviet guns. After the guns ceased the bombers would come over and attack for anything up to an hour; then there would be another short burst of shelling before an infantry and tank attack was launched. These attacks, for the first five days of the offensive were, however, only slight feeler movements aimed at finding out which points in the line were weakest. The first big attack came towards Taipale on February 8, and continued unabatedly till February 13, but it was held up on the ice of the wide Vuoksi River near Lake Ladoga. It was apparently intended as the right arm of a pincer movement, the left arm of which was to bite into the low ground around the Summa sector.

Against Summa the heaviest artillery fire had been directed. The concrete forts were pounded continually, but they stood up to it well. Then the Russians tried a new method. They began to shell the ground immediately to the front and to the side of the pillboxes. After tens of thousands of shells had been fired, the ground was so smashed up that the forts began to tilt. They were literally being prised out of the ground.

On February 10 the main attack on Summa was launched. An hour after dawn the barrage lifted, and the bombers came over, smashing the lines for half an hour. Then the tanks pushed forward towards one section where aerial photographs had shown the Soviet High Command that the Finnish forts had been thrown over almost on their sides. The men in them could not work the 75s, and the heavy machine-guns were difficult to keep in position. At the head of the Soviet thrust came 35-ton tanks—

heavier than any used till then. They were followed by medium tanks dragging a new weapon—armoured sledges protected by steel plates four to five feet high on the sides. They held ten to fifteen men. They were dragged to the edge of the Finnish trenches. There the men jumped out and the sledges were slung round to get a fresh load across No Man's Land.

Farther back came the regular infantry. These were men from three first-class divisions, the 100th, 103rd and 49th. They soon showed that they had a thorough knowledge of infiltration tactics. They were fully equipped with snow capes, and their patrols not only had skis, but knew how to use them. The Finns, already exhausted by the shelling, found that this time they had a far tougher enemy to deal with. In many places the Finns fought with bayonets, hand grenades and with their knives when their machine-guns were no longer of any use. But they had nothing to check the larger tanks. They had few anti-tank guns; their artillery was scanty; and grenades and land mines were of little value.

On February 13 the break came. Officers holding this sector had been told that they must remain till they had lost three-quarters of their effectives. Close to Summa a reserve battalion, brought up to the line only the day before to replace troops worn down by the fortnight of shelling, gave way and retreated. But through the gap they left the Russians poured in every man and tank they could summon. By evening they had definitely forced a gap in the line. Radio Moscow announced that night that they had captured sixteen Finnish concrete fortifications. This meant a break of some half a mile in the line. Into this gap the Finnish High Command hurled their crack regiment, the Tavast light horse, now dismounted and serving as an infantry unit. They fought throughout the days of February 14 and 15 till they were almost completely wiped out. Other counter-attacks failed, and the Russian advance swept on, regardless of their casualties. Every night the front-line Russian troops were relieved by others, who carried on the terrific pressure. These were the tactics laid down by Voroshiloff, the crescendo offensive, the ever-increasing pressure. By February 15 it was clear that the line was breached, and that the Finns must retire.

On February 13 the Finnish communiqué announced, "In the area east of Summa the enemy have succeeded in capturing a few of our most advanced positions". It was the first of the bulletins of gradual defeat which were to come steadily, day after day, till the end of the war.

The Russians did not slacken for a moment. At Taipale they kept up their attacks, but with little result. But into the Summa break they poured fresh troops, and more tanks. The crack in the line became a definite gap.

The break through had not been caused by the destruction of the Finnish forts. It came because the Finns were exhausted. They were shell drunk, automata moving into position. Had they had reserves, the positions might still have been held. But they had none available, so all they could do was drop back, towards a rear which was almost as dangerous as the front.

For against the area behind the lines the Soviet air force was working with deadly effect. On February 5, raids were launched all day against Viipuri. Over 400 bombs were dropped by forty-seven planes. On February 20 came another terrible raid. Twenty separate formations smashed at the city for two hours and twenty minutes. Building after building was reduced to ruins. The railway station was hit, but was able to continue working. The Knut Posse Hotel where we had stayed was levelled to the ground. Almost every modern building in the city was smashed. Only one church remained undamaged, and fire ravaged the entire city. The 5,000 people who had remained out of the 83,000 inhabitants of peace-time, were hastily evacuated, and the city left absolutely empty except for troops. On Friday and Saturday, February 4 and 5, Sortavala's turn came. It was bombed for twelve hours by ninety-two different machines. At the end only fifteen people were dead and forty-four injured, but the town was one great sheet of flame, with fire brigades doing what they could in the intense cold to check the blaze.

On the ground the offensive rolled on. After the failure of the attacks on Taipale, the Russians gave up for the moment this wide flank attack. They decided to turn the Summa offensive into a narrower pincer movement by attacking just ten miles to the right, in the Aayrapaaea corridor, a narrow strip of land between two lakes on the extreme west of the Isthmus. On the last week of February they attacked here violently, while they pushed on up the coast past Summa. By February 23 the Russians could claim to have conquered and occupied twenty-seven forts. By February 25 they were on the land peninsula opposite the great fortress of Koivisto. The Koivisto guns were still hammering at their communications, but by February 26 the Russians claimed that they had captured it, and on February 27 the Finns confirmed this. The keystone of the Finnish defensive system on the right flank of the Mannerheim Line was broken.

Most of the defenders of the fortress had been killed and its 11-inch batteries had been hammered night and day for at least a week by Soviet guns. There were in all ninety men on Koivisto island in addition to the regular garrison. Their food and supplies were raced across the ice by lorry from Sakkijärvi every night at high speed. There was always danger of the ice cracking. This lorry was, incidentally, driven by an Italian from Trieste, who had been living in Finland for seven years. From time to time the Russians were dropping parachutists on the ice to try and capture these supply lorries, but they never succeeded. The only two who ever attacked were shot dead by the Italian, who saw their dark shapes clearly against the white ice.

The guns and equipment of the forts were carried out by the troops on the night of February 26-27 on specially-constructed heavy sledges. They had an exciting night. The ice cracked under the weight of the 11-inch guns and the men found themselves on an ice-floe adrift in the Gulf of Finland. They waited until the early morning, when the ice re-formed in the chill of dawn. During the whole of this time they had been only two kilometres away from the Russian listening posts on the mainland at Viberlati.

All this time Viipuri was under Russian artillery fire. Since February 22 the Russian guns had been shelling the outskirts of the city while their masses of tanks and infantry poured up. The total of men used by the Russians was, the Finns estimated, between 120,000 and 150,000.

The right wing of the Mannerheim Line was gone, but the Finnish position was still not desperate. They had still the magnificent natural defence of the Gulf of Viipuri. This Gulf with its wide expanse of ice should thaw in March.

Behind Viipuri City, to the north, Finnish engineers were

already busily constructing a reserve line. This would have linked up with the line of the Vuoksi down to Taipale. Instead of running south-west from the junction of Heinjoki, the line would have followed up the valley of the Vuoksi in the direction of Imatra, curving down to meet the Gulf of Viipuri through Juustila. It would have been in many ways an easier line to defend, because the open ground was much less than in the Summa sector. In all there would not have been more than fifteen miles of open country to be held. General Badoux, the Belgian officer who had helped construct the Mannerheim Line, had arrived out by plane from Brussels to advise on the building of this new position. In this reserve line the small forts were being built, like those at Summa, but strengthened with concrete "aprons" four feet wide, and ten feet below ground, to prevent them being levered out again. With truth, the Finnish High Command stated that their position was strong and that they still had a chance of holding out—if their men could get a spell.

But before they retired to this line the Finnish General Staff had to make one of the main decisions of the war. Strong as this new line might be, had not the experience around Summa shown that in the end their troops would become exhausted again, and have to give way? Might it not be better to fight a purely delaying action on the new position and then abandon the line altogether, retreat behind the central lake system and get the Russians out in the open?

Swedish officers with whom I spoke in Stockholm, early in March, were of the opinion that the best thing the Finns could do would be to draw back and let the Russians advance into Central and Southern Finland, as they had allowed them to advance in the north. Then, on the roads, they could ambush them and try to cut their communications. But this brought many serious complications. It meant that the Finns must decide to give up, if necessary, Helsinki and the thickly populated southern areas of the country. It meant great suffering for a huge mass of civilians and mass immigration behind the central lake system. It meant that the Finns north of Ladoga would be outflanked, and that the whole area in which the army had been fighting, with considerable success, would have to be given up. They would have to drop back to a line behind Joensuu and Nurmes.

Yet, even so, influential Finnish Generals were in favour of it. General H. V. Oestermann, peace-time Commander-in-Chief from whom Field-Marshal Mannerheim took over on the outbreak of the war, and who had been in command of the Mannerheim Line during this fighting, was one who wanted to drop back. But Mannerheim threw his weight against the idea. The Line was his Line. He was convinced that the war would be won or lost there. He was determined to stay there and fight. So General Oestermann gave up his command of the Isthmus front and General Hendriks took over. At the same time General Oesch, who had been Chief of the General Staff, gave up his post there, and took over a command in the field. He was said to be worn out by the strain of staff work. It is certain that he was exhausted. But it is significant that his place was taken by Colonel Airo, later promoted a General. He was a brilliant staff officer, who believed in a war of position and who believed that if the Mannerheim Line was lost, all would be lost. With this change the Finnish decision had been taken. They were to stand or fall on the Line.

These reasons for the reshuffle came to me from German sources in Helsinki. They were later indignantly denied at a Press meeting in Helsinki, but the fact of the changes themselves has never been denied. The Germans were convinced that their version was true and the Germans had proved very right about other military matters in Finland. It is only when we see the archives of the Finnish General Staff that we will be able to find out definitely the exact way in which the dispute was worked out.

At this moment another significant change was made. General Wallenius was brought down from the Salla front to the Isthmus. This move had two reasons. A command had to be found for General Linder, the chief of the Swedish Volunteers, who had now taken over on Salla to allow the Finnish troops there to be moved down. Mannerheim, too, perhaps thought that Wallenius, who had snatched victory out of defeat in the north, might be valuable in this tight situation in the south. He was given a command on the Isthmus front on the Bay of Viipuri.

CHAPTER XXXV

BREAK THROUGH

So FEBRUARY DREW to its close and yet the Soviet offensive did not slacken. Every day in Helsinki the Press Department announced more and more attacks. Military experts, grabbing at every possible straw of optimism, pointed out that the Soviet were running into increasing difficulties. As their lines of communication lengthened the supply question became more of a problem. Their ammunition dumps were clearly being used up. Their troops must be growing weary. Their losses in material had been enormous. In one week alone, the first week of the offensive, the Finns claimed to have knocked out over two hundred tanks. Could the Russian troops go on for ever charging over the dead bodies of their comrades into the teeth of Finnish machine-gun fire? Would the thaw come or snowstorms which would check the Soviet air activity? But steadily, day after day, the advance continued. What was more important, there were no signs of the thaw beginning. The freeze-up in the Bay of Viipuri became vital. There the ice was no thicker than usual—about 3½ feet—but it was locked together, instead of being a mass of split, drifting ice-formations. And as March came in it remained like this. Winter had gone over to the Russian side. This freeze-up doubled the length of the Finnish line behind Viipuri and put twice the work on to the tired Finnish army. They had now all this huge expanse of ice to watch.

As the army grew tired, its efficiency fell enormously. Men who when fresh were willing to tackle tanks with hand grenades were now too exhausted to move and the tanks had infinitely more effect. The raw troops flung in to fill the gaps had to face the full force of the offensive before they could learn, as their comrades had learnt in December, that the Soviet tanks could be stopped by determined men with grenades. The defeat was getting under way.

In the last three days of February and in the first three days of March the Russians continued their pressure, chiefly against the centre and left wing of the Mannerheim Line. On their own left flank between Koivisto and Viipuri they were massing troops for the final battle of the war—the battle of Viipuri Gulf. They brought up, over railway lines hastily repaired and over the Isthmus roads, fresh divisions and great supplies of material. They brought up light tanks which were concentrated on the peninsula north of Koivisto and on the Island of Trurinsaari, and the other islands that made a great archipelago along the eastern shore of the Gulf of Viipuri. The Finnish troops fortified positions in the islands on their shore, the western shore, and hastily constructed a line on the shore itself between Viipuri and the coastal town of Virolahti. It was in this sector that Wallenius had his command. By Monday, March 4, this new offensive was under way. Russian troops with tanks at their head were attacking the islands on the western side of the Gulf. On March 6 their main attack was launched. Soviet columns of troops in sledges headed by tanks pushed out across the bay and hit at the shore at a dozen different points. At the same time, right out on the ice of the Gulf of Finland, the Soviet carried out an audacious strategical manœuvre which showed that their General Staff was now willing to take real risks. From Koivisto a column moved thirty-four miles across the ice and attacked the coast at Virolahti forty-five miles on the Helsinki side of Viipuri. At the same time, another column moved fifteen miles from the island of Hogland in the middle of the Gulf, more than half-way between Leningrad and Helsinki, and attacked the Finnish position on the Haapasaari Island. Both these attacks were thrown back by the Finns and the Russians suffered heavy losses, particularly round Virolahti. But they had their effect. Finnish troops had to be rushed back from the immediate line round Viipuri to watch the entire length of the coast, for it was impossible to foresee where one of these Russian flying columns might hit next.

At the same time the Russian offensive against the island inside the Gulf of Viipuri was beginning to tell. For the next three days and nights fighting went on there, but by March 7 the Russians had secured positions on the island in the Gulf. Russian artillery worked from positions on the ice in the bay, shelling the Finnish troops. Russian aircraft pounded unceasingly at the Finnish lines and at their communications behind. The Finnish Air Force, now considerably strengthened by bombers from Great Britain, made bombing flights against the close-packed enemy units on the Bay of Viipuri. They machine-gunned advancing Soviet troops, hit at their tanks and blew up the ice to hold up the advance. But it was no good. By Friday the 8th the Russians had a foothold on the island on the western side of the bay, in the very sector commanded by Wallenius. A few days later Wallenius was back in Helsinki, deprived of his command. It was later announced that he had been dismissed from his rank as General and from the army. No official explanation has even been given exactly of what happened. All we knew was that he appeared to be definitely in disgrace when he returned to Helsinki. He avoided the dining-room in the Hotel Kamp and spent most of his time sitting in the rooms of journalists.

On March 9 the Finnish High Command announced that the enemy had secured "a restricted foothold on the north-west shore of the bay" and had "captured some islands". It was the most vital sentence in any communiqué of the war. Not merely the first, but also the second Mannerheim Line had been turned. It was no easily-won success. In these last bitter days of fighting the battle was more intense than at any time in the whole war. The Finnish army communiqués of this period tell their own story. Consider, for instance, the one dated March 8. It runs:

"Army. On the Isthmus enemy pressure against the north-west shore of the Bay of Viipuri continued on March 7. Fighting on the capes at the mouth of the bay continued until the evening with our troops still holding their positions. Attacks against our positions on the island were repulsed. Our artillery destroyed several tanks and at least eight guns of the batteries brought by the enemy on to the ice. Between the bay of Viipuri and Vuoksi the enemy launched several local attacks which were repelled; seven tanks and two armoured cars were destroyed in these attacks. In the direction of Paakkola over 400 enemy dead were left lying in front of our lines after the fighting the previous day. South of Vuosalmi enemy attempted to advance across the Vuoksi River but was beaten back. An attempt at attack at Taipale was repelled. North-east of Lake Ladoga enemy attacked at Kollaanjoki but was beaten off. About 2,000 enemy dead remained on the field. On other sections of the land front artillery activity and local attacks which were repelled.

"Naval and Coastal defence. In the course of March 7 a couple of enemy detachments again tried to cross over the ice in the direction of the Haapasaari Islands and Virlahte archipelago but were driven off.

"Air Force. On March 7 our aircraft continued their reconnaissance and bombing flights. Close-packed enemy units, transport vehicles, tank and troop columns and artillery batteries crowded on the island and ice of the Bay of Viipuri were bombed and machine-gunned. Enemy aerial activity was concentrated chiefly on the Kotka Säkkijärvi and Bay of Viipuri areas. Elsewhere in the country only slight enemy activity was observed. According to confirmed reports six enemy planes were shot down, in addition to which there are two unconfirmed cases. An enemy plane was yesterday found shot down, the destruction of which had not been previously reported."

Out on the ice of the still frozen Gulf of Finland the Soviet continued, for the remainder of the war, to make their daring long-distance raids against the Finnish coast. From Haapasaari Island they launched attacks against Kotka, half-way between Viipuri and Helsinki. Apparently they even landed planes on the ice outside Helsinki, for we heard the coastal batteries at Helsinki, go into action several times. Civil Guards were hastily mobilised in Helsinki and in other towns along the coast and drafted up to begin a long line of coastal watching. This further weakened the already minute Finnish reserves. Thousands of men who might have been in the trenches at Viipuri were standing on lonely capes along the shore watching for Soviet columns. Strategically it was a brilliant success for the Soviet. The last act was almost over. The end was nearer than the world imagined.

CHAPTER XXXVI

PEACE TREATY

SOON AFTER MIDDAY on Thursday, March 7, as the exhausted Finnish troops on the shores of the Gulf of Viipuri were facing yet another Russian attack, a Swedish passenger plane touched down on the airfield at Moscow. Four men stepped out, and were greeted by the Chief of the Protocol Department of the Russian Foreign Office. The four men were Risto Ryti, the Finnish Premier; M. J. K. Paasikivi, who had been Finnish delegate in the previous talks in Moscow; Professor Voimaa, President of the Finnish Diet Committee on Foreign Affairs, and a historical expert on Karelia; and General Rudolf Walden, a magnate of the Finnish pulp industry, and a close friend of Mannerheim. They had come to talk peace.

In London in mid-February I had been told by a British Communist that the Russians would offer peace the moment they had got to Viipuri. Stalin realised the danger of the growing interventionist movement inside Britain and France. Once at Viipuri the Russians would have broken the Mannerheim Line, and they could have restored the prestige of the Red Army.

This move was not as surprising as it later seemed. Throughout the time of the great offensive indirect peace negotiations had been in progress. On January 29, before they launched their attack, the Russians sent a note to Sweden saying that they were not in principle opposed to a settlement with M. Ryti's Government in Finland. This was a step of the greatest importance, for it meant virtually that Stalin was willing to let Kuusinen drop. Till then the whole Soviet attitude had been that they recognised only the Kuusinen Government, not the "clique of White Guards and bankers" sitting in Helsinki. From that day onward peace became an immediate possibility. The war changed from being one for the introduction of Communism into Finland into one about borders and fortresses—much easier things in which to get agreement. Ever since the start the Finns had maintained that they were willing to make peace, on the assumption, implied in their offers, that the Russians let Kuusinen drop and recognised the Helsinki Government once again as the legal Finnish Government. Ryti said in his speech to the Finnish Chamber on March 15: "The present Government which came into power on December 1 last, a day after hostilities had broken out, has regarded as its chief task the restoration of peace." The outside world, fascinated by the spectacle of Finnish resistance, had indeed tended to forget this fundamental fact that Finland had never deliberately chosen to fight rather than give way on the question of Hango or frontier revision. It had been allowed no choice. It had simply been attacked and it was willing to make peace the moment it could be sure of the one thing on which it would not give way—that Finland should not go Communist.

Ryti explained how on the outbreak of hostilities the U.S.A. had tried to secure a settlement, but the Russians had refused and had, on December 4, recognised Kuusinen. On December 15 Tanner, in a broadcast, had openly approached Molotov and offered to resume negotiations. But the Russians were still unconvinced that they could not win a quick military victory, and they made no reply. On January 29, however, their view had changed. Before they launched the summer offensive, an offensive which they knew was going to claim the lives of many of the best men in the Soviet army, they had sent via Sweden their offer to negotiate.

The Swedes handed the offer on. In it the Russians had stated that they must get at least all they had demanded in their previous negotiations, plus several other "guarantees". The Finns replied that they would negotiate on the basis of what they were willing to accept before war began and to cede further territory on the Isthmus and "neutralise" the Gulf of Finland. They asked, too, for compensation for territory ceded. The Russians refused, and the offensive was launched.

As events showed, the Finns would have been wiser to accept the Russian offer. But their cautious reply was understandable. Their military position was considered sound. Few of their military experts believed the Russians could break the Mannerheim Line before the thaw came. If they hung on they might lose more men, but they would get much better terms. New material, too, was flowing in.

In mid-February, once the Russians had broken through at Summa, they made another peace offer. In London the Soviet Ambassador, M. Maisky, asked the British Government to act as intermediary and put forward the Soviet demands. These were much more extreme. They included all the Isthmus up to Viipuri, the area north of Ladoga including Sortavala, Hango, the islands in the Gulf of Finland. It was a shrewd Soviet move. It tended to spike the growing demand from inside Britain for intervention in the Finnish war, for Britain, if she once urged Finland to accept these terms, could hardly at the same time prepare a force to fight the Russians if they were not accepted. But Mr. Chamberlain refused, and preparations for the Anglo-French expeditionary force were hurried on.

In the meantime, during the critical first fortnight of February, indirect peace negotiations had in effect been going on through Madame Kollontai, the Soviet Minister in Sweden; the Swedish Foreign Minister; and M. Tanner. Christian Gunther, the Swedish Foreign Minister, told the Swedish Riksdag that he had been in constant touch with Madame Kollontai ever since late December. On February 5 M. Tanner had come to Stockholm and asked if the Swedes would object if Finland ceded Hango. The Swedes refused to have any opinion. For two weeks after that, the two weeks of the Summa offensive, in the words of M. Gunther, "both parties were active with the object of attaining a basis for negotiation, the question of Hango still remaining in the forefront".

On February 20 the Russians, faced with Mr. Chamberlain's refusal to act as mediator, turned again to the Swedes, and handed over to M. Assarson, the Swedish Minister in Moscow, the new Russian terms, including Hango, Karelia, and north Ladoga. The Finns, trying frantically to secure Allied aid now, and to get Allied troops a free passage through Sweden, refused to accept any discussions on these terms. The Swedes tried to get the Russians to ask for less, but were told that these were the minimum demands essential for the defence of Leningrad. But already the Viipuri front was cracking. On March 4 the Russians were across the ice, the Finnish ammunition was low, and the army exhausted. On March 5 M. Erkko, Finnish Minister in Stockholm, asked the Swedes to let Moscow know that Finland would talk on the basis of the Russian terms, and asked for an armistice.

The Russians refused the armistice, so on the night of March 6 the Finns, informed by Mannerheim that the situation was desperate, sent off their delegation to Stockholm, where they took plane for Moscow. On March 12 peace had been signed. Fighting was to stop at 11 a.m. the next day. The war was over.

CHAPTER XXXVII

FOREIGN AID

It was over only by a hair's breadth. At the moment when the Finnish delegates bent over the conference table in the Kremlin British and French forces were waiting on transports in north Scottish ports, ready to sail for Norway en route for Finland. At midday that very day the British had presented a last demand to both Sweden and Norway to allow the passage of their troops. The world trembled on the brink of a move which might have led to war between the Soviet and Britain, the engulfing not only of Norway but Finland and Sweden in the world war, an early precipitation of the German offensive against the Maginot Line and Belgium. It trembled, but halted. Russia had won her war against Finland in the utmost nick of time. She had snatched her stronger frontiers just before she was involved in widespread world war.

Ever since the start of the Finnish war there had been a growing demand for intervention by Britain and France in Finland. Public opinion, angered by the bombing of Helsinki, roused by the successes of the tiny Finnish army, weary with the inaction on the Western front, listened readily to those people who wanted to help the Finns. These were divided chiefly into two groups—those definitely anti-Soviet who saw, in this, a golden opportunity to get the mass of British people to march against the Soviet; and those who were convinced that neither the Maginot nor the Siegfried Line could be broken, and that the only way to defeat Germany was to attack her through Russia, via Finland and Baku.

As early as December 7 Mr. Chamberlain had announced that thirty fighter planes were being sold to Finland. On December

11 the League was called together and showed, considering its reluctance to help any aggressed Power when China or Spain were attacked, a strange haste in urging that all aid possible should be given to the Finns. On December 27 and 28 the British and French Governments, taking this as their text, informed the Swedes that they proposed to give "indirect assistance" to Finland. This was to take the form of the despatch of a technical mission and material. The Swedes agreed to help the transit of material provided the fiction was maintained that all material sent should be material purchased by the Finns, and that any volunteers who went in should go as private individuals, not as bodies of troops.

From then on till mid-February quantities of British and French arms poured into Finland, along with some material from Italy and other countries. High British air force officers visited Helsinki and discussed with the Finns the type of machines needed. Young British pilots flew bombers over from Britain after the Finns had crashed two on the way owing to their inexperience. M. Daladier, defending his policy on Finland on March 12 in the French Chamber, gave an imposing list of material sent. It included: 145 planes, 496 guns, 5,000 machine-guns, 400,000 rifles, 200,000 hand grenades, and 20,000,000 rounds of ammunition. Four hundred thousand rifles—think of what they could have done against the Germans if they had been handed to the people of Paris in June 1940.

All this was non-intervention on the classic lines adopted by Germany and Italy in Spain. It went on throughout January, but in February it came suddenly up against a snag. For the whole policy had been based on the assumption that the Mannerheim Line could hold without mass intervention by foreign troops, or at least with the intervention of Swedish troops only. But now the Line was broken, and the Swedes were refusing to send regular troops, both the Finns and the Allies had to reconsider their policies. Were the Finns to run the risk of being drawn into our war by appealing to us for open aid in the form of troops? Were we to run the risks of a second Gallipoli, and worse still of adding the enormous power of Russia to our enemies, by sending an army to Finland?

Both the Finns and ourselves dodged the decision for some time. At the end of January Mannerheim stated that all Finland required in the way of troops from the Allies was 30,000 men at the beginning of May, when the rivers would unfreeeze and the fronts become more difficult to hold. He may have based this figure on a belief that the Finns could fight alone till then; he may have believed the Swedes would in the eleventh hour always come to his aid. But the Swedes from the start had said "No" and they stuck to this "No" though a great section of Swedish opinion was madly for intervention, even to the point of war.

Throughout the months leading up to the war, and during the war itself, note after note passed from Helsinki to Stockholm appealing in more and more desperate terms for aid. During October it had been merely appeals for diplomatic aid during the negotiations; this was readily given. The Stockholm conference, called on October 18 and 19, gave full diplomatic support of all Scandinavia to Finland. At the same time a Finnish request for Swedish aid to defend the Aaland Islands was turned down and the Finns told plainly that they could not count on help from Swedish troops during any war with Russia. Twice Sweden made démarches in Moscow asking the Russians to go slow. Then when war came they again turned down a Finnish request for help to defend the Aaland Islands.

But they gave considerable indirect aid. Credits were granted to the Finns; funds started; and great quantities of war material, up to one-third of the material of the Swedish army, sent to Finland. The trickle of volunteers began. By January 6 aid had reached a sufficiently large total to bring a protest from the Soviet Union to the Swedes. And on January 13 they agreed to a British request to allow British volunteers to pass through, provided they went unarmed, without uniforms, and without being on active service with the Allied armies. They were to follow a specified route. But that marked the limit of Sweden's concessions. From then on it became clear that the type of aid that Finland needed was so substantial that Sweden could only let it pass at grave danger not only of getting into war with Russia, but of being attacked by the enemy of Britain and France, the German Reich.

On February 1 the Swedes turned down a direct request from the Finns that volunteers should be sent in whole units—in other words, that sections of the Swedish army should be sent to Finland at once. The request was repeated on February 13, and again refused. And on February 19, when it was clear that the Mannerheim Line was broken, and that nothing short of an Allied army could prevent a Finnish defeat, the Swedish King himself stated publicly that Sweden would never allow the open passage of volunteers across her territory to Finland. The next day came the Soviet's peace offer, and her new terms. The Finns, before considering it, asked again for Swedish aid, and asked if the Swedes would let the British and French through. Again the Swedes refused, though they agreed to send more volunteers of their own. The Finns had now only one choice before them. Either they asked openly for British and French aid, or they admitted defeat. Their General Staff had already turned down the other course of dropping back behind the lakes and fighting another of the "Great Wrath" wars that had devastated Finland in the past. The British had already told them that they would get the help, and substantial help, if they cared to ask for it. But to the Finns this would only be feasible if the Allied troops were sure of a smooth passage through Norway and Sweden. If they had to fight their way through there, probably against German as well as Swedish and Norwegian troops, they would arrive far too late to be of any value, even if they got there at all.

By this time there were some five hundred British volunteers in Finland. They were sent after the Allied Supreme War Council decided on February 3 to help the Finns with men as well as arms. They had been selected partly from British army units, sent to Chamonix to be trained in ski-ing, and sent in civilian clothes through Norway and Sweden to Lapua. It was hardly tactful to choose Lapua, the traditional centre of Fascism and reaction in Finland, as their training centre. Russian propaganda, if the war once started, could have made great use of the fact. But both Finns and British seemed to feel that it was past time to worry about details like that.

These five hundred men could serve as the nucleus for any larger British force, and provide a substantial part of its officer cadres. For the first time since the start of the war British uniforms were seen in Helsinki.

On March 2 the British and French told the Swedes that they might be sending substantial forces to Finland, and guaranteed "extensive military assistance to Sweden and Norway" should the arrival of these troops expose these countries to "a strong

German reaction". Once again the Swedes said no, and the King wired direct to M. Daladier appealing to him to hold his hand. At the same time the Swedish Foreign Minister warned M. Erkko, the Finnish Minister in Stockholm, that this was Sweden's attitude and that if the British and French tried to come through Sweden she would have to keep, because of her own added danger, much of the material she would otherwise send to Finland. This is probably the conversation in which the Finns claim that the Swedes said that if the Allies sent troops she would be unable to send any more ammunition to Finland.

Four days later the peace talks opened in Moscow. But inside Finland there still existed a powerful group who regarded the Russian terms as impossible, and who wanted to fight on. They believed that the Swedes had brought pressure to bear on the Finnish Government to make peace, and perhaps brought it to bear at Germany's request. The Swedes angrily denied this.

On Monday, March 12, as negotiations reached their final vital stage in Moscow, both Mr. Chamberlain and M. Daladier came out with their open offers of aid to Finland if she cared to demand it. Questioned in the House on whether this meant that we were going to war with Russia, Mr. Chamberlain replied airily, "We have not arrived at that yet."

When the news of Mr. Chamberlain's offer reached Helsinki, I was having a drink with General Wallenius. I asked him what he thought of it. He replied, "There is only one question—can your troops get here before the German armoured divisions are on the Isthmus or at least before their planes are smashing every railway in Finland? No, of course they can't. It's too late."

Mr. Chamberlain may, of course, have been only trying to strengthen the Finns' hands in the negotiations in Moscow. If apparently assured of our aid, they might be able to buy peace at a lower price from Moscow, who certainly did not want any war with Britain on her hands. Many people thought that in Finland that day. But in Stockholm the British Minister was making yet one more démarche which apparently showed Mr. Chamberlain meant business. Once again he went to the Swedish Foreign Office and this time said that the Finns had asked them to make an urgent appeal for permission for British forces to pass through. The Finns, it seems, were still ready to accept British troops provided it did not mean war with Germany. Or perhaps, too, they were just bluffing in order to strengthen their hand in Moscow. The Swedes, knowing how far the negotiations in Moscow had gone, said they would let the Allies know the next day. At midnight that night the peace was signed. The Finns had never, despite the desperate position their army had been in, asked directly for military aid in the form of troops from Britain and France.

CHAPTER XXXVIII

WHY PEACE CAME

THE FINNS MADE peace because they were beaten in the field. Straight out military defeat was the main factor which caused Baron Mannerheim to tell Premier Ryti to go to Moscow. The Finnish armies, drunk with fatigue, were no longer in a position to defend southern Finland the moment the Russians had turned the second Mannerheim Line by crossing the Bay of Viipuri. They were desperately short of ammunition. I spoke to men who held the last line in front of Viipuri till the end. They had five rounds of ammunition per man, and the spare machine-gun belts were kept jealously in reserve till the Russians actually attacked. The flower of the army had been killed or wounded, the highly-trained men who in the first two months of war had caused such havoc among the advancing Russians. The older men and the boys who were now being put in the Line had nothing of the same fighting power. As a result their losses soared up. The older, shrewder, stronger troops had been able to cope with tanks by the fury with which they attacked them. But these raw reserves could not do this, and were mown down right and left. In the last week of the war men were being killed on the Finnish side at the rate of 1,000 a day, chiefly because of weariness and shortage of ammunition. This meant that within five days the Finns lost more men than in the whole first month of the war.

Weariness was almost their worst enemy. The same men went into battle again and again without sleep, without even rest. By day they were attacked. At night the Russians bombed them. At the rear, as at the front, there was no rest. The men were "shell drunk", "bomb drunk". The roads were machine-gunned by planes that dropped from the clear blue March sky. Their field kitchens were bombed and their supplies of hot food stopped. Their field hospitals and base hospitals were smashed. Men and officers fought on drunkenly, woodenly, against troops who were every day relieved, and who had ever more tanks, ever more shells and planes. The Five Year Plan was bearing its fruit. The materials that Magnitagorsk and Stalingrad and Dniepestroi produced were wearing down even the iron will of the Finnish army.

The Finnish material was worn out, too. They had started the war with a park of 200 guns. This had been considerably increased by purchases from Britain, France, Sweden, and by material captured from the Russians. But it had been worked to death. At the end hardly a gun on the Isthmus was in condition. They all had been fired so continually that they needed reboring. They also lacked any really heavy artillery and large anti-tank guns which could face the heavier Russian weapons.

In the nightmare of that last fortnight on the Mannerheim Line men went mad with the strain of endlessly firing machine-guns into the masses of charging Russians. Men fell exhausted by the roadside, unable to march farther though they knew that certain death awaited them, while others fought forty-eight, sixty hours without sleep.

In all, the Finnish army, according to their latest official figures, lost 27,000 men killed and 40,000 wounded in the war. By far the greatest proportion of these fell during the last month of the fighting. In the first two months, despite all the battles in the north, it is unlikely that more than 10,000 men at the very most were killed. Above all, the losses among the reserve officers were very great. Platoon and company commanders were simply exterminated.

At no time did the Finns have more than 120,000 men on the Isthmus front. Against them they had twenty-seven Soviet divisions, some half-million men in all. The Finns had taken their deadly toll of the Russians, it is true. The Finns estimate the Russian dead as at least 250,000, and claim there must have been some 300,000 wounded. Most military observers in Helsinki were prepared to believe the total of Soviet dead was at least 100,000. Molotov claimed that 75,000 Finns had been killed and only 58,000 Russians. These figures must have been meant primarily for home consumption, for it is out of the question that in a war like this in which the Russians did the bulk of the attacking that they should have sustained fewer casualties than the Finns. No foreign military observer was willing to put the total Finnish dead as higher than 40,000. The 75,000 mentioned by Molotov would mean that one man in five out of all their mobilised Finnish force was killed—a total which, if true, would have brought the war to a standstill much earlier than it did. Nor can one take 58,000 as an accurate figure for the Russian losses. Around Suomussalmi, Kuhmo and Lieksa alone the Russian losses, at the most conservative estimate, were at least 15,000. Add to this the divisions destroyed at Tolvajärvi and north of Ladoga; the losses at Kemi River and before Salla; and the blood-letting on the frozen lakes of the Mannerheim Line through December, and throughout the great offensive of February and early March, and the total leaps up towards, if not past, the figure of 75,000 to 100,000.

But in the end sheer weight of both men and material had counted. The Russians could put one division into the line for three days, throw it into attack, replace it, rest it, and send it in again against the same tired Finnish troops. The Russians employed in the whole war, the Finns estimate, 47 divisions, 1 army corps of light and medium tanks and 2 brigades of heavy tanks. They used from 7,000 to 8,000 batteries of field artillery of 4 guns per battery, and 50 batteries of heavy artillery. They employed over 3,000 planes. The Finns started the war with 90 planes, and finished with approximately 300 planes.

This sheer defeat was the main factor in making the Finns willing to talk peace; but it was not the only factor. For the Spanish Republic was defeated in the field just as soundly at least twice in the Spanish Civil War—once in November 1936 and once in March 1938, when Franco was on the outskirts of Madrid and when he broke through to the sea and cut off Catalonia. But they fought on. Many Finns would have willingly fought on. They would have retired behind the central lake system and fought a long bitter war of attrition. But two other factors prevented this.

The first was undoubtedly fear of being caught up in the other war, the war between Hitler and the Allies. The *Altmark* incident played its part in forming this view. It showed the Finns, and all Scandinavia, that our tempers were rising, that we were prepared to throw aside some of our scruples to get at the Germans. That alarmed Scandinavia, made the Norwegians and the Swedes even more cautious, and the Finns more worried.

We owe the Finns—and certainly the Swedes—a great deal for not inviting us in. For the whole subsequent failure of the Norwegian campaign shows that we would have almost certainly run into disaster if we had tried to push an expeditionary force through into Finland. We would have had to capture Narvik first, and there is very good reason to believe that already German marines were waiting there hidden in iron-ore vessels. We would have had to transport our expeditionary force, and revictual it by the one-track electric railway that ran through Narvik and down to Boden. It would have taken at least three weeks, even given good conditions, to get the first detachments on to the Isthmus. All the way they would have been exposed to air attack by the Germans and Russians. Petsamo was blocked, and was little use anyway. It is appalling to think of the type of catastrophe that we were close to at this moment, when Mr. Chamberlain was replying to a question in the House whether we were at war with Russia, "Not yet".

Fear of being drawn into the other war was, however, only one of the extra factors that made for peace. A second, which the Finns realised vividly, was that if the war continued they would have the whole industrial belt along the upper Vuoksi River smashed, and above all they would have their forests burnt by incendiary bombs in the summer. By late June it would have been dry enough for the Russians to set fire to great tracts of Finnish pine forests, as the Germans had done in the Basque country in Spain, by dropping incendiary bombs. This would have wiped out Finland's greatest source of material wealth, her green gold. It takes forty-five years for a pine tree to grow to full maturity; much of the timber which had reached that stage of development would be ruined. The moment the fighting spread to the back of Viipuri, too, the pulp and manufacturing plants along the Vuoksi would have been in the centre of the fighting zone, and would certainly have been smashed. There is no doubt that a great section of Finnish business interests preferred to cut their losses, let the Russians take some territory, and save the rest. They certainly took losses. One British concern alone was to lose a quarter of a million pounds' worth of forests and plant north of Ladoga.

We must remember, too, that the Finns had won one of the wars they were fighting—the war to keep out Kuusinen. Kuusinen had been dropped right out of sight. Not a peep had been heard from him in Moscow. Stalin had pushed him into the background as quickly as he had produced him. For the time being, at least, private property and the whole social system built on it was safe in Finland. The bankers would still have their banks, the industrialists their plant, the peasants their land. Some of these may have gone to Russia; but in the parts that remained the private property system was still upheld, and no one was dangling from the lamp-posts. Russia may have won her war against Finland, but the Third International had lost hers.

CHAPTER XXXIX

THE LAST DAY

ON THE SECOND day that the Finnish delegation was in Moscow they were called to the Kremlin and given a map of eastern Finland with a quarter-inch line drawn in ink, straight as if with a ruler, from the Gulf of Finland just west of Virolahti to a point half-way between Lake Ladoga and Lieksa. It was the new frontier. It was almost exactly that which Peter the Great had drawn when he made peace with Sweden in the Treaty of Nystad in 1721.

I later saw a photostatic copy of the map. It was an old Russian type, with some of the new towns which had grown up since the war, like Enso, marked only as tiny villages. The line went through them gaily, indifferently, regardless of whether it cut off one half of a town from another, or a village from the land or roads around it.

At the next meeting with the Russian delegates M. Paasikivi raised this question: "That line represents an area at least half a mile wide. Can we not define it more exactly, or we will have endless difficulties?" Molotov shrugged his shoulders. "It is the way we settled Poland with the Germans," he said. "It worked all right there. It can work again here."

The Russian negotiators were M. Molotov, M. Schadanov, the party boss of Leningrad, and General Vasilievsky, commander of the Leningrad High Command. Stalin, who had played a considerable part in the earlier negotiations, made no appearance. His absence may have been a sign that he was far from pleased with the way things had turned out. "The war has been your pigeon. You straighten out the mess it has brought," he seemed to be saying to Schadanov and Molotov.

M. Paasikivi later told us in Helsinki something of the talks. From other delegates I learnt further details. There was little drama about them. The Russians had their minds made up on exactly what they wanted; the Finns had no choice but to give way, or accept Allied aid, and their minds seemed clear. It was simply a question of detail.

Paasikivi, a burly figure with a flushed red face, heavy spectacles, and hair that stood shock upright, looked like a small-town German lawyer as he sat at the head of the Press table when he returned to Helsinki. He seemed cheerful, almost jovial about the whole business. He may have been just hiding his true feelings, but it was a strange note to strike amid this city of men and women weeping in defeat. From the airport the delegation had been taken to the building in the Rue Dostrovsky which the Soviet keeps for visiting diplomats. Here the Allied military delegations stayed during their futile visit to Moscow last summer; here the Turkish Foreign Minister had spent ten days kicking his heels in the autumn; here the Finns had stayed during the earlier negotiations.

They were comfortably housed. The only drawback was a little too constant attention from the G.P.U. The building, built by a rich "bourgeois"—Paasikivi smiled as he pronounced the word —before the war, was very comfortable. The service was "brilliant"; there was both fresh and pressed caviar (we were forbidden by the Finnish censor to mention this detail) and the cooking very good. "Russian cooking has always been recognised as very good, though it is a little rich for my taste," went on the delegate.

On the night they arrived there had been a chilly and formal prise de contact between the delegation and M. Molotov in the Foreign Office in the Kremlin. The next morning the delegation got the detailed Russian terms; in the afternoon discussions began on them. There were few incidents. Schadanov provided most of them. He got furiously angry at times with the British and French warmongers who had incited Finland to war. To emphasise his points he spat occasionally on the floor. He alone of the delegation wore a high Russian shirt. Molotov kept to his collar and tie throughout.

The Finns demanded compensation for the great slice of territory they had lost. They pointed out that Peter the Great had allowed compensation. "Many things have changed since the days of Peter the Great," replied Molotov. "That is hardly logical," objected one of the Finns. "It is the logic of war," came the reply.

Kuusinen's name was mentioned, it seems, in passing, but both sides avoided any open reference to the strange fact that the Russians had suddenly lost sight of this Terijoki Government with whom they had signed a treaty of alliance, and were now making peace with a Government which they declared did not exist. More significantly still, there had been practically no reference by the Russians to the possibility of British and French intervention at the eleventh hour. "They touched on the question of Allied aid, but they did not seem to regard it of any importance," said Paasikivi. From other sources I understand that Schadanov sarcastically referred to Allied attempts to aid the Finns, then pounded the table and said, "Now do you see why we had to fight, and make our frontiers secure?"

There were in all five sittings of the commission. The Russian demands differed from the first proposals by two important facts. The news of a railway across north Finland to Haparanda, via Kemijärvi, had not been in the first treaty, and there had been no question of change of frontier opposite there. The Russians also stressed their desire for better trade agreements with Finland. They had lost the Finnish market, an important market in Tsarist times, principally in the face of British competition. Now they wanted it back. The mass of people in Helsinki knew nothing of what was afoot till the Monday morning. From my window in the Hotel Kamp I watched them running, ever disciplined, ever determined, for the shelters as alarm followed alarm those final days of the war. On the Saturday morning a lorry drove up before the hotel, unloaded three workmen and a supply of timber. The men began to board up the statue of Runeberg in the square outside. The sun sparkled on the snow. The gun crew stood by their machine-gun on the roof of the building by the harbour, swinging their arms to keep warm. In the great Helsinki sauna soldiers back on leave dived in the heated swimming-pool, luxuriating in comfort after the horrors of the Isthmus.

I had been back in Helsinki for ten days. I had come back from London the moment I realised how serious the threat to the Mannerheim Line had been, but I had had to waste almost a full precious week in Stockholm before I could get on the Vaasa plane. It was packed with volunteers going in. I had had two days of reporting fighting and then suddenly the story had become another one entirely—peace.

That night of the 12th of March I walked round in the blackout, past the heaps of snow piled by the footpaths, to the Press Room. It was crowded. Every correspondent knew that to-night we would probably hear something definite. At their radios up and down the country the Finnish people were waiting, too. The delegation kept the Finnish Cabinet informed by cable through the Swedish Legation. But virtually they had complete power, and acted as they wished. M. Tanner, back in Helsinki, was not convinced that the treaty was signed even at midnight on March 12, when the ink on it was already well and truly dry. Indeed the first word permanent officials and Press officers of the Finnish Foreign Office had was when they heard Haw Haw giving details of it from Hamburg that same night.

I shall never forget that night. For a week an almost visible tension had hung in the air of the government circles of the capital. It was one of the hardest week's work I have ever done. Ever since the first report of the negotiations leaked out in Stockholm on the Thursday we had been working night and day checking rumours, reports, denials. Mannerheim was ill and had been taken to Stockholm; no, that proved to be false. He was still at headquarters. Svinhufhud was in Berlin. Yes, that was true. Then he was going on to Rome. What was he doing? Actually he was trying to get the Germans to restrain the Russian demands, and he was trying to get an Axis guarantee for the truncated

Finland that was left. It was not till the Sunday that we got even an official announcement that Ryti was in Moscow, and when the terms came out they seemed unbelievable.

I looked round the Press Room that night, at the green-covered tables with files of translations from the Finnish Press, the photos of Suomussalmi on the walls, the heavy curtains drawn for the black-out. Here I had heard the first communiqué of the war read out; here I had seen Miss Helsinkis, the pretty Finnish girl who acted as chief secretary, looking eagerly every night for the figures of Russian planes brought down. I asked her now what she felt about it all. She gave a half smile. "I live in Viipuri. Last week I saw on a news-reel my flat, smashed to pieces by a bomb. But I don't mind that so much as stopping the fight now when we have suffered so much."

Soon after midnight, Captain Zilliacus, one of the chief Press officers, came in with a slip of paper in his hand. "Fighting will stop at eleven to-morrow," he said. "It means peace." His voice was that of a man at a funeral. For a moment no one spoke. Then slowly the room emptied, as correspondent after correspondent went to type out his message telling the world that Russia had won. The day that followed was ghastly. I had been through Prague's suffering when the terms of Munich became known, and I knew only too well the atmosphere of defeat. This was Prague all over again, in almost every respect except we did not have that dreadful tick, tick, tick which had been the interval signal on the Czech radio, and which sounded there between the announcements from every loud-speaker in the streets like a death knell.

Tanner was to speak at midday. That was to be the first knowledge the Finns got of what had happened. The papers in the morning had carried nothing. Out in the streets people walked along in the sun, wrapped in their fur-collared coats, still absorbed with the duties of war. Queues stood in front of the tobacco shops. There were even groups down saying good-bye to men leaving on the Viipuri train.

When Tanner spoke I was in the hall of the Societetshuset Hotel, the chief hotel of Helsinki. The dining-room was already crowded with army officers and women and business-men. The manager switched on the radio, and after a few seconds Tanner started. From the kitchen the staff and the waitresses crowded to the doors of the room. A grey-haired Lotta who had acted as air-raid warden, shepherding guests to the cellars during alarms, stood stiffly beside them. Men sat at their tables, their hands still. Remorselessly, painfully the voice went on. Tanner spoke first in Finnish, then in Swedish. I could not follow the words, but the tone was clear. He went through the whole story of the war—the small country attacked, the lack of aid from outside, the negotiations. Then he came out with one sentence, and paused. Two of the maids began to weep. On the face of an officer at the next table tears were openly showing. The Finn I was with said, "He has just said—the treaty of peace was signed last night."

He went on to give an outline of the terms. Every name came as a blow. "Virolahti—then that means Viipuri is gone." I thought of the fair girl on the ski jump in Rovaniemi, who had fought so willingly because she wanted to get back to Viipuri. "You should see the sea there in the evenings in the summer," she had said. "Sortavala, Kaksisalmi, Hango." On, on went the names.

Suddenly the Lotta burst into tears, her shoulders heaving. I slipped out through the door. Outside, around a car, its radio going, a group of men stood—two soldiers, the chauffeur, two street sweepers with their snow shovels. Their eyes, too, were red. The chauffeur suddenly shouted, "No, no." In the cafés nearby other people sat listening tensely.

I walked round to the main boulevard. On the wooden covering of one shop window street sellers were posting up a special edition, just one sheet, with the terms. When the newsboys appeared with the afternoon papers they were almost mobbed.

In the streets, in the corridors of the hotel, Finns stared at us, with our yellow Press arm-bands, angrily. A strong race, they resented anyone seeing them in this hour of sorrow. They resented the outside world which had given them so many words of sympathy, so little real help. In the dining-room of the Kamp at lunch-time it was like a funeral.

On the fronts the news had come as an equally great shock. At Kuhmo one company, warned that they must stop fighting at eleven o'clock Finnish time, had hurled themselves against a Russian position at dawn in their anger, and had fought till almost every man was wiped out. At Viipuri a Finnish icebreaker, sent in to try and crack the ice of the bay and cut off the Russians on the western shore—a brilliant strategic move—kept moving after eleven o'clock. Russian guns fired on it, killing seventy men. At Taipale, the Finns who had held their posts on the lakeside cliffs unchanged since the first day of the war, in face of countless attacks, thought that the Cease Fire meant they had won. They stood and cheered. Defeat seemed impossible after all that they had been through. In front of Viipuri troops lying in the shallow trenches that were all there had been time to dig were not told of the armistice till, suddenly, at eleven o'clock the Russian guns ceased firing. The Finnish officers thought this meant a great attack was coming. They issued out their reserve belts of munitions. A minute later the message came through that it was peace.

In Viipuri itself the blue-and-white flag of Finland, which had remained till the end flying from the old castle, was dipped to half mast, then raised again. North of Ladoga the peace saved the lives of at least 6,000 Russians of the 168th Division, surrounded and trapped in mottis by the lake shore. At Kuhmo the 54th Division, besieged and hungry in their stockades, heard of the news over the radio. Some of their men rushed out and tried to embrace the Finnish soldiers; others began playing accordions and dancing. Farther east, the Finns hung white flags from the trees, and sent forward their officers under white flags to arrange the terms of the Russian withdrawal. At Salla, and many other points on the front, fighting went on long after the armistice hour, for men had been sent out on patrol days before and could not be reached.

Back in Helsinki I got a Finnish journalist to go out and talk to people in different parts of the town, asking their reactions. "It's terrible, but what else could we do?" was the general feeling, instinctively they knew little could be gained by fighting on. Those who wanted to fight on, regardlessly, were, I found, chiefly girls or older men. Men who had been through Viipuri and the Isthmus fighting were bitter. "Why so much suffering, and then defeat?" they argued. But then they would add, "But it was terrible there, terrible in this last week."

The mass of the people were simply stunned. They went through the streets in groups, talking glumly. It was a difficult fact to realise, this fact of defeat, for the real seriousness of the situation on the Isthmus had never been fully explained to them. They knew only that on every other front they had been winning. Now, in a flash, had come utter defeat.

One section of the Finnish leaders had been afraid that the army might not accept this peace; that the Generals who wanted to make a guerrilla war inland would try to fight on. But the army was both exhausted and disciplined, and it had great faith in Mannerheim. They trusted him as a soldier; they knew he would make no peace with the Soviet unless it was essential; and from the moment that he spoke on the radio, the next night, and told the country that it was at his demand that peace was made, there was no question of internal trouble.

That evening the last communiqué of the war was published. It read:

Army High Command Communiqué
13.3.1940., noon.

Army

On March 12 the enemy launched several attacks on the north-west shore of the Bay of Viipuri, all of which had been beaten back by counter-attacks by the morning of March 13. Twelve tanks were destroyed. About 60 tanks put out of action by us during the past few days of fighting have been abandoned by the enemy on the ice of the bays of the rivers Mahujoki and Vilajoki. Enemy attacks on the suburbs of Viipuri were repelled. Between Viipuri and the Vuoksi the enemy made local attacks, but was thrown back everywhere, at some points by counter-attacks in the night. In the direction of Paakkola our artillery broke up an enemy attempt at an attack. In the Vuosalmi area a fierce infantry and artillery battle raged all day. Enemy attacks were repelled and 3 tanks destroyed. Between Vuosalmi and Lake Ladoga harassing artillery activity. At Taipale an enemy attack was repelled. North-east of Lake Ladoga enemy attacks were repulsed at Uomas and Kollaanjoki. At Kuhmo the enemy launched several attacks, which were all repelled. On other sections of the land front patrol activity. On the morning of March 13 the enemy continued to attack and our troops to counter-attack on the

THE LAST DAY

Isthmus, north-east of Lake Ladoga and at Kuhmo up to 11 a.m., when both sides ceased hostilities.

Air Force

On March 12 enemy aerial activity was directed chiefly against Northern Finland, where Kemijärvi, Pelkosenniemi and certain other localities were bombed. According to confirmed reports our anti-aircraft arm shot down 4 enemy 'planes, in addition to which the fate of three other 'planes is uncertain. Of the unconfirmed cases reported on March 12, four have been confirmed by the discovery of the wreckage of the 'planes. On March 13 our own aircraft went out of action at 10 a.m., having previously carried out several flights. According to the reports received by noon, the enemy dropped bombs this morning at least on Rovaniemi and Kemijärvi, causing injuries to 3 civilians.

I was in a small café near the railway station when it was read over the air. Soldiers in uniform, Lottas, porters from the station, ordinary people were sitting there.

As the announcer said, "Here is the last communiqué of the war," everyone rose to their feet. The soldiers stood at attention, women put down their bundles and stood by them. Slowly the voice went on ". . . enemy attacks . . . artillery activity."

I watched the faces. Every man's eyes were red. One great soldier with the high-boned Mongolian face I had seen so often in North Finland was weeping openly.

When the announcer read the last sentence of the raid made just before zero hour on Rovaniemi, injuring three civilians, something like a gasp rose from the whole room. Then the announcer's voice stopped and almost embarrassedly the people settled down round the tables.

One more of the wars of history was over. Outside the station clock, lit up for the first time since November 29, glowed against the sky, a twentieth-century sign that peace had come.

CHAPTER XL

HANGO

ACROSS THE ICE that made an endless snow plain of Hango harbour four lorries moved. They swung along the well-marked roadway, past the pile of rocks just off the pier, came in through the gap in the barbed-wire entanglements along the beach, and reached the shore just where the obelisk to the German Division stood. In red granite, with a German steel helmeted figure carved on the side, this column stood on the spot where Von Der Goltz and the 10,000 men of his Baltic division landed in April 1918 to attack the Left Government of Helsinki from the rear.

Now another army was about to land at Hango. Under the peace treaty Hango and the greater part of the peninsula on which it stood were to go to Russia on a thirty years' lease. The Finns had ten days in which to move out. These lorries, piled high with boxes of ammunition, machine-guns and stores, came from the two fortress islands off-shore Rusaro and Hastobuso, the great Hango fortresses which were the Soviet's richest prize. The fortresses themselves and the guns in them were to be handed over as they stood; only the moveable army gear was to be taken away.

Along the main streets where the lorries now passed lines upon lines of trucks and cars were parked. They had been sent in from all over southern Finland to evacuate people and property from the peninsula area which was also going to the Soviet. Hango town, a seaside resort (it was the Isle of Wight of Finland), as well as a harbour and naval base, had had 23,000 inhabitants in normal times. Only 2,000 had remained during the war, but the others were swarming back now to take their furniture and their personal possessions away before the Red Army troops moved in.

I walked through the crowded streets and out along the foreshore where the summer cottages of the well-to-do of Helsinki were built among the pines, side by side with a big wooden casino. Outside one of the cottages a group of soldiers were nailing wooden boxes together. Underneath the cottage a deep cellar had been cut into the rocky soil and there, in a tiny room no bigger than a cabin on a destroyer, sat the commander of the Hango fortresses. This cellar, perfectly camouflaged by the innocuous cottage above, was his headquarters. From here he had directed the firing in the only naval battle of any importance in the Finnish war, the fight between the Hango batteries and the Russian cruiser *Kirov* on the second day of the war, December 1.

"We have in all thirty different guns in our coastal batteries here," he said to me. "They are either French guns, or American. The largest are 30.5 heavy naval guns. One battery of these are the old Russian guns which were here in Tsarist days, modernised and refitted; the others are completely new, for the Tsarist officers, when they left the forts in 1917, after the revolution, smashed up one battery beyond repair.

"I had installed the new guns myself, and trained the greater part of the gun crews since I took command here in 1922. The men were all, except for some reserves drafted in since the war, long-service members of the permanent army, serving a fifteen-year spell. They lived in peace-time here in Hango with their families.

"It was almost exactly ten in the morning of December 1 when our reconnaissance posts on the islands in the archipelago in front of the fortresses wirelessed back that the *Kirov* was in sight. She came up to a point eighteen kilometres from the shore, with three destroyers with her. She was comfortably within range, for our guns have a range of twenty-three kilometres. I was amazed to see her come in so close. I think the Russians must have believed that we had still the same armament in the fort as in Tsarist times, when the longest guns had only a range just under eighteen kilometres.

"We opened fire at once with our heaviest batteries, and got in sixteen shots within a quarter of an hour. Firing was difficult because there was a double mirage, and the first shots sent up columns of water at least 200 yards into the air. But we got results. We certainly sank one destroyer and hit one other badly. On the *Kirov* herself we scored at least one direct hit with one of the heaviest shells. Our observation posts, which were within a few kilometres of the ships, saw that clearly.

"In return the Russian ships fired about thirty-five shells at us, but they did no damage except throw up a lot of dirt, and knock over one of my lieutenants. After a quarter of an hour—sixteen minutes to be exact—the *Kirov* moved off, and the two remaining destroyers followed her. That was all—the only fight we had in the whole war."

The freezing of the Gulf of Finland put a stop, of course, to naval warfare by mid-December. Yet Finland's navy, and above all, her coastal artillery, played their full part in the war. The Koivisto batteries had not only taken part in the great struggle for the Mannerheim Line. They had had, in early December, a fight too with Soviet warships. The Russian battleship *October Revolution*, accompanied by cruisers, had moved up the coast bombarding Finnish positions around Koivisto from the sea. The Koivisto batteries had replied. They claimed to have badly damaged the *October Revolution*, and to have hit at least two cruisers.

The moment the war broke out the Russians declared a blockade of the Finnish coast; the Finns replied by declaring the blockade ineffective and by fortifying the Aaland Islands by landing marines and some guns there. The Russians also seized the three chief islands in the Gulf of Finland, Seiskari, Lavansaari and Suursarri (Hogland).

In the three weeks of sea warfare that then followed the Russians lost at least six submarines, almost all of the small 250-ton type. The Finnish sailors stated that they were good vessels but that they had to keep coming to the surface every two hours to prevent the mechanism of the periscope from freezing up. They were sunk by depth charges dropped from submarine chasers and trawlers; one was hit by a bomb from the Finnish coastal planes. On Lake Ladoga the small submarines which the Finns had built—99-ton models made to keep under the 100-ton restriction on war vessels on Lake Ladoga—went into action once against Russian barges, but they were soon sealed up in their ports. The rest of the winter the navy spent preparing launches and pleasure boats for use as motor-torpedo boats in the spring. The remainder of the navy, laid up in ice-locked ports, was manned in the latter part of the war only by skeleton crews. Every man that could be spared was drafted ashore and sent up to fight on the Isthmus front in the infantry or the artillery. I met two young officers who had been on the famous windjammers of the Ericksson fleet based at Marienhamm, who fought to the end of the war as officers in the trenches before Viipuri. One of them had American parents who, in the last war, had left their child in Finland while they made the risky voyage across the Atlantic. They were torpedoed, and drowned, and the son lived on to grow up a Finn. He too had been torpedoed once, by a German submarine in the North Sea. He was returning from running the first cargo from Finland through the German blockade of the Baltic. He had got out of a German prison camp only just in time to see the war start in Finland.

The Finnish coastal artillery was, the Finns claimed, the most powerful in Europe. Its main difficulty was that, having been remodelled at intervals, it was made up of guns of eighteen different calibres. This did, however, give it added range and effectiveness. Batteries on the Viipuri—Helsinki coast played their part in repelling the Russian attempts to land across the ice towards the end of the war.

The Hango batteries, now in Soviet hands, were passed over with every item of their equipment intact. Stalin had secured one of his main objects. Shore batteries on both sides of the Gulf of Finland now had intersecting arcs of fire; they could stop any fleet of any size steaming through the straits by daylight. Leningrad was now safer than it had been at any time since 1917.

CHAPTER XLI

THE RED ARMY

IN FINLAND THE modern Red Army had its first large-scale test. Since the close of the wars of intervention at the beginning of the nineteen-twenties the only actions in which the Red Army forces had been engaged had been in the fighting with the Japanese in the Far East in August 1938, and, to a limited degree, in Spain during the civil war. Now for one hundred and forty days the Soviet forces had been engaged in a struggle which, if it started out as a minor campaign, had developed into a full-dress modern war. On the battlefields of the Finnish forests and the Isthmus, the army which for twenty years had been one of the mysteries of Europe stood forth for the first time in the eyes of the world.

The first impression made by the Red Army in Finland was certainly not flattering to the Soviet régime. Smashed tanks, captured guns, prisoners with their toes protruding from rotted boots, clad in filthy, thin uniforms, were seen and photographed on every front. The Soviet advance was held at every point except in the unimportant region of Petsamo. Division after division was trapped in the forests. Casualties mounted steeply. These things were all true, yet they gave a false picture of the Red Army. For many of these forces employed were second-rate troops and, more important still, the Soviet High Command showed a willingness to learn from its errors so that in the end it emulated the habit usually ascribed to us of losing every battle but the last. Just as in the Boer War we recovered ourselves and worked out tactics suitable for the country after we had suffered disaster upon disaster by sending troops in scarlet coats in close formation over the open veldt, the Russian commanders worked out their way of bringing the great ponderous weight of the Red Army machine against the elusive enemies in the Finnish woods.

Finnish troops and Finnish newspapers used to say often enough that one Finn was equal to ten Russians. Lisin, the Tass correspondent in Helsinki before the war, wrote a despatch on November 17 complaining that this appeared again and again in the Helsinki dailies. But for the first two months of the war this statement was generally true. It was true, I believe, not only because the Red Army was sent into Finland with its aim wrongly defined—to occupy rather than conquer—but because its equipment was faulty and its tactics ill-suited to the type of country in which it had to operate. The army built primarily for defence of the great plains of the Ukraine and White Russia, built for a struggle with the mechanised forces of the industrial countries of western Europe, was found to be of little use when it had to fight on narrow roads in thick forests in terrible cold. It was as if an ordinary British division fitted for fighting in, say, Flanders were suddenly shipped to the

Sudan and told to fight a summer campaign there with the same clothing and gear.

The uniforms which rotted on the backs of the Red Army infantrymen in the snowstorms of December and January were not bad uniforms—for normal weather. But in Finland where the men could not change them because they were so cold that they had to wear every garment they had, they got sweaty, filthy and worn. The boots that were all right for muddy roads split and broke when men tried to warm their frozen feet around camp fires. When I came back to England in February, I remember suddenly coming face to face on the Channel steamer with a French poilu coming home on leave. I stared closely at his clothes. They were certainly no better than those of the prisoners at Suomussalmi. But he had been wearing them on the banks of the Saar, not in the forests around the Arctic Circle.

Similarly the Russian equipment, though mechanised and modern, was not fitted for forest fighting. On the narrow roads of north Finland tanks were right out of their element. The fighting there showed that the tank, or at any rate the light or medium tank, is no weapon in a position where it cannot manoeuvre easily and where its opponent has cover. Look at what happened again and again on those forest roads in north Finland. The road, perhaps a shade wider than most, had always a deep ditch of snow on either side. This ditch was sufficient to overturn a light tank, and at least to trouble other tanks unless they crossed it at right angles. Beyond the ditch was a thick forest in which the Finns could lie invisible in their white capes until the tank was almost alongside. Then they could throw hand grenades at it or rush forward and thrust an iron bar in between the caterpillar and the wheel. They could also bombard it with Molotov cocktails, which they made of tar and petrol with a fuse attached. These cocktails did not, incidentally, produce very good results in Finland. The weather was actually too cold for their effective use. Later, too, the Finns had anti-tank rifles, including the British model, and anti-tank guns. Of course, the Russians were dealing with men of more than usual courage. One other method, for instance, which the Finns employed against tanks was to dig a hole six feet deep by the roadside. In this a man stood with an anti-tank grenade—a half-pound high-explosive bomb—in his hand. Branches were put over the top of the hole and covered with snow. As the tank came along the man pushed aside the branches and flung the grenade. He then crouched down at the bottom of the hole. He was in a very safe position, for the tank's fire could not be directed down into the hole, and the Finn's colleagues lying in the bush nearby could open fire on anyone who tried to get out of the tank and deal with him.

In the intense cold of the North, too, the tanks frequently had to stop through engine trouble. The moment the crews emerged to try and fix this trouble they were attacked by the Finnish patrols.

But the chief Finnish anti-tank weapon was the land-mine. They laid the mines, which were rather like soup plates in appearance, on the roads and covered them with snow. The snow froze quickly, giving a perfectly smooth appearance to the road. Again and again these traps, which could be laid in a matter of seconds, were put across roadways behind the Russian lines by the Finnish patrols. Lorries and tanks moving up were blown up again and again. On the Isthmus a great number of anti-tank mines were laid in front of every position. They are the chief reason why the Finns claim to have knocked out or captured 1,635 tanks during the war.

The other great blunder the Russians made in the North was that they did not have their troops trained in ski-ing. Only later in January, when Siberian troops were brought in on the Kuhmo front and when crack troops came up on the Summa front did the Russians produce any good ski patrols at all. Again and again Russians, equipped with skis, were found carrying the skis because they could not manage them. Their ski instruction books were also short-sighted in many details. Published only in September, they were clearly the work of a man who had never had any real experience of ski fighting. Diagrams showed men kneeling in the snow on their skis with one knee resting on the snow preparing to hurl a hand grenade. That picture always amused the Finns, for it is an impossible position. If you try it your knee sinks into the snow, and you overbalance. They showed men, too, bayonet fighting and charging on skis. This is very difficult, because the skis in Finland were used chiefly in forest regions where they became actually a drawback to manœuvre in a very small space. The Finns used skis almost entirely as the cavalry use horses, for getting themselves from place to place. When they fought, even when they fired, they usually kicked their skis off and got a firmer foothold with their shoes.

Lack of ski troops crippled the Russian troops' skirmishing power, but even more it blinded them. For without them the Russians had practically no means of reconnaissance. In the North in the thick forest in the long dark winter days aviation reconnaissance was of very little value. The Russian planes could not spot the Finnish troops moving up through the forest, and usually, in December at any rate, the clouds were so low that they could do very little in the way of observing or photographing the rear of the Finnish army. Lack of these patrols, too, meant that the Russians had to keep to the road. They could not turn out into the woods like the Finns, for their men could not move through the snow. They could not throw out adequate screens to protect their flanks.

The failure of the Russian attack in the North, however, must not blind us to the fact that their divisions were very well equipped with modern weapons. The troops at Kemi River, for instance, had two telescope rifles to every squad of ten men, one light Djegtjarew machine-gun and one automatic rifle for every ten men. Their regimental artillery had also slightly more guns proportionately than is usual in the British or French armies. They also had light anti-tank rifles using a magazine of twenty steel-tipped bullets and excellent 3.7 cm. anti-tank guns. Every Company had one section of heavy machine-guns, each with two guns, attached to it.

They had tanks in abundance. The Finnish reports stated that the Soviet 7th army had 981 tanks for its operations on the Isthmus. At Petsamo the 14th army had 141 tanks. The 13th army operating just north of Ladoga had 96 heavy tanks, 96 medium tanks, and 90 light tanks.

On the Isthmus every section of fourteen men in the Soviet infantry was equipped with one new automatic rifle, the remainder of the men, apart from those working the light machine-gun, being issued with the new Russian 1939 rifle. This was a weapon which the Finns admired greatly. It was much superior to the rifle the Russians sent to Spain, which was usually just a 1914 model rebored. On the Isthmus, too, the Russians produced electric digging machines and rollers to smash tanks, as well as the effective armoured sledges.

This wealth of equipment is one of the definite characteristics of the modern Red Army. It is the army of a country with a substantial war industry. It not only has masses of men but apparently masses of material. It is fundamentally a big army, with the advantages and defects of its size. It may be clumsy in the use of both—men were certainly poured into action on all fronts with an almost Oriental disregard of human life—but that lack of economy in the use of force must not hide the fact that the force is there. If the Reichswehr comes into conflict with the Soviet—or rather when the Reichswehr comes into conflict with the Soviet—the Germans will find that for the first time they are up against an army which outnumbers them both in men and machines. The test will be whether the Russian High Command, and indeed all the Russian officer corps, can use these men and machines with anything like the efficiency of the German war-lords, and of their officers and N.C.O.s. For there were definite weaknesses in the command of the Soviet forces in Finland. The drastic reorganisation which has been carried out inside the Red Army since the Finnish war is proof itself of that. Discipline has been greatly tightened, officer's badges of rank have been restored, saluting reintroduced and the whole elaborate political commissar system swept away.

Lack of initiative was undoubtedly among the faults shown in the first weeks. Swift action taken on the spot might have won the battle of Suomussalmi for the Russians if the 44th Division had, for instance, pushed ahead instead of standing on the defensive, or even if they had immediately drawn back over the frontier and made sure of their communications step by step as they advanced again. Vinagradov, however, was unwilling to take responsibility for recommending either of these. He turned again and again to the commanders above him, in a manner which gives a hint that some of the fears of the purges still existed in his mind. There can be little doubt that the Red Army which moved into Finland was still feeling the effects of the reorganisation after the purges. You cannot take out many of your high officers at one sweep unless you have—as Hitler had—young well-trained men prepared to take their places.

On the other hand, as the war went on, the Soviet commanders appeared to gain greatly in confidence. The attack on the Isthmus, for all its enormous cost in men and material, was the product of good staff work and, in moves like the tank raids up the ice of the Gulf of Finland, showed real strategic boldness and imagination.

The Soviet High Command was also willing to learn from its mistakes, and to experiment with new methods when their old proved disastrous. The "motti" technique which they adopted in the North was the best way out of the difficulties into which their rash advances into the country had led them. The field defences they built in the mottis were, too, well constructed and well sited. On the Salla front the lines they built at Märkäjärvi were solid and formed a good base for the new offensive which they were planning for the summer if the war had continued. The troops there learnt to ski as the weeks went on, and their patrol work in the woods became steadily better. On the Isthmus the change over in the tank formations, bringing the heavier tanks to the fore on the German model, and the use of armoured sledges showed adaptability and improvisation. The Red Army made mistakes in Finland, but it had something which not all armies have—a willingness to learn from its errors.

The staff work in January surprised every observer. They had only five roads and two lines of railway on which to bring up their supplies to the Isthmus and mass their troops for the attack. They had at least twenty divisions on the Isthmus. These were moved up into position and changed over repeatedly without a hitch. During a great part of the period no brigade fought on the front for longer than three days at a time. This staff work was the point at which most military calculations on the future of the war went wrong. I understand that military attachés in Moscow were in the habit of taking, as a ratio of efficiency in the Red Army, the ratio of efficiency in the Soviet industry as compared with industry in the West. Industrial experts stated that the average Soviet factory was only 60 per cent as efficient as the average British or American factory. So it was reckoned that Soviet staff work was probably only 60 per cent as efficient in dealing with things like railways as the corresponding staff work elsewhere.

Yet this proved a complete underestimate. Ammunition was piled up for use by guns which were firing at one time 300,000 shells a day. This ammunition flow was maintained and the intense fire, though not always at this rate, continued during the forty-six days of the offensive. This alone is a formidable piece of staff work. One suggestion put forward is that German officers supervised the Russian offensive on the Isthmus. There was no proof of this, and it seems to me unlikely. For even if the Germans drew up the general plan the execution of it would have to fall on the shoulders of the Soviet officers and N.C.O.s.

The Russian staff had, of course, considerable advantages in planning this attack. They knew the Finnish air force was so weak that they could build up huge munition and supply dumps with little fear of them being bombed. They could use their railways day and night without interruption. They were preparing for an attack against an enemy who, whatever his defensive powers, had no chance to attack. Against the full force of a fully equipped modern army they could not hope to achieve the same results. But for all that they showed thorough organisational ability.

The political commissars, now abolished, were attached to every regiment in Finland, and to many battalions and companies as well. They had first been instituted by Trotsky, to survey the politics of the Tsarist officers whom he took into the Red Army during the wars of intervention. Dissolved by Lenin, the Corps of Commissars had been reinstituted by Stalin, to check over the loyalty of the officers and maintain the morale of the men. It undoubtedly made for strain in many cases, though in others it seemed to have worked well enough. It must have been nerve wracking for an officer, every time he was faced with a serious decision, to know that he had standing at his side a man who might describe any mistake as sabotage. Yet the major who told us the story of Suomussalmi said that if the commissar concentrated on his own job of maintaining morale and looking after the men's comfort, and left the officer free for the purely tactical side of affairs, it worked well enough. The Finns claimed from time to time that commissars were shot by their own men, particularly in the hard fighting north of Ladoga. I could never get any definite confirmation of this, though often enough prisoners shook their heads and muttered angrily when they were asked their opinion of their commissars. It would not be surprising if there were minor mutinies of this kind, for to maintain morale on a place like the Rattee Road among starving men could have been no very easy job.

The commissars at times told their men some odd tales. They always stated that it was no good surrendering, for the Finns shot all their prisoners. To the best of my knowledge this was quite untrue. Any prisoner who was taken and drafted back was safe. But whether all men who offered themselves up as prisoners in the forest were actually taken is another matter, for there, in the animal-like stalking of man by man, it was very definitely a question of shooting first and asking intentions later. In the North, too, the Russian infantry were told they were fighting a defensive war inside Russia long after the front had moved deep into Finland. There were no villages or peasants to give the lie to this, for all had gone as the Finns retreated, burning the cottages as they went. Others were told that the British and French had built a secret Maginot Line in the woods of the North, which stopped the Russian advance.

With its man-power the Russian High Command was prodigal. They certainly suffered from none of the worries about slaughter on Verdun lines which had dominated so much military thinking in Western Europe since the last war, and which was so strong in the mind of, for instance, Marshal Pétain. Again and again they pushed their men on into the teeth of murderous machine-gun fire, with an almost Oriental disregard of the cost in human grief it would bring, with the iron will of men who were going to get what they wanted at whatever cost, and with all the confidence of commanders who know that they have a 180,000,000 population to draw from. This is a factor which must be reckoned with in any new war into which the Soviet comes. She has got men to lose, if the Finnish war is any test. No great skill was devoted in any of the battles to keeping down casualties. On the Isthmus the Finns declared that Soviet tanks, pushing forward, fired into trenches where their own men were locked in hand-to-hand fighting with the Finns. Perhaps we who saw this war were over-impressed by the cost it brought in human life to the Russians, for those miles of roadway in the North strewn with bodies were a sight that I for one will never erase from my mind.

There was no lack of courage among the Russian troops, for all this slaughter. Men came on and on over the frozen lakes where the bodies of their comrades already lay heaped in great dark swathes, moving forward into the same machine-guns which still poured forth their fire. Every Finn was impressed, almost at times appalled, by this courage of the Russian infantry, even though it seemed to spring from fatalism rather than fanaticism.

What of these Red Army men who, in their grey peaked caps with the dull red star above the brow, and their grey uniforms, suffered and fought this war? My knowledge of them comes inevitably chiefly from prisoners. I spoke, through interpreters, with scores of men in prison camps in different parts of Finland during the war. I am well aware that you must not judge an army by the prisoners its enemy takes. The worst type is most liable to surrender, and even the best had been through a terrible psychological shock in the process of their capture. But they give some clues as to the Red Army men. Most of the prisoners I saw were chiefly peasants, many often of poor physique. Numbers of them were small men with narrow shoulders and stunted frames, the bodies of men who have carried on their shoulders one great war, a long civil war, a gigantic social experiment, the strain of the food troubles of 1933, and now yet another war. There was a marked difference between the peasants and the townsmen. You could tell a man from Leningrad or Moscow the moment he walked into the room. He was usually a finer, sharper type, often a trained workman or truck driver who had been called up in one of the specialist arms.

All the prisoners I saw maintained a considerable natural dignity. Again and again I saw parties of them brought into a room at a barracks or a police station to be interviewed by the Press. Never once did I see one cringe or try to insinuate himself into the good graces of the Finns. They stood there, answering questions easily enough, and after a time usually were very cheerful and interested in what was going on. They were fascinated by cameras and always asked to see the Press photographers' gear. I am certain they took this as all part of the crazy doing of the capitalist world. They assumed that it was a place in which strangely dressed men and women were fools enough to write down every sentence you said in little notebooks and to let off innumerable flashlights to take your picture.

Some, of course, were terribly depressed by the strain of the war and at being away from their homes, but many were as cheerful as children.

Another marked fact was very rarely was any one of them outspokenly antagonistic to the régime in Russia. At Viipuri we talked with one man who seemed very glad that the Soviet was meeting with difficulties. He was the son of a man who was a prisoner in a timber camp in north Russia. His attitude was understandable. Even though many of the others must have realised that they might ingratiate themselves with the Finns by attacking Stalin or Communism, they did not do so. Perhaps fear of the G.P.U. kept them silent. But the impression they gave was that they did not regard this war as the particular fault of Stalin or anyone. It was just one of those evils that occurred, and the great thing was to survive it, to get out of it as soon as possible. Certainly none but the occasional members of the Communist Party who were among the prisoners saw it as a crusade, though some sincerely thought it necessary for the defence of Russia. To most of them it was a thing of great discomfort, into which they had been drawn, they were told, because wicked Finland had attacked Russia. Above all they knew they had been intensely cold, and very near death, and they wanted to get back to their families as quickly as possible.

The enormous human cost of this war in suffering inside Russia was writ large on every battlefield. Everywhere we picked up letters from wives, mothers and children, telling of their terrible sorrow and unhappiness during the war. True, the Russians may be given to the expression of melancholy, but very very rarely, if at all, were any letters found in which the families seemed to believe that this war was worth while. Here is one, written in a child's handwriting on a slip of paper apparently some sort of form to be filled in. I picked it up from the body of a dead man.

"Dear Papa,

I go to school and I get good marks, but I am very lonesome for you and I see you often in my sleep. Please buy a guitar. I am waiting for you and it seems terribly long. I am lonely and I wish you could come home if only for a visit.

Greetings from Uncle, from Leona, from Sada and Grandma. I send you all my love, my beloved Daddy."

The guitar is interesting. Perhaps someone from that collective farm went to fight in Spain and came back with a guitar and the child associated guitars ever since with war. In the same man's pocket was a letter from his wife saying that she wept for him every night and that the children wept too and that she was short of money. It was typical of thousands. At Suomussalmi the Russian field post office was captured. It was full of letters from wives and children, almost all in the same unhappy tone. Many of the letters written by the men were requests for money to be sent to their families or for care to be taken of them.

Here is a page from the notebook in which I wrote impressions of my first talks with a group of prisoners at Rovaniemi:

"Prisoner, narrow shoulders, flat chest under grimy cotton shirt, artilleryman, aged 27, wife, two children, wants to go home; tractor driver paid 250 roubles a hectare for ploughing in peace time, says bread costs 80 copecs for two and quarter pounds on collective farm, clothes are bad there; was in army that went Poland; came north October 1, told war would last only twelve days, then they would go back by ship to Leningrad. Only political commissars allowed to listen to radio in their camps; they then handed on, explained news. Asked 'Have you lice?' he grinned 'Of course'. Had no gloves; never issued with any. Another, worker from southern Russia, had close-cropped hair, lively humorous face; had been told Finland was always breaking treaties making attacks across border, must be punished. Asked if he had butter at home, said no but he'd seen some in shop window on way through Leningrad. Said there wasn't enough vodka in army though food was sufficient. Another clearly member Communist Party began very intelligent argument about war. When an American reporter said what did he think of Roosevelt's appeal to Stalin to make peace said 'Can't be true. Roosevelt can't appeal Stalin, because he's not head Soviet Union. Would have appeal to Kallinen'."

Women as fighting troops were never used in Finland. All stories about Amazonian detachments were unconfirmed. The only ones who fought were the medical students and nurses of the 36th tank brigade.

Sorting through this detail, I have tried to work out an answer to the main question about the Red Army—can it stand up to the Reichswehr? Most military writers, and most of the experts who watched the Soviet forces in action in Finland, are of the opinion that the advantage is definitely on Hitler's side. It is dangerous, though, to deduce from the Soviet's blunders in Finland that it would make the same errors in a war in the Ukraine or the plains of White Russia. For on the steppes the Red forces would be fighting on the terrain for which their army has been devised; they would have the advantage of interior lines of communication; they would be fighting a defensive war, easy for the Russian peasant to comprehend, rather than a war which left him bewildered; and their High Command could meet Hitler with his own weapons. The Russians have parachute troops in abundance (the Germans took the idea from them); they alone in all the world have a greater tank strength than the Germans; and they have the weapon of internal Communist revolution, if not in Germany at least in occupied countries like France, to use against Hitler. But for all that it is an undoubted fact that the Red Army which fought in Finland was not in training or methods the equal of the Reichswehr which burst into Flanders. The Russians, even on the Mannerheim Line, never used to any extent the new methods of war which Hitler employed on the Western Front. They did not use dive bombers working with their tanks, or parachute troops in mass (even though they had them). The war they waged on the Isthmus was chiefly of Great War type, with artillery used in the orthodox fashion, and tanks working closely with the infantry instead of a lone raiding column. Their officers did not show in action the machine-like precision of the Germans. So that if it comes to war in the Ukraine the Soviet will have to rely on the great size of their forces to equalise the superior German skill. That size becomes, however, more and more important with every raid the R.A.F. makes against Hitler's tank factories and munition centres.

CHAPTER XLII

THE RED AIR FORCE

THE FINAL BATTLE of the Finnish war was won on the ice of the Bay of Viipuri. But equally it was won in the air above the Isthmus and above the Gulf of Finland. Russian superiority in the air was one of the decisive factors, if not the decisive factor in this war. Soviet planes smashed the Finnish front line hand in hand with the Soviet artillery; Soviet planes smashed the Finnish lines of communication, prevented ammunition and food reaching the troops at the front; Soviet planes harried and exhausted the weary Finnish troops along the whole length of the Mannerheim Line.

Throughout the war the Russians easily dominated the air above Finland. The Finnish air force, numbering at the most only ninety planes at the start of the war, was never able to put up any effective opposition against the Soviet planes. For this reason there were few spectacular air battles fought in Finland. There were no dog-fights of any importance witnessed by any correspondent. Air battles, apart from the air attacks on cities, played little part in the stories sent by any reporters. But that did not mean that the Red air force was not playing a vital rôle. It was as important as any domination of the sea has been in any great war.

In the early part of the war, however, the Russian air force did not play any extremely important rôle, because the Russian General Staff did not allow it to. There was no consistent bombing of the rear. On the front there was little opportunity for the planes to do a great deal, for in the Isthmus the Finnish positions were strong enough to stand up to heavy bombing, and the weather was generally bad then.

Even in the later offensives the Soviet planes played no very great part as "mobile artillery" on the front. Dive bombers do not seem to have been used at all, and the Russians did not try the tactic of sudden bombing attacks, with their accompaniment of fearful noise, working hand in hand with tanks. The bombing carried out on the Isthmus to back up the artillery was still a support for shell fire, not a substitute for it, as was the German bombing in the Low Countries.

But if the Soviet air force was not used to the full on the actual fronts, it was used with terrific effectiveness against the rear, and particularly at the immediate rear of the Mannerheim Line. Throughout February every road and every village and troop position behind the line was bombed and machine-gunned almost daily by planes which seemed to fill the cloudless blue sky. Here the weather, too, was against the Finns. Usually in mid-February heavy snowstorms come on the Isthmus, but this year they never came. Cloudless day followed cloudless day throughout the month. The day on which I visited the west side of the Summa sector we spent half our time getting off the roads into the woods to hide from planes. The Finns took at first far too many precautions against planes above their roads. Convoys would be stopped or turned under trees. But in the end, as in London, they let things run "regardless", but not until great losses of men had already been caused. In the final stage of the war on the Isthmus the rôle of the Red air force became increasingly important. Their ceaseless machine-gunning and bombing of the roads dried up the supplies, particularly of munitions, which the Finnish troops needed so badly. The blows at munitions centres and arms factories added to this strain, which undoubtedly led to the final breakdown of munition supplies which was one of the final decisive factors in the war.

In the industrial centres, too, the raids told steadily on the "man-hours" of the Finnish war production. Again and again in the last month the sirens went in Helsinki, Lahti, Tampere and the other chief factory centres, sending workers streaming out to shelters. The Russians, who had little to fear in the way of Finnish fighter defence, made a point of sending their planes, even when they were going to bomb a distant objective, over as many towns as possible on the way, so as to get the sirens sounded. To meet this a system was worked out under which workers in factories were graded into groups according to the war importance of their jobs. Those whose jobs had to be kept going remained at their posts; those who did less vital work remained at their benches and desks until a roof spotter signalled planes overhead; those whose work was of slight importance took cover the moment the sirens went. But even with this, the strain on the civilian population became increasingly evident. People got weary of rushing to shelters, and their weariness grew with a leap the moment it became clear that the battle of the Isthmus was being lost. On the last day of the war in Helsinki I went into a shelter outside the Hotel Kamp. A girl waiting there joined in a discussion on the chances of peace. "Well, if it does come, at least we won't have to spend all day in these shelters," she said. Then she paused and looked round hurriedly, as if feeling suddenly guilty at making such a remark. But the other people nodded. They were prepared to hold as firm as the troops on the front so long as there seemed to be any hope of victory or at least a good peace. But now that that hope was gone, let the air raids go too. Civilian morale under air bombardment depends enormously on two factors, I believe—a firm belief in ultimate victory, or a very clear conviction that the cause for which they have gone to war holds in it some hope for a better future.

This steady bombing of the rear was aimed also at the railways. Yet here it had surprisingly little effect. At no time did the Russians succeed in holding up train services on any Finnish main line for more than twenty-four hours. The average interruption was much less than that. This was chiefly due to the fact that Finland is a very flat country, with few viaducts or big bridges which could be destroyed. For this reason the Russians concentrated their attacks chiefly against junctions. Riihimäki, the junction of the north-south and east-west lines, became a favourite target in the last month of the war.

At Tampere, the great industrial centre, which was frequently attacked, the station was hit and the main station badly damaged, yet the trains continued running. Around the station you could see in March lines of burned-out houses and factories that had been struck by bombs, but the main lines were restored and working. In this continual battle to rebuild cut lines the extraordinary organising power of the Finns had full play. In the bombardment of Riihimäki on February 22, gangs continued throughout the day to rush out and continue repairs the moment the bombers had gone. When I went through the junction early in March the yards were a mass of rusty burnt-out lines. Houses all around the station were burnt and smashed. The side of the low concrete station had been torn away and patched with wood, yet the main line sidings were open, supply trains moved past by the ruined sidings. In the station ravintola, which I shall always remember for its excellent cabbage soup, quiet-faced Finnish women were working again, though boards covered a hole in the wall and one side of the room was still blackened with smoke.

The Finnish air force was never, till the last fortnight, strong enough for more than slight strategic bombing on the front. No fighter squadrons protected the cities. There was never anything but a "token" fighter defence of Helsinki. The real defence there was entirely confined to anti-aircraft guns. The air force, though only some ninety machines at the start of the war, was made up of modern planes and included twenty Bristol Blenheim bombers. Their chaser planes were chiefly Fokkers, and they had British Whitworth coastal hydroplanes. After the war had got under way they were strengthened in the North by Swedish fighter planes (chiefly Gloster Gladiators) and some bombers, but these never numbered at the most more than twenty in the Salla region. Two ancient fighter Fokker biplanes fitted with skis used to circle over Rovaniemi. I wondered how the pilots could stand the terrible cold in the open cockpits. But they did not have to stand it long. Both planes were shot down within the month of December. The three bombers which were stationed at Rovaniemi were used by the Finns on the Salla front to attack Russian bivouacs on moonlight nights. All were ultimately shot down.

Gradually new planes came in from outside, from Britain, Italy, Holland and France. But the variety of types brought difficulties. It meant the need for an equal variety of repair shops, and for mechanics trained to deal with machines completely different in design. The Italians sent some pilots, chiefly men whom they wanted to get experience in cold weather flying, and some mechanics with them, and there were occasional volunteer pilots from Holland and Belgium and Spain. But it was not flyers that Finland wanted. What they needed was ground crews and tools.

The Finns claim to have brought down during the war 684 planes. I believe this figure. Of the planes that they claim all but 250 were checked by the British Military Attaché or his assistant and were found to be absolutely correct. We must remember that in Finland weather conditions were very difficult and many Soviet planes crashed with ice on the wings. These were listed by the Finns as machines destroyed. The Finnish anti-aircraft was also very effective. They had first-rate Bofors Swedish anti-aircraft guns and very good Vickers machine-guns which they used for anti-aircraft work, all manned by first-class men. Their fighter planes found also that the ordinary Russian medium FB bomber could be attacked from the lower right-hand side, from an angle of forty-five degrees, with deadly effect. It was completely blind at that point. One pilot over Viipuri shot down seven bombers in a row, attacking them one after another from behind.

In the North the aeroplane played no great part in the war. There was little bombardment of the Finnish front lines of communication, except on Petsamo and Ivalo, where bombs were poured down with a lavish wastefulness. On the Arctic Highway cars and lorries were repeatedly machine-gunned from the air and chased with bombs, but the rough country made the aeroplane in the North of no great value. The Russian aeroplanes were operating from temporary bases without arrangements for night landing, and except for a night raid on Oulu and Rovaniemi in the moonlight there was no night air activity in the North at all.

The daylight in the first two months of the war was also very short, lasting only from nine o'clock to four o'clock at the utmost. By waiting for dusk, and by operating in small groups on skis, with sledges for transport, moving in the shelter of trees, the Finns could avoid any interference from any enemy aircraft. There were no great marching columns to disperse, no lines of tanks or lorries, just these men moving in Indian file by the roadside and an occasional lorry tearing along a sheltered part of the road. Often as I went through those woods I thought of the open roads leading to Madrid or the plains of Flanders and northern France, which seem made by nature as playgrounds for the bomber and the fighter with its machine-guns blazing. Finland was another type of warfare altogether.

Parachute troops were used by the Russians in very small numbers. The usual formation was of two or three men, dropped during the fighting on the latter stages of the Isthmus, with the specific task of attacking communications or blowing up a bridge. There were no mass parachutist attacks on the rear, such as were made by the Reichswehr in Holland. Some of the cases of sabotage carried out by parachutists were effective. In Oulu, for instance, the telephone line between the chief observation post on the water-tower outside the town and the main A.R.P. post in the town was cut just before an air raid. This is believed to have been the work of a Finnish-speaking parachutist. The alarm was never given and the town suffered severely in the raid. To deal with parachutists the Finns formed a highly mobile shock corps, rushed from place to place wherever parachutists were reported. But they did not have a great deal to do. This was probably due to the wide, wild nature of so much of Finland. It was of little value to drop men in an area where the only thing they could do was blow up a stretch of railway which, over flat frozen ground, could be easily repaired.

CHAPTER XLIII

THE FINNISH ARMY

THE RED ARMY in Finland was not only up against great difficulties of terrain and weather. It found itself face to face with one of the best armies of history. The Finnish forces that took the field in autumn 1939 were a model of what can be done by a General Staff that studies and makes use of every natural defensive feature its country offers, trains its army to fit in with its environment, and combines a clear war aim with good organisation, efficient discipline, and high morale.

In all the Finns mobilised about 325,000 troops. Of these probably 125,000 were all the time engaged in transport and supply work, and never fired a shot. Yet with these they held up the Red Army for 140 days. They had little artillery, no air force to speak of, and at the start few anti-tank weapons. But they allied themselves with the natural forces of their countryside, and made allies of these. Their white capes and skis made the snow worth whole divisions to them; their special fighting gloves, with a tiny slit through which the trigger finger could be thrust, their knee-length leather boots with a toe-cap that made bindings unnecessary on skis, and kept the feet dry and warm, their fur-lined coats and caps, were not only cheaper than tanks, but in the snow in the North more effective. For in them they could continue to fight, while the frozen, hungry, lost Russians could not do so with any effect.

Unable to afford artillery, the Finnish command had concentrated on the problem of maintaining a high degree of fire power from its ski patrols. For this they evolved a very effective weapon, the Suomi machine pistol. This weighed only ten pounds, could be easily carried on patrol, and fired a circular magazine of seventy rounds, or a smaller straight magazine of thirty rounds. It was simply a forest Tommy-gun, and was used with deadly effect in the woods of the North. With it a Finnish scout could creep up, silent on his skis, invisible in his white cape, to the outskirts of a Russian camp-fire and wipe out a whole section of troops before they realised his presence. The Finns had also an excellent army rifle, with which their men were very efficient, and a light machine-gun, the Lahti Saloranta 7.62 mm. gun, which weighed only twenty pounds.

For other material the Finns drew liberally on the Russians by using the guns and rifles they captured at Suomussalmi and in the other battles. The bores of the main Finnish weapons were the same as the Russians. This was partly intentional, for the Finnish General Staff hoped in any future war to capture material, and partly an unintentional result following from the fact that when Finland first broke away from Russia in 1918 the only material available was the old Tsarist army supplies.

The Finns had an almost Prussian sense of discipline in their army etiquette. If an officer, for instance, entered a restaurant every soldier there junior in rank to him stood up and bowed as he passed. There was a great deal of heel clicking and saluting —almost too much, I thought often. In the field this strictness fell away because of the essentially individual nature of the fighting, but it came back again when one got into the sphere of headquarters.

Their officers were intensively trained, and proved in this war to be the great strength of the fighting army. It was the commanders of isolated companies in the forest who led their men in the first attacks against tanks with grenades, and who built up in them the fiercely aggressive spirit which made their defensive action such a brilliant thing. For the whole secret of the

Finnish successes was that throughout the war in the North they retained the initiative and attacked repeatedly. Suomussalmi, Kemi River, Tolvajärvi were victories only because the Finns refused to take up a static defensive, and flung themselves into a war of movement which called for skill, courage, and great organisation. Any officer knows how difficult, even in open ground, it is to co-ordinate scattered groups of troops in attack. Yet the Finns did this in dense woods which made all fighting practically fighting in the dark, where every direction had to be found by compass, and where signals between different parts of a force were practically impossible.

Courage was a steel fibre which ran through the whole of this organisation. It was because men went for tanks with one or two grenades, standing up close till their own limbs were sure to be smashed by the explosion, rather than let this tide of machines flow into the land where their farms and homes lay, that the first Soviet advances were stopped. It was because men held on in positions which many other armies would have abandoned that the Mannerheim Line held as long as it did.

Good organisation fed these skilled, brave men, moved them at the right times to the right places, informed them of the enemy's movements, got ammunition and supplies to them—till there were no more. On all the forest fronts the troops had hot food every night, cooked in field kitchens on sleds and drawn up by pony to the front in the dark. They slept in warm tents, where they could dry their clothes. The village saunas behind the lines provided them with baths practically on the front. Of course there were defects, breakdowns, delays, muddles in this army as in any other, but they were comparatively slight. From a military point of view it was a formidable sight, this spectacle of a force avoiding at least some of the confusion which tends to make of war, as George Steer has pointed out, an affair of mistakes in which it is the side which makes the fewest wins. And linked to its technical efficiency as an army was the fact that the men themselves wanted to win. They wanted to keep the Russians out of their country, and with this clear aim in their minds they threw themselves into the fight with all the strength of the hard, buffeted border race that they are.

CHAPTER XLIV

THE PROPAGANDA WAR

THE FINNISH PEOPLE fought the Russians heart and soul. That is one of the chief facts of the Finnish war which must be recorded before history. Kuusinen's propaganda, backed by the whole force of Radio Moscow and by all the forces of Soviet publicity, did not at any time split the Finns' unity. At no time was there any effective Fifth Column inside Finland. Despite the fact that in 1918, and again in 1932, Finland had been split from top to bottom by social trouble, by a conflict between Right and Left, she fought as one united country against the Russians during the invasion of 1939–1940. It is a fact of equal importance to the Left as to the Right.

I told this to Communists in England when I returned from Finland in February. They queried my right to say it. They asked me what knowledge I had of working-class movements inside Finland. I admitted that I had been for the most of my time there on the fronts with the army and that I had not spent any length of time in places like Tampere, the great working-class centres. But when I went back to Finland in March, I made a definite point of investigating this question. I spoke with Finnish M.P.s of the Left who defended the Soviet Union. I spoke with Finnish police officials; I spoke with Finnish Communists who were then supporting the war. I talked to Army Commanders and asked them their opinion. The reply of one officer, I feel, sums up the situation best. He said to me, "How do you imagine that these men of mine who are fighting every night alone or in parties of twos and threes in the forests could keep on with this terribly bitter struggle if their hearts were not in it? What would be easier for them than to desert? They have only to walk over to the Russians and give themselves up. They know that there they would get good treatment, if only for propaganda purposes. But they did not do so. You ask me if I have Communists among my men. I tell you frankly, I do not know. I have never bothered to ask."

I found the same thing again and again. I asked officers on the front if they had Left-wingers among the men. They regarded the question almost as superfluous. Some answered angrily, "There are no classes now in Finland." Others just shrugged their shoulders. No doubt officers kept their eyes on men of known Left views from time to time. But on the Isthmus front to the end, officers asked for men from the working-class districts of Helsinki because they found they stood up to the strain of modern war better than the peasants. There was no question of drafting just the peasants into the army and keeping the workers out. All classes went equally. All classes suffered equally in the fighting.

I spoke to Aleksi Aaltonen, the former Social-Democratic M.P. who had stood with Kuusinen in the ranks of the Finnish Red Government in 1918. He is now Secretary of the Social-Democratic Party in Finland, having been pardoned under a general amnesty in 1927. We talked in his room in Helsinki, hung with portraits of Karl Marx. Volumes by Marx stood on the shelves on the walls. Clearly if Left-wing persecution took place under this Government it was not directed against this room. Aaltonen told me that to the best of his knowledge there were five hundred members of the Communist Party in Finland before the war. Most of the five hundred were rounded up the moment war started. There were as well several thousand adherents. These had almost all dropped away after the first air raid, and after the attack had begun. "How can you expect people to remain loyal to a cause which dropped at the same time pamphlets offering peace and bombs bringing death?" he said. "After the first air raids on Helsinki, we had scores of angry people coming in here bringing pamphlets, putting them down on the table and saying, 'Look at that. How can the Soviet do a thing like that?'"

Aaltonen, a great block of a man who had clearly suffered in his life, told me that the Communists had made two attempts to bring out illegal pamphlets in Helsinki immediately after the war started, but both printing presses were discovered by the police. After that there had been no attempts inside the country at propaganda. The pamphlets which appeared were all dropped from Soviet planes. Among the men arrested was Mauri Ryoina, a former Communist M.P. Statements were made abroad that he had been brutally maltreated. This was denied by the Government on March 6.

The Soviet radio propaganda was on the whole inept. They jammed the Finnish news every night at 10 p.m. This itself operated as good pro-Finnish propaganda. You could always hear the news; but as well you were conscious of the irritating whistle of the jamming. The sole influence was not to make you stop listening but to make you angry with the Soviet. When the war started, their first line of propaganda was one of inducement to revolt. The Finnish workers were being told to come over and join the happy ranks of the Soviet Union. But this was done clumsily. On the Isthmus front, Finnish soldiers were told that if they joined the Soviet they would get hot meals six days a week. At this time, the six-day week still operated in Russia, although, of course, it did not in Finland. The Russians had apparently overlooked this fact. The Finnish troops, who were getting seven hot meals a week and who knew from the Russian prisoners that nothing like that was being obtained by the Soviet forces, just laughed at this kind of talk.

When this failed, and it was clear that the Finnish army was not splitting internally, the Russians tried another kind of propaganda, that of intimidation. One of their broadcasts on this line was tactless in the extreme. They said to the Finns, "We advise every Lotta to carry two pairs of shoes with her. She will need them. For she is going to march to Siberia side by side with the Finnish soldiers for taking part in the struggle against the free Finnish people and the Soviet Union." Imagine what a message like that meant to a Finnish soldier, hearing it from a loud-speaker under shell fire, just after a Lotta had risked her life to bring him his food or perhaps his ammunition. He immediately felt determined to go on with the fight. I met many Finnish soldiers who spoke bitterly of that particular broadcast.

The first Soviet pamphlets dropped, too, were long-winded and, on the whole, ineffective. Here is one of them:

"Finnish labourers, factory workers, the Finnish army and soldiers! The bloody crimes of the tyrants Mannerheim, Ryti and Tanner are continuing ceaselessly. Not enough that they drove Finland into criminal senseless war against her great neighbour, the Soviet Union. Now they have started a war against the Finnish people themselves. Peaceful populations have been forced out of towns and villages by the Civic Guards. The guard and their officers have destroyed many villages in Karelia with fire, at the order of Ryti and Tanner. These stupid Government officials simply do not seem to be aware that the Soviet are within twenty-four hours of Viipuri, Abo and the other towns of Finland. And the tyranny of these perjurers, robbers and gangsters is almost over. Do not let them destroy your homes. Come to the side of Otto Kuusinen. Down with the bloody butchers, Mannerheim, Ryti and Tanner."

That pamphlet was dropped in the Finnish lines on the Karelian Isthmus on December 9. The troops who picked them up had themselves burnt the villages on the frontiers. They knew why they had burnt those villages. They had done it to check the Soviet advance. They were the last people likely to be impressed by such propaganda. Nor were the people who had fled from the villages likely to be interested. All they knew was that the Soviet had invaded and that their Government was fighting back. They did not believe that the village burning was directed against them.

The Kuusinen Government put out a paper called the *Kansan Sana* (The People's Word) which was dropped by Soviet aeroplanes over the Finnish lines. It reached the number 44 before the war ended. I saw a copy, No. 41. The leading article ran:

"Finland's workers, peasants, civil servants, intellectual workers and soldiers! You are violently banished from your native places; you are thrown out under the sky. Your homes are burned, your property is destroyed, your whole life is ruined. Your mothers, your wives, your sisters, your children are made homeless beggars. In one hit the results of the long work of the people have been annihilated. The Finnish culture, centuries old, has been unsparingly destroyed."

These were words with which every Finn would agree. But he would put the blame for them on the Russians. His astonishment when he discovered that he was asked to blame his own Government for them was natural and strong. The proclamation continued:

> "Join the people's government led by Otto Kuusinen. Soldiers, turn your weapons against those who destroy your homes."

That was precisely what the Finnish troops were doing. They were turning their weapons against those who destroyed their homes, who were, so far as they were concerned, the Russians.

I asked Aleksi Aaltonen what he remembered of Kuusinen. He said that Kuusinen had been at one time a teacher in the Democratic Party School in Helsinki which he had attended. Later they had been fellow M.P.s together. Aaltonen himself had come back to Finland in hiding early in the 1920's. He lived in Abo, hiding in his wife's flat. Once he had to go to Helsinki for an eye operation. Coming back with his face bandaged so as to be unrecognisable, he got into a first-class carriage. As he sat there, another man got in and sat in the opposite corner, bowing to him stiffly in the normal Finnish way. He bowed back. The man was Field-Marshal Mannerheim, who would have willingly signed his death warrant at that time. Now he and Mannerheim were standing side by side in this struggle.

The war had brought one thing to the Finnish trade unions which they had not had before—recognition. Sir Walter Citrine had made this a condition for the British Trade Union's support of Finland. The eight-hour working day remained valid throughout the war, but industry was carried on with a tremendous amount of overtime work which was paid at 50 per cent additional rate for the first hour and 100 per cent for the next hour. Until early March, the Finnish workers were not paid for the time they had spent in bomb-proof shelters. After that, under a new agreement between the trade unions and the Employers' Association, the workers were to be paid for the time they spent in the shelters. But if it was possible, they had to make up the time spent in the shelters by overtime work, unpaid, up to two hours. After that they were paid overtime.

Of Kuusinen, Aaltonen said, "He is an entire foreigner to Finland now," bringing his hand down smack on the table. "We do not know him and he does not know us. He does not know anything of the political and social development of Finland during the last fifteen years. He has never wanted to know it. His agents here have had to send him fake reports of bad news about Finland, just as the Russian Minister, Dereviansky, has sent fake reports to Stalin. Dereviansky moved only in circles where he always got news about dissatisfaction and antagonism to the Government."

I asked him his opinion of Mannerheim.

"He is a good soldier," Aaltonen replied, slightly smiling.

Again and again, in visits to factories in different parts of the country, we met men who said that they had been staunch Communists before the war but were now definitely prepared to fight to the end to prevent the Soviet winning. There were also Communists who took the opposite view. Marte Huysmans, the daughter of the great Belgian Social Democratic leader, told me that she talked in Helsinki with a Communist who said that he was glad the war had taken place and that he was prepared to support it to the end. But he was a very rare type. And Finland's gigantic war effort showed what little effect his view had.

I cannot claim to have had an intimate knowledge of the Finnish Left-wing movement. I did not speak Finnish and I was too busy with reporting the fighting to have the time to investigate it as thoroughly as I would have wished. The only thing I can say is that it showed no outward signs of taking any anti-war line, nor did any of the Left-wing M.P.s in Parliament, many of whom were positively pro-Soviet, despite the war, admit that there had ever been anything in the nature of real effective pro-Soviet activity inside the country. Finland was as united in this war as any country has been in any war.

CHAPTER XLV

COST OF DEFEAT

THE FINNS LOST, under the Treaty of Peace, one-fifth of their country's industry, one-tenth of their country's farming land and forests and the homes of one-eighth of their population. Under the Treaty, the Russians took over Hango on a thirty-year lease. They took over all of northern Ladoga, and all the Karelian Isthmus right up to Virolahti. Round Viipuri and Imatra the Finns lost many of their best pulp mills and part of their cotton industry. At Sortavala, which went to Russia too, there was an important timber and pulp industry. Much of their best tourist country was in the forests north of Lake Ladoga—in forests, too, where grew the pick of their timber. On the Karelian Isthmus they lost enormous resources of Karelian birch. They lost 40,000 farms, over 400 different industrial establishments, employing over 20,000 workers and using 100,000 horse-power, with a gross output of over £2,000,000. The great Rouhiala 132,000 horse-power hydro-electric power station was ceded to the Soviet.

Under the terms of the Treaty the Finns were to leave all the fixed property, taking only their movable gear. In the Gulf of Finland, the Russians got all the islands, strengthening their strategic position there enormously. There were interesting changes in the North. The Russians kept the line they had at Märkäjärvi, thus making a great bend into Finnish territory, so as to give the Russians the strategic strong points of Salla and the country behind it. The Finns agreed to construct with the Russians a railway line running from Kemijärvi to Kandalaksha. This would give the Russians a much greater military advantage in northern Finland, for they would always have a railway to rush in troops in the case of any new war, and it would give them more rapid approaches to Sweden and the north of the Gulf of Bothnia. It also had enormous economic advantages for them. The Russians agreed to hand back Petsamo, but kept the Peninsula, which gave them a complete strategic stranglehold on the Petsamo area. The Finns agreed to demilitarise the Arctic waters of Petsamo and to keep there no armed vessels or warships of more than 100 tons and a maximum of fifteen war or other armed vessels, the tonnage of which might in no case exceed 400 tons.

Strategically, the effect of the Treaty was to put the Finns completely into the grip of Russia. The Mannerheim Line was smashed. The forests north of Ladoga, which had operated as its logical extension, had gone. Russian armies could now build a new line at Viipuri, which would form a solid position of defence. They would have this as a base from which to launch any attack against Finland in the future. From Hango, with its two great harbours of Hango and Lappvik, they could land troops in Finland's rear. And they would have an air base from which Helsinki could be bombed in a few minutes. Their guns could shatter the entrance to the Gulf of Finland. Round Hango they took over all the islands within a radius of five miles to the south and east and three miles to the west and north. This was done under the terms of the Treaty specifically to establish a naval base.

The Finns, the moment the first shock of defeat was over, wasted no time in moping. They turned all their attention to evacuating the areas they had to give up. The day after peace was signed the trains pulled out of Helsinki for Viipuri crowded with people going back to collect their belongings. But none of them got back. For the Russians, who under the Peace Agreement were to leave an area a kilometre wide between their lines and the Finnish lines—the Finns were to retire at least a full half-kilometre—poured into Viipuri and took over the city before anyone got back. That, at any rate, is the official Finnish version. The Finns claim that thousands, perhaps millions of pounds of private property in the form of jewellery, silver, pictures and furniture which might have been removed were captured by the Soviet in this way. There were isolated clashes in the streets between the advancing Russians and the Finnish troops.

Into the other areas from which property and individuals had to be evacuated the Finnish swarmed with their ant-like efficiency to carry out the task. On the roads from North Ladoga and the Isthmus long lines of peasants jammed the way beside the retreating army. I watched the evacuation of Hango Peninsula. It was one of the most incredible sights of the war. Cars, buses and lorries poured in from the surrounding country and from Helsinki, bringing in people who had been evacuated from this much-bombed city—it had seventy-five different raids and 282 alarms and had once had an alarm for four days without cease—to get their property. Yachts were dug out of the frozen harbour, put on trolleys and hauled overland to the Finnish area. People jammed on to the trucks everything imaginable—deck chairs, children's toys, old tin cans, household furniture, clothes. I saw one woman pile the coffin containing the body of her son, which had been sent back from the Isthmus for burial, on to a sledge and have it taken onto Finnish soil. One man right on the frontier found that the line went through the middle of his house, so that his kitchen was in the Soviet and his front door in Finland.

At the station they were loading Bofors anti-aircraft guns on to railway trucks and boxes of ammunition marked in English, "Danger, do not expose to an open flame." In one house we found a woman baking bread. She said, "My oven is so good, it breaks my heart to leave it, so I'm baking in it once more before I go." Mannerheim himself had a house at Hango which he had sold only just before the war: it, too, was being cleared by its occupants.

In his office in the Town Hall I spoke with the young mayor of Hango, Elim Wennstrom, a Swedish Finn from the Aaland Islands. He was packing away the usual gaudy portraits of Town Councillors. This man had stuck it in Hango right through the terrible bombardments, through the continual raids, and the peace had come as a terrible shock to him. He had been in Helsinki at the time, arranging for the preparation of deep shelters to be blasted out of the granite rocks near the town. The calendar on the wall still stood at the day 13, the fateful 13th of March on which peace had been signed. On the 22nd of March, Good Friday, he had to hand over to the Red Army. Now, amongst the crowds of busy lorry drivers and householders, he showed us the town. The centre part was smashed and burned by explosive and incendiary bombs. But the damage was, comparatively, very small.

On the 22nd the Russians arrived at Hango. G.P.U. troops landed by aeroplane on the ice of the bay, advanced into the town and met the Finnish officer who remained to greet them. A detachment was told to go and take up their positions at the new frontier, a barrier of barbed wire across the road, half way to the next town of Ekenes. On the Finnish side of the frontier the Finns in their grey army caps and grey uniforms waited. Three or four onlookers stood with them. Down the long avenue that led towards Hango, two figures appeared. They came closer and closer. They were Russian guards in admirable blue uniforms, with warm caps. They marched up to the Finns, saluted them and took up their position by the barrier. They grinned in a friendly way at the photographers. They could afford to do so. Hango was theirs.

CHAPTER XLVI

THE PRESS AND FINLAND

THE REPORTING OF the Finnish war has been continually attacked and criticised. From Russia itself, from many groups in England and America there was a terrific barrage of criticism during the war, and this continued later, accusing the Press of distorting the whole course of the war, of exaggerating every criticism of the Red Army and every victory of the Finns. The public, surprised by the first Finnish victories, and sceptical of their extent, listened the more readily to these attacks when the sudden Russian victory in March appeared to prove that all along the situation had been far different from the versions given in the papers. In America the Left-wing critics grew increasingly vehement. In *New Masses* George Seldes wrote a series of detailed articles on the American correspondents in Finland, attacking points both in their past careers and in their stories from Finland.

To all this the reply is, that in the Press work on the Finnish war there was a considerable amount of exaggeration and faking, particularly from the Scandinavian reporters—but so is there in every war. A big section of the Press jumped at every news item that could be used as propaganda against the Soviet, and played up this type of news in huge headlines, behind which you could almost see those men who hated the Left rubbing their hands and saying, "What luck to have this stuff to write about the Soviet at last." When I first got back from Finland and saw the way some papers had presented, as truth, every rumour from Stockholm or Copenhagen that could harm the Soviet, I was staggered. Papers which had passed over the mass bombings of Barcelona in March 1938 as being small beer, played up the Soviet bombings of Finland in the largest type. All that is true. But it happens in every war. And it was only one side of the picture. For at the same time there were reporters in Finland who, throughout the war, turned out as careful, well balanced reports as are possible in any war. If one-tenth of the stuff written from France during the "head in the sand" period of Maginotitis of the winter of 1939-40 had been as honest, we might have been forewarned of the disaster that was to come in May. Walter Kerr, for instance, of the *New York Herald Tribune*, showed himself as one of America's outstanding newspapermen by the honest, cautious despatches he sent from Finland. Leland Stowe reported the scene of the Tolvajärvi battlefield in what is one of the best pieces of modern journalistic description. George Steer, working under conditions of the greatest difficulty, covered the fighting on the Mannerheim Line in the same encyclopædic, reasoned, and well written way that he had described the Abyssinian and Spanish wars.

Another factor of the greatest importance, which tended to make the reporting of the Finnish war lopsided, was certainly not the fault of newspapermen. It was the direct result of the power which complained most about mis-reporting—the Soviet. For Russia, by refusing to allow foreign correspondents near the fronts in the Finnish war, made this the first war in recent times which was "covered" from one side only. In the Spanish war, the Abyssinian war, in every modern campaign there have been reporters with both armies, and their two versions have usually been available to the thinking man to allow him to make up his mind fairly. But in Finland this did not happen. British correspondents in Moscow who asked permission to go to the front were told they must rely on the reporting of Russian observers. But these observers reported very little until the final stage of the fighting on the Mannerheim Line.

I have seen enough of the movement of events in this world

to know how vitally important it is for the functioning of any sort of democracy—or of any sort of government, for that matter—to have accurate information. For that reason I agree with much of the criticism about the Press in Finland. But what I do not agree with is that many of the people who make the attacks have themselves any right to speak up, for the version of the war which they want accepted is as far from the truth as the wildest fakes which came out of Helsinki. It is one thing to say, for instance, that the destruction of the 18th Division was reported several times over, so that it looked as if at least five different divisions had been knocked out there instead of one. But it is quite another thing to declare that the division was never destroyed at all—which was what Moscow stated.

George Seldes, in his *New Masses* articles, attacked the reporting of the first raid on Helsinki, and declared that, compared with what happened to Barcelona, Helsinki had been very lightly treated. That is true, even though Seldes' figure of 28,000 casualties in Barcelona is an exaggeration itself. But that is not the point. The point is, did the Soviet bomb the crowded civilian centres of Helsinki? And the answer is—yes. No amount of accusations against correspondents for writing the way they wrote of the bombing can deny this fact.

When I first went to Finland I realised that this war would arouse enormous controversy. From the start, therefore, I kept detailed notes and piled up all the evidence I could on the points most likely to be in dispute. It was from those notes that my stories at the time were written, and it is from them, checked as far as they can be in this bombed world, that I have written this book. And no amount of denials or indignant articles by people in London or New York can wipe from my mind the pictures I saw sculptured by war and frost throughout fighting Finland.

For the faking the Scandinavian journalists must bear much of the responsibility. They were, on the whole, bad journalists. Perhaps it is because their countries have mixed so little in world affairs in recent years that they have not needed high standards of foreign reporting. Personally courageous, charming and intelligent, they have very loose standards of what constitutes accurate news. They had a curious idea about competition. In the British Press, competition means getting the story of what is happening more rapidly and more efficiently than your colleagues. In Scandinavia, it means, so far as I can see, getting a different story from the one your colleague has. Again and again I saw reporters of Swedish and Danish papers leave a spot where obviously the news was hot, to go somewhere else, just to have something different from their colleagues. And if news is short—well, do some thinking. They bombed Kronstadt day after day, when the Finns had hardly a bomber that could go into the air; they wiped out civilians right and left; they advanced into Russia, rolled back Russian attacks, laid out line after line of Soviet tanks and aeroplanes. They did this cheerfully, believing that they were helping Finland. They felt that this was good pro-Finnish news. In effect, it did Finland infinite harm. They built up, inside Sweden particularly, a belief that the Finnish army was winning the war without any need of help.

There were, of course, exceptions to this reporting. Barbara Alving, of the *Dagens Nyheter*, is, I think, one of the best and most responsible journalists I have ever met, and her reports did much to correct inaccuracies in other papers. Ebbi Munck, who worked for a leading Danish paper, must also rank among the best correspondents in Europe to-day. From Stockholm, too, the London *Times* correspondent had kept up a steady stream of cool, unbiased articles, summing up at intervals the course of the war. History owes him a definite debt for his work during this period. But these men and women were exceptions. The carelessness and irresponsibility of the Swedish Press was demonstrated to the world at large when we started to fight the Germans in Norway. Everyone remembers the flood of false reports they sent out about our fighting in Bergen Fjord; about our landings at Stavanger; about our repeated defeats of the Germans. The same sort of thing had happened in Finland again and again.

It would have been less serious had these reports gone no farther than Scandinavia. But, as in the case of the Norway campaign, they were sent on inevitably as reports from the Swedish Press to the outside world and they were printed in other papers.

I do not say that the Scandinavians were the only ones who faked reports. In the Finnish war, as in any war, there were reporters whose whole approach to the campaign was utterly biased, who were either sensationalists at heart or pro-Fascists who saw this as the great revelation of the utter rottenness of the Left, and who rushed round collecting every minor point of detail that could show that the Soviet was tottering to its inevitable crash. Some of them were second-rate men who had hastily been called in because many papers were keeping their first-class men for reporting the war in France. Reports which anyone with experience of war corresponding would never have sent out, such as the statement that Polish women and children were chased ahead of the Russians in the Isthmus to blow up the land mines, or the repeated report that the Russians were locked in their tanks, were repeated and published all over the world.

One masterly fake came at the time of the battle of Suomussalmi. A French correspondent had said that the Russians had lost the battle because their secret weapon had failed there. This was a torpedo boat on skis which was to manœuvre on the frozen lakes. What on earth a torpedo boat on skis was going to torpedo on empty frozen lakes no one seems to have considered. I suppose it failed because the Finns had built no boats on skis to be torpedoed. I heard this report come over the B.B.C., quoting a French paper, when we were on the front at Suomussalmi. We listened, in a tent full of Finnish soldiers, while the Press Officer with us translated it for them. Their laughter nearly broke the beaverboard walls of the tent.

But again, I repeat, this was only one side. The truth was there for all who cared to look for it, written by men who ran considerable personal danger and endured considerable discomfort to discover it.

Finland was a huge country with great difficulties of communication. News courses, as a result, tended to divide themselves into two groups. Correspondents worked chiefly from Helsinki and from Rovaniemi away in the North, which led at times to duplication of reports. A reporter would, for instance, hear in Helsinki of the rout of a certain division, and send a message to that effect. A special correspondent at Rovaniemi would perhaps hear of it only the next day, and then send his message which might also be printed by his paper. To the general public, confused with long Finnish names, and with a strange country, it looked as if two divisions instead of the same one had been wiped out, as they read their papers hastily in the Tube or bus-ing towards the office. Then the special correspondent would probably go down and see the ruins of the division. His report would appear a few days later. Again the ordinary newspaper reader who was not following the events from day to day would perhaps think that yet another division was wiped out.

The blame for this cannot lie entirely with the papers. It must lie to a large extent with the public which wants the news quickly and is not prepared to read any lengthy digest or to acquire the background fully to appreciate the day-to-day stories. But all the main London papers—my own certainly—did, at intervals in the war, carry summary articles which balanced up the recent fighting and which put events into their accurate proportion as they developed.

We worked in Finland also in the face of considerable difficulties. We were able to see and learn, it is true, far more of the war than any of the correspondents did of the swift-moving war on the Western Front in the spring of 1940 or of most wars. That was because it was a smaller war, far slower, and one in which you could get into direct contact with the Generals and officers who had fought the various battles. But there was none of that happy hunting of news and of watching battles from front-line positions that came the way of correspondents in Spain. The Finnish Army Command disliked the Press. Many of their officers, fundamentally Fascist, regarded newspapers as annoying things which in peacetime were usually criticising soldiers, and which gave publicity to far too many unpleasant facts in this world. Their own correspondents were mostly old men who were allowed to see very little. The foreign correspondents they regarded either as fools or spies. General Wallenius in the last days of the war told me frankly that he had, from the start, taken the view that I must be a British Army officer sent to spy out the war in the North, and that he took good care to keep me away from as many facts as possible, until such time as he felt it was safe to let the information out.

The Finns were always impressed by broadcasters, particularly those working for the American companies, and tried to give them special facilities. On the Isthmus on New Year's Eve this produced unexpected results. Warren Irvin of the N.B.C. had arranged to do a talk from a post on the Mannerheim Line, and he asked that if any guns were fired they should be fired then, so that the sound would come in the background of his description. The Finns, intrigued, ordered two batteries close by to fire throughout the three minutes Irvin had arranged. This sudden outburst of fire, however, on a front that had been virtually dead quiet for the last few days, alarmed the Russians. They thought some kind of attack was coming and hastily told their own guns to open up. "They threw everything but the Kremlin at us for about half an hour," Irvin said later. The Finnish High Command was furious. For thousands of troops a night's rest had been lost, yet they could not deny it was their own fault for providing the gunfire. They must have guessed it would draw a reaction. And even this fact never stopped anyone who could claim he wanted to do a radio talk getting better facilities than most correspondents there. The radio gear, with vans and microphones and all the rest, seemed to impress them enormously. After all, there is little that is impressive about a reporter walking about writing things down in a note-book and asking annoying questions.

To get anywhere near the front we had to fight endless tussles with Press officials. It certainly cost me more energy to get permission from Lieutenant Leppo in Rovaniemi to go to Salla or Petsamo than it ever cost me to report or investigate the battles themselves. Leppo's attitude can only be explained, I believe, either by some curious personal dislike of the Press, or by his having received definite instructions from the Finnish High Command to prevent our seeing any actual fighting. But he would do anything to keep us from the front. He would promise us trips and fail to arrange them. He would avoid you and go out ski-ing just when you wanted to arrange something. He would listen to a suggestion you made—as when, early in January, I suggested that an American and I should be allowed to go over the frontier with one of the ski patrols into Russia— say it was a good idea, and then send some other correspondent or one of the agency reporters on your own idea.

With a curious amateur approach to the Press the Finnish Press officers, too, tried to give people scoops. They would take one man on an exclusive story which was of little value to him alone, and which simply irritated every other correspondent. I cannot personally complain. By moving North early, I had a good break, and saw a great deal before any of my colleagues got there. Later, perhaps by making an appalling nuisance of myself—I hate sometimes to look back on the arguments I had —I got many good trips to the front, to Joutsijärvi, Petsamo, Salla, and Viipuri. But they were always reluctant to show us any actual fighting. They regarded the Press as a combination of ghouls and schoolgirls who wanted to see the Finns and Russians locked in a death struggle just for sensation, but who ought not to be allowed to take any risks. In the Finnish war, as in every other war I have reported, I have found few newspaper men who were not willing to take the same risks as the officers conducting them. Newspaper men, after all, are war correspondents partly because they earn their living that way. They know they get a better story and will make more money if they go nearer to the front. But as well they are usually men who are intensely interested in the story they are covering, who are passionately anxious to discover the truth. They hide this under a jesting cynicism; they joke about their stories in bars and laugh in the midst of other people's suffering. But that is often because they see so much of suffering that they have to build up some sort of defence. But the Finnish Press Bureau did not see us like that. They disliked most of us. We were nuisances. They were running their own war and they did not want propaganda except on their lines. We tried to argue with them that the truth was the best propaganda, but only a few of them ever realised that. Many officers in the Press Department, like Lieutenant Mackinnen and Captain Zilliacus, realised our point of view and did everything they could to get the Finnish Command to give us facilities. But they were men without influence. Against them the whole weight of the army machine was thrown. This does not mean that their reporting was inaccurate. For in any war you get your news after the fight has taken place, and not at the time. You get it from the records of the Commanders and from their word as much as from anything you see. All the events you see only give you a certain amount of local colour. Walter Kerr, of the *New York Herald Tribune*, whose reporting from Finland was certainly in the very highest class of newspaper work, wrote one dispatch in which he pointed out the enormous difficulties under which correspondents were labouring in Finland, and in which he debunked much of the sensational stuff which had been written. This dispatch did, I think, a great deal of good, but it also needed to be generalised. For in no modern war except in Spain have the correspondents really seen much. The Finnish war was no exception, but because of the political atmosphere surrounding it the reporting of it was more carefully scrutinised than that of any other modern war.

Reporting in Finland, as in France, suffered from the military theory that strongly fortified lines are practically impregnable. The Finnish High Command, and most foreign military observers in Finland, were extremely optimistic in January that the Mannerheim Line could be held. This meant that the Finnish victories in the North appeared much more important than was later shown to be the case. The spotlight had been on them too much. Once the Mannerheim Line was smashed Suomussalmi, Kemi River, Tolvajärvi fell back into their true perspective as side campaigns, brilliantly conducted by the Finns, and very important locally, but still just sideshows compared to the decisive struggle on the Isthmus. As I read through the newspaper cuttings of my stories of the war in the North there is little now that I would alter. They give, I believe, a thoroughly fair picture of the fighting there. The battles on the Salla front, the Kuhmo front, the Suomussalmi front did take place as I described them then. But I realise that, though accurate in themselves, their stories gave, to some extent, an inaccurate general impression of the war. For to balance them I should have been saying continually, "But despite these victories we must always remember the huge weight that Russia can fling against the Finns, that with her tanks and planes she must win soon". I did not say so—though I did point out repeatedly that the northern war proved only that the Red Army was no good in the snow, not that it was under all conditions no good—because I did not believe it. I could not see where the tanks and planes were to be used. They were hopeless in the North. The ruins of the 34th Tank Brigade, the wreckage on the Rattee Road, proved that beyond doubt. And the experts told me that they could not break the Mannerheim Line. So I took the experts' word for it, and let the spotlight dwell on the war of movement in the North, too little on the preparations for the Summa offensive which was to prove the experts so utterly wrong

In one place I have said that at first few first-class reporters were sent there. This should be—few star reporters were sent there at the start by British papers, though later one after another of the first-rank war correspondents arrived. Webb Miller came first, on the last war assignment he was ever to have; then William Forrest, who had been the great supporter of Soviet policy in Spain, and who was to be its great opponent in Finland; Langdon Davies; Virginia Cowles, and for the B.B.C. came Edward Ward, who gave the first really alive news broadcasts the B.B.C. has ever given about events abroad, and who scooped us all on the signing of the peace. The Finnish war was particularly outstanding in one journalistic way. It produced some of the best news photography of our times. The snow, the unusual costumes, and above all the fantastic battlefields of the North, with their massed tanks and their dark, twisted figures of the dead, provided magnificent picture material. Karl Mydens of *Life*, Frank Muto of the I.N.S., Arthur Mencken of Paramount News, were all early in the field making a first-class record for America. For Britain Eric Calcraft of *Planet News* made series after series of photographs which were both news and art. Calcraft, a slight, bearded figure with merry eyes, came on to Finland from Poland, where he had secured the only pictures of the attack on Warsaw, and where his jaw had been broken by a piece of flying wood thrown by an exploding bomb. He seemed oblivious to danger—when Rovaniemi was bombed he stood out in the open photographing away until a bomb explosion knocked him over. His photographs, which portray many of the scenes I have described, I am fortunate to have as illustrations for this book. They tell more than my words.

CHAPTER XLVII

PERSONAL VIEW

So it was all over. I drove out with Walter Kerr to the airport at Helsinki—the first time I had been allowed to see it since the war started. The buildings were still camouflaged and seemed undamaged. In the hall was a Finnish pilot I had met in the first days of the war. He had just come back from

Stockholm where he had been sent to collect some Bristol Blenheim bombers.

"If only they had arrived a month sooner," he said bitterly. On the field outside a Fokker reconnaissance machine was just taking off. We got into the Junkers plane, piloted by one of the two brothers who had run a service unfailingly, night and day, from Abo to Stockholm throughout the war. We took off. Below us, black and white amidst the snow, was Helsinki. We looked down on the camouflaged factories—and I must admit they looked like nothing else than camouflaged factories. There were the streets where I had walked so often from the Hotel Kamp around the centre of the town. There was the area near the docks, the Technical High School where the bombs had fallen. There, by the post office, you could still see the houses scarred by that other bunch of bombs in that first raid.

I picked out with my eye the little lake near which I had been ski-ing the Sunday before. It had been a perfect day, sunny, with the snow crisp underfoot. We had ski-ed on the slopes around the little house, eaten a big lunch cooked for us by the Finnish peasant woman, and sat in the sun afterwards.

Out there in the snow I had worked out what I thought of this war. My views have changed little since. I realised that day, in Finland, that I believed the Soviet were quite right to have demanded from the Finns bases to strengthen their defences around Leningrad. They knew already what we have learnt since—that Hitler is a dangerous maniac who wants to dominate the world. They knew that they must bolt and bar every approach to their country against him—and Finland formed one of these approaches. However much the mass of the Finnish people might have been against any use of their country as a springboard against Russia, there were plenty of men in high places in Finland who were very close to the Germans, whose mentality was at bottom, if not Fascist, certainly violently anti-Communist. These men would certainly have tried to bring Finland into any German war against Russia which should be proclaimed as a crusade against Communism. If they did not, it mattered little. Hitler would have forced their country to do his will anyway.

In face of this situation the Russians took the chance that the war in the West offered, to strengthen their defences at Finland's expense. They were not going to have any Norway adventures in which they were beaten by the Germans to the strategic strong points. All that I felt was reasonable.

It was the Russian method which I felt was wrong. It was not only wrong in that the Finns were not given any final chance of avoiding this terrible blood-letting by being presented with a final ultimatum to give up the bases or fight. For to launch war against people, to bomb their cities when there is still a chance of getting what one wants at the conference table seems to me simply an evil. But also the Soviet attack, launched, as I have said, on what appears to have been faulty information, was made behind the façade of a revolutionary war. It was ostensibly to shake off a ruling minority and put into power a leader, in exile in Russia, whom the Finnish people longed for. This was shown by events to be false, events which made a mockery of the whole early Soviet propaganda, and which gave the Russian move an appearance of utter hypocrisy. Had the Russians come out bluntly before the whole world with the hard truth that they were fighting to defend their own boundaries in a world where no state, however huge, and whatever pacts it signs, can be sure of safety they would not only have had more support, but they would have got some of that support where they wanted it most —inside Finland. For the Finnish people, who fought wholeheartedly to keep out of their country a neighbour from whom they had won freedom only twenty-two years before, who fought partly for their lands and belongings, partly for the right to run their own affairs, would not have felt so enthusiastic about a war for one or two naval bases. No honest man can say that in truth there was any real difference between the way Kuusinen was put forward as a premier by Stalin and the way Quisling was put forward by Hitler in Norway.

This action had, too, blunted one of the weapons of their own defence—the sympathy of masses of workers in western Europe. Events, and particularly the full horror of the Hitler terror, will sharpen that weapon again, as people in a slave Europe look to Russia as a country which may one day come to their aid. But that it was blunted at the time of the Finnish war cannot be denied; the support which could be raised for intervention in Finland alone shows that.

Perhaps, of course, I belong to a generation who have been unfitted by their training for the world which is now before us.

For I have had instilled into me a belief that war is a fundamental evil to be undertaken only where a great good can result, and undertaken then only as a last resort. I could not free my mind from the fact that this blood-letting, this suffering that the Finnish people had been through, was essentially evil. But perhaps I was just shrinking from reality. Perhaps progress is only made in this way, at terrible human cost, and we must not hesitate about wastage of lives in this expenditure, even if they run into hundreds of thousands.

Then I realised that the sun was shining, that the snow was crisp, and so I gave up this thinking and turned for home.

Back at the hut I leant on my skis and stared round. How good life could be in Finland. The woman who had cooked our meal sang as she washed up. We asked her what she felt about things. She said, "All I know is my husband is coming home. I've given up trying to work out things like politics".

Children in their red caps and sweaters tumbled about in the snow. The sky was very blue. "You'd never think they had the highest rate of T.B. in the world. God knows how they get it. Someone tells me there aren't the proper food properties in the grass, so that the butter and milk lack vitamins. Someone else says it's just that a wave of T.B. hits countries at different times," said Rex. But I saw only the snow and sky and the children and refused to take in this new note of gloom.

We motored back to Helsinki in the dusk. The street lights were on for the first time. In the restaurants a new Helsinki was appearing. Women whom I had never seen in anything but ski trousers and sweaters were there in high heels and evening dresses. Officers were back from the front, laughing, drinking. Even in defeat, this place meant relief from the terrible strain of war. Not to have relaxed would have been inhuman. Outside the shops many of the wooden hoardings which had hidden the windows had been taken down. Helsinki suddenly became much more full of colour and of beauty. Children's voices rang again in the parks. In the Hotel Kamp they took down the black-out shutters and even opened a window—the first, I am sure, that had been opened on the ground floor for at least four months.

The aeroplane droned on towards Stockholm. We passed over the frozen bays beyond Abo, out over the Gulf of Bothnia where the first ice-floes were already stirring. Below us, from the plane, frozen sea had given way to frozen land.

In front were the yellow buildings of Stockholm. Stockholm, and the route back home, to a future where German marines were lying waiting for the signal in the holds of their vessels in Narvik, where German forces were massed on the Danish frontier, the Dutch frontier, the Belgian and the French frontiers, where all the world as we knew it was going to be reshaped.

Slowly the plane circled and swooped down, down towards the white, snow-covered surface of the airport at Stockholm from which I had taken off for Finland that chilly morning on November 30, 1939, only three and a half short months before.